Casimir Pulaski
Cavalry Commander of the American Revolution

Know that as I could not submit to stoop before the sovereigns of Europe, so I came to hazard all for the freedom of America, and desirous of passing the rest of my life in a country truly free, and, before settling as a citizen, to fight for liberty.

—Casimir Pulaski
to the Continental Congress
19 August 1779

GENERAL CASIMIR PULASKI, 1745-1779

Artist Tytus Maleszewski (1827-1898) captures the image of a sorrowful man, reflecting the tragic life of Casimir Pulaski as a freedom fighter in Poland and America. (Courtesy of Marek Skorupski, Editor-in-Chief of Photography, Polska Agencja Informacyjna-S.A., Warsaw)

Casimir Pulaski
Cavalry Commander of the American Revolution

Francis Casimir Kajencki

Francis Casimir Kajencki (signature)

Southwest Polonia Press
El Paso, Texas

Casimir Pulaski: Cavalry Commander of the American Revolution. Copyright © 2001 by Francis Casimir Kajencki

FIRST EDITION

All rights reserved. No part of this book may be used or reproduced in any manner whatsoever without the written consent from the publisher, except for brief quotations for reviews.

Published by Southwest Polonia Press, 3308 Nairn Street, El Paso, Texas 79925-4126.

Printed in the United States of America

Cataloging-in-Publication Data

  Kajencki, Francis Casimir
    Casimir Pulaski: Cavalry Commander of the American Revolution

    Bibliography
    Includes index

    1. United States—History—The American Revolution, 1777-1779

    2. Poland—History—Insurrection of the Confederation of Bar against the Russian-occupying Forces in Poland, 1768-1772.

    3. Biography—Casimir Pulaski

  Library of Congress Control Number: 00-135024
  ISBN: 0-9627190-5-6

To the Officers and Men of

THE PULASKI LEGION
An Intrepid Unit of the Revolutionary Army

And to Their Descendants

"*As he was valiant, I honour him*"
—SHAKESPEARE

Books by Francis Casimir Kajencki

Star on Many a Battlefield:
Brevet Brigadier General Joseph Karge
in the American Civil War
1980

"Uncle Billy's War":
General William T. Sherman's Changing Concept
of Military-Civilian Relations during the
Civil War—from Staunch Civilian Protector
to "Cruel Plunderer"
1989

Poles in the l9th Century Southwest
1990

Across the generations:
Kajencki Family History
1994

Thaddeus Kosciuszko:
Military Engineer of the American Revolution
1998

Casimir Pulaski:
Cavalry Commander of the American Revolution
2001

· **Preface** ·

When Casimir Pulaski arrived in America, he was an accomplished military leader. He had developed his skills as the young commander of the Army of the Confederation of Bar, a movement of patriotic gentry that attempted to evict the hated Russian-occupying forces in Poland during the period, 1768-1772. Because of Russian superiority, Pulaski developed and executed successfully "hit and run" tactics that kept the enemy off balance. In America, he studied the generalship of George Washington and concluded that to engage the British in general battles was counterproductive. Washington had suffered a disastrous defeat at the Battle of Long Island in 1776 and at Brandywine and Germantown in 1777. The strategy of waging general battles played into the hands of the better equipped, trained, and led enemy forces. The British sought to fight large battles in which they were confident of defeating the Americans and ending the rebellion quickly. Pulaski told Henry Laurens, President of the Continental Congress, on 5 July 1778: "It is certain that the English must risk every thing for the present, or entirely abandon America." Pulaski concluded that "our great object should be, not to risk every thing on the fate of one general engagement, but, by many detachments, observe the movements of the enemy, disconcert them whenever possible, cut off their divisions at favorable opportunities, rather than attack them with our whole army." When Washington took advantage of a "favorable opportunity" to strike an unsuspecting force of Hessian mercenaries at Trenton and Princeton, he scored satisfying victories.

In addition to being an astute military analyst, Pulaski was a bold and experienced cavalry general. He was aghast to find General Washington wasting the capability of the cavalry on menial tasks of messenger service and ceremonial escorts for generals. Washington did not understand the value of cavalry nor did he care for it. He boasted that he could recruit and equip three infantrymen for the cost of one cavalryman. Pulaski advocated a powerful cavalry corps operating as Washington's eyes and ears and thrown into battle at critical times to insure victory. Pulaski was 100 years ahead of the Americans. Not until the Civil War did the Confederates States field the magnificent cavalry corps of General Jeb Stuart.

Historian Charles Francis Adams observes that when Pulaski landed in Massachusetts in July 1777, the Revolutionary War had entered its third year, and the cavalry still remained "undeveloped." Adams concludes: "It thus devolved on a Pole and an exile to make the first serious attempt to give form to a systematic American cavalry organization for actual use in practical warfare." When Congress appointed Pulaski "Commander of the Horse" on 15 September 1777, Pulaski took command of four under strength cavalry regiments. He found the Americans, although normally good horsemen, lacking the fundamentals of cavalry tactics and maneuvers. He began a vigorous training program for all personnel, from the colonels down to the lowly privates.

Pulaski could not have arrived in America at a more inopportune time. The American commissioners in Paris, Benjamin Franklin and Silas Deane, recruited many foreign volunteers, mostly adventurers, who expected high rank and glory. Thus, these foreigners displaced Americans who expected to advance to the higher positions themselves. Most American officers seethed with resentment against the foreigners, and Pulaski also had to suffer this resentment. In addition, Pulaski did not speak English and this drawback inhibited him from mixing freely with most of his officers. Only on the battlefield could Pulaski's zeal and bravery evoke the respect of Americans. General Washington praised Pulaski's bravery on several occasions. Nevertheless, the continued opposition of officers within his own cavalry brigade, coupled with Washington's frittering away of the cavalry's capability, induced Pulaski to resign as "Commander of the Horse" and request Congress to authorize his independent legion. Experienced foreign officers flocked to his new command. When petitioning Congress for an appointment in the Continental Army, they specifically asked to be assigned to the Pulaski Legion. In the Middle Atlantic area, Pulaski's independent command had little opportunity to demonstrate its capability. However, in the Southern Theater of Operations, the Pulaski Legion performed in an outstanding manner. Only a chance mortal wound at the Battle of Savannah, 9 October 1779, stopped Pulaski from fighting to final victory. During his more than two years of service in the American Revolution, Casimir Pulaski upheld the noble Polish tradition—"For Your Freedom and Ours."

—FRANCIS CASIMIR KAJENCKI
El Paso, Texas

· Acknowledgements ·

The author expresses his deep appreciation to individuals and staffs of libraries and historical societies for invaluable help in providing data and other documents during the author's period of intensive research. In particular, the author would like to thank his daughter Dr. AnnMarie Kajencki, Professor of English at Bismarck State College, North Dakota. She reviewed my manuscript critically. My son Anthony joined and assisted me during two weeklong field trips to the Philadelphia area and Savannah, Georgia. My cousin Marzena Piasecka of Sopot served ably as a contact with scholarly institutions in Poland.

I would also like to thank Brigadier General Thaddeus W. Maliszewski (Retired) of Jupiter, Florida, for generously turning over to me many published essays on Casimir Pulaski and letters from *The Writings of George Washington* by editors Jared Sparks and John C. Fitzpatrick. This ready source of data shortened my period of research.

The list of assisting individuals and agencies is shown in Appendix D.

—Francis Casimir Kajencki
El Paso, Texas

· Contents ·

Preface	xi
Acknowledgements	xv

CHAPTERS:

1. Soldier of Liberty in America	1
2. Commander of the Horse	19
3. Pulaski Attacks British at Haddonfield	37
4. The Pulaski Legion	57
5. Betrayal at Little Egg Harbor	79
6. Mis-Assignment to Minisink	99
7. The Long March to Savannah	113
8. Pulaski Saves Charleston	131
9. The Siege of Savannah	143
10. French-American Assault on Savannah	161
11. Demise of The Pulaski Legion	171
12. Evaluating General Pulaski's Service	187

APPENDICES:

A. Balancing the Books	201
B. Pulaski's Military Experience	211
C. Pulaski's Burial Site	219
D. List of Acknowledgements	223
Notes	227
Bibliography	253
Index	263

· Illustrations ·

COLOR PLATES: *following page* 74
    Moravian Sisters Present Pulaski with Legion Banner
    Pulaski Legion Banner
    Pulaski Legion Banner (obverse side)
    Pulaski Banner Marker, Bethlehem, Pennsylvania

PHOTOGRAPHS:
General Casimir Pulaski	*Frontispiece*
Marquis de Lafayette	4
Monument in Honor of Casimir Pulaski, Brandywine Battlefield Park	15
Casimir Pulaski Marker near Brandywine Battlefield Park	16
Memorial Arch at Valley Forge National Historical Park	32
List of General Officers on the Memorial Arch at Valley Forge	34
Brigadier General Anthony Wayne	47
Henry Laurens, President of Congress	59
Colonel John Laurens	60
Letter of General George Washington to Committee of Congress	65
Pulaski Legionnaire (Infantry)	73
General Pulaski Monument, Mystic Island, New Jersey	94
Inscription on the Pulaski Monument	95

Street Sign "South Pulaski Boulevard," Mystic Island, New Jersey	97
Street Sign "Kosciusko Way," Mystic Island, New Jersey	97
Document of Congress Appointing Lieutenant James de Bronville in The Pulaski Legion	100
Major General Benjamin Lincoln	128
Major General Augustin Prevost	135
Pulaski Monument in Savannah, Georgia	174
Two Historic Markers at Pulaski Monument	177 & 178
Historic Marker in Honor of Pulaski and Sergeant William Jasper	179
Fort Pulaski National Monument	194
Equestrian Statue of Pulaski, Washington, D. C.	197
Author Visits Former Pulaski Gravesite	220

Maps:

Battle of Brandywine, Situation, 3:00 P. M.	10
Brandywine, The Battle Erupts	12
Pulaski Strikes British at Haddonfield	48
Movements of American Units & British Squadron	85
Little Egg Harbor & Environs	85
Pulaski's Camp at Little Egg Harbor	89
Planned Route of the Pulaski Legion	127
Assault on Savannah, the Allies Prepare to Attack	156
Poland in 1768	214

Figures:

1. Officers of The Pulaski Legion (September 1778)	68
2. Organization of The Pulaski Legion (March 1779)	124

Casimir Pulaski

Cavalry Commander
of the American Revolution

· I ·
SOLDIER OF LIBERTY IN AMERICA

CASIMIR PULASKI landed at Marblehead, Massachusetts, on 23 July 1777. His ship, the American brig *Massachusetts,* commanded by Captain John Fisk, had sailed from Nantes, France, on 7 June 1777. While crossing the Atlantic Ocean for forty-six days, Pulaski developed several plans to help the Americans gain independence. However, not knowing the vast geography of America nor the temperament of its people, most of the plans turned out impractical. One did become a positive accomplishment—the formation of an independent legion capable of striking quick and unexpected blows at the enemy, a capability that later culminated in the great Confederate cavalry in the American Civil War and in the thrusts of the armored divisions of World War II.

The thirty-two-year-old Pulaski carried a letter of recommendation to General George Washington from Benjamin Franklin, American commissioner in Paris. At first, Franklin hesitated to write a letter, knowing little about Pulaski and his military background. At the same time, Franklin was overwhelmed by the requests of many foreign volunteers who sought promotion and glory in America. Coming to his aid, Pulaski's friends in France convinced Franklin of the Pole's ability and valuable experience.

Franklin, therefore, penned a favorable letter to the Commander-in-Chief, 29 May 1777:

> Count Pulawski of Poland, an Officer famous throughout Europe for his Bravery and Conduct in Defence of Liberties of his Country against the three great invading Powers of Russia, Austria and Prussia, will have the Honor of delivering this into your Excellency's Hands. The Court here have encouraged and promoted his Voyage, from an Opinion that he may be highly useful in our Service. Mr. Deane has written so fully concerning him, that I need not enlarge; and only add my Wishes, that he may find in our Armies under your Excell[enc]y, Occasions of distinguishing himself.[1]

After debarking at Marblehead, Pulaski left immediately for Boston and called on Major General William Heath, the American commander. Pulaski dined with Heath at his headquarters, where the Pole got an overview of the military situation.[2] He also became painfully aware of the great disadvantage of not knowing the English language. Despite his handicap, he obtained information from those American officers who spoke French. In Boston, Pulaski examined the fortifications and observed the appearance and behavior of the soldiers. He wrote of his impressions to French historian Claude de Rulhiere: "Their artillery is in good order, but the soldiers are not well trained as they should be and the native officers lack experience." He added that the tactics of the Americans are not well developed, and he lamented their recent defeats. He was caustic of General Philip Schuyler's abandoning Fort Ticonderoga in the face of General John Burgoyne's British Army on 6 July 1777. "General Skala the commander," he wrote Rulhiere, "deserted the position at Tekundroko, abandoned all his equipment and retreated without giving the slightest opposition."[3]

Pulaski's visit to Boston was short. On 3 August 1777 he left to report to General Washington at his headquarters on Neshaminy Creek, twenty miles north of Philadelphia. In his diary, Surgeon Albigence Waldo describes Pulaski as a "Man of hardly middling Stature, sharp Countenance, and lively air." The Pole very likely wore the uniform of a Polish hussar [generally consisting of braided fur-lined dolman sleeves and pelisse, an outer garment trimmed with fur, close fitting trousers, and a tall fur hat with a bag hanging from the top over the right shoulder]. In addition to carrying letters from Franklin and Deane, Pulaski brought with him a letter from Adrienne de Noaille de Lafayette, wife of the Marquis de Lafayette, and delivered it to the marquis.[4] Pulaski's thoughtful deed became the occasion for an early meeting with Lafayette and led to a growing friendship.

Pulaski arrived at a time of deep resentment of American officers against foreigners. Washington and his officers had grown weary and irritated with the large number of foreign volunteers, many of them incompetent and unable to speak English, but all seeking high rank and glory. Historian Rupert Hughes writes that "the nations of Europe began to empty on Washington all their adventurers. They came speaking any language but English. They were all heroes and all zealots for liberty—with a commission. Anything less than a generalcy was an insult." The American officer corps was still furious over the Philippe du Coudray affair. Earlier in Paris, Silas Deane had promised this French officer the rank of major general and the post of chief of artillery of the Continental Army. If granted by Congress, Du Coudray would rank two senior Americans, Major Generals Nathanael Greene and John Sullivan, as well as displace the current chief of artillery, the respected Brigadier General Henry Knox. The pending Du Coudray confirmation caused the three generals to submit their resignations and provoked Congress into anger. Although the problem was resolved satisfactorily, it nevertheless caused Americans to view all foreign volunteers unfavorably. Historians R. Ernest Dupuy and Trevor N. Dupuy write that "many Europeans flocked to the American cause, but again a sharp division in motivation separated the comparatively few generous souls—like France's Lafayette, de Kalb, and Fleury; Prussia's von Steuben; and Poland's gallant Kosciuszko and Pulaski—from the horde of soldiers of fortune who gravitated from overseas to America, seeking their own advancement...and Silas Deane in Paris was dangling

CASIMIR PULASKI

MARQUIS DE LAFAYETTE OF FRANCE
Major General of the American Continental Army and staunch friend of General Casimir Pulaski. Lafayette supported the Pole with Congress and General George Washington. Pulaski arrived in America carrying a letter for Lafayette from his wife, Adrienne. The thoughtful act sparked the beginning of a lasting friendship. (Portrait by Charles Willson Peale in 1781. Independence National Historical Park Collection)

generalcies in the Continental Army with spendthrift generosity."[5]

Pulaski was fortunate to have the strong backing of Lafayette, who introduced the Pole to the Commander-in-Chief and his staff. Washington listened carefully to the Marquis, for Washington was very favorably impressed with the young nobleman. Becoming convinced of Pulaski's capability, Washington wrote a letter of recommendation to John Hancock, President of Congress, 21 August 1777:

> Sir: I do myself the Honor to inclose you a Copy of Doctr. Franklin's Letter in favor of Count Pulawski of Poland, by whom this will be handed to you. I sometime ago had a Letter from Mr. Deane, couch'd in terms equally favorable to the Character and Military Abilities of this Gentleman.
>
> How he can with propriety be provided for, you will be best able to determine; he takes this from me, as an introductory Letter at his own request.[6]

The thoughtful Lafayette also penned a letter of support for Pulaski who carried it to Philadelphia. Lafayette addressed the letter to James Lovell of Massachusetts, member of Congress and the Committee on Foreign Applications. Lovell, who spoke fluent French, often served as interpreter for the French volunteers seeking commissions from Congress. Lafayette told Lovell:

> The bearer of my letter is the Count de Pulaski, who will be in your department as a stranger officer asking the leave of fighting for our liberty. Though I did not know him, as I received a particular account about him, I think proper to acquaint you with it. He was one of the first members of the Confederation of Poland, the most distinguished officer and the most dangerous enemy of the tyrants of his country. He derived a great reputation by his bravery and intelligence in the war, and his noble and fiery conduct after the destruction of the unhappy Poland.[7]

In Philadelphia, Pulaski presented the letters from Franklin, Deane, Washington, Lafayette, and his own of 24 August 1777 to Congress. Pulaski referred to his military experience in fighting Russians over a period of four years. "I commanded in Poland 1800 men in different battles," he explained. "The sieges and attacks of Places which I have managed give one a title to be counted among men of military experience." He concluded with his purpose of coming to America: "I have passed hither from Europe to do myself the honor of being admitted among worthy Citizens in the defence of Their Country and Their Liberty."

Pulaski proposed to Hancock that he initially be given command of one volunteer cavalry company and commissioned a rank that would entitle him to command a division "when I shall merit it." He also proposed an arrangement of command strikingly different from current American thinking. He advocated that he be placed directly under General Washington and be subject only to the orders of the Commander-in-Chief. He realized, though, that his idea was radical and would probably not be accepted. "If that cannot be, yet joined to the Marquis de La Fayette," he said, "I would take pleasure in sharing his labours and executing the orders of the Commander-in-Chief as subaltern of the marquis."[8]

The Committee on Foreign Applications reacted negatively to Pulaski's proposal for an independent command. The members concurred with Lovell that to accord Pulaski a status second only to Washington and Lafayette would be "contrary to the prevailing Sentiments in the Several States as to the Constitution of our Army, and therefore highly impolitic." Wary of extraordinary demands of foreign officers, Congress was suspicious that Pulaski could be contemplating a large and autonomous unit. Although Congress did not reject Pulaski's proposal, the members needed time to study it.[9]

General Washington had his own priorities of combat arms. Relying on the infantry and artillery, he considered cavalry as playing a secondary role in the war. Notwithstanding, when the Continental Army was established, four individuals recruited cavalry regiments: Theodorick Bland and George Baylor of Virginia, Elisha Sheldon of Connecticut, and Stephen Moylan of Pennsylvania. Their regiments were all under strength, ill-equipped, and ineffectively employed. The generals took units of the regiments for ceremonial and protective escorts or had them serve as messengers, and occasionally to gather intelligence on the enemy. Washington dealt individually with the four colonels, although it was apparent to him that he must shorten his span of control by placing the four regiments into a brigade and assigning a brigadier general to command them. (Washington initially offered the command of the cavalry to General Joseph Reed, who declined). Evidently believing that none of the four colonels was deserving, Washington did not recommend anyone of them for promotion to brigadier general. Nor would Washington "degrade" the capability of the infantry by taking away a competent general and assigning him to the cavalry. As he told President Hancock, "I have not, in the present deficiencies of Brigadiers with the Army, thought it advisable to take one from the foot, for that command. The nature of the horse-service with us being such that they commonly act in detachment, a general Officer with them is less necessary than at the head of the Brigades of infantry." Still, Washington needed a "commander of the horse," and the timely arrival of Pulaski seemed to solve his problem. However, the authority to grant a commission and assign the officer to the cavalry brigade rested with Congress.[10]

While Pulaski waited for Congress to act on his application for service, he closely followed the developing British threat to Philadelphia. General Sir William Howe had sailed from New York with an army of 15,000 soldiers, 23 July 1777, and disappeared over the horizon. He reappeared a month later in the upper reaches of Chesapeake Bay, landing at the Head of the Elk, Maryland, some fifty miles south of Philadelphia. His objective was to capture and occupy the largest American city and the seat of the rebellion.[11]

Cooling his heels in Philadelphia, Pulaski grew restless as he sensed the approach of a great battle. He decided that he must return to the army where he could assist the Americans in some way. He explained his decision to President Hancock:

> I have Tought it not my Duty to stay here any longer, in as much as I have heard; that his Exy Genl Washington is gon to meet the enemy; wherefore I will go to the Army...I can not do

much, but Hover I will shew my good will. I depend upon His Excelly and leef him my Memorials.[12]

Pulaski departed immediately for army headquarters at Wilmington, Delaware, where he again pressed his case with Washington. The Commander-in-Chief listened carefully to the Pole's fervent pleas. Paul Bentalou, an officer in Pulaski's Legion, wrote that Washington became impressed by the "inherent ardour of his warlike spirit, his habits of activity and the desire of efficiently serving the cause which he had so warmly embraced." Washington invited Pulaski to join his staff as a volunteer officer.[13] Meanwhile, he took an important step in giving Pulaski an assignment in the army. Although Washington previously had left the proper appointment for the Pole in the hands of Congress, he now formally proposed that Pulaski become the first commander of cavalry of the Continental Army. In his letter of 28 August 1777, he wrote President Hancock: "Having endeavored, at the solicitation of the Count de Pulaski, to think of some mode for employing him in our service, there is none occurs to me, liable to so few inconveniences and exceptions, as the giving him the command of the horse. This department is still without a head." Washington admitted that "a Man of real capacity, experience and knowledge in that service might be extremely useful." He pointed to Pulaski's considerable experience in cavalry operations in Poland and the way that experience could benefit the Continental Army. He stressed that "as the principal attention in Poland has been for some time past paid to the Cavalry, it is presumed this Gentleman is not unacquainted with it." Before Congress acted upon Washington's recommendation, however, the Battle of Brandywine was fought.[14]

The British Army departed the Head of the Elk on 28 August 1777, marching in two grand divisions, the larger force under General Charles Lord Cornwallis and a smaller one under the Hessian General Wilhelm von Knyphausen. The army marched northeast toward Wilmington and then north for the Nottingham Road that led to Philadelphia. Meanwhile, Washington's Army of

13,000 soldiers took up a strong defensive position along Brandywine Creek at Chad's Ford, 9 September 1777. The main road to Chester and Philadelphia crossed the Brandywine at Chad's. The Commander-in-Chief posted Major General Nathanael Greene's division and Brigadier General Anthony Wayne's brigade of Pennsylvanians at Chad's. About one-half mile below at Pyle's Ford, Brigadier General John Armstrong commanded some 1000 militia. North of Chad's Ford, Washington deployed the divisions of Major Generals Lord Stirling, Adam Stephen, and John Sullivan. These three divisions formed the army's right wing under the overall command of Sullivan. As a further precaution against possible British crossings further up Brandywine Creek, Washington ordered Sullivan to place outposts at Painter's, Wistar's, and Buffington's Fords. Colonel Theodorick Bland and his cavalry were located at Painter's. (The cavalry was not under Pulaski's command, as Historian Christopher Ward incorrectly states).[15] (See map, page 10).

Although Sullivan guarded his right (north) flank on the Brandywine, Washington did not count on Howe possibly conducting a very wide envelopment of the American Army. The grand division of Cornwallis, however, marched north up the Great Valley Road as far as Trimble's Ford on the West Branch of Brandywine Creek and still further north to Jeffries' Ford, crossing the East Branch of the Brandywine. Cornwallis thus passed around the most outlying American units. Meanwhile, Knyphausen marched his division of 5000 soldiers straight to Chad's Ford where he began to cannonade the Americans as a feint for a preparation of the main attack. As Washington waited, Cornwallis crossed the Brandywine and now marched south on the road to Dilworth. Soon he would be in the rear of the Americans and in position to inflict a disastrous defeat.[16]

Nevertheless, the march of Cornwallis' grand division did not pass undetected. Colonel Moses Hazen sent word to army headquarters, at about 9:00 A.M., 11 September 1777, that an enemy force was observed marching along the Great Valley Road to Trimble's Ford. Washington notified Colonel Bland to keep the

Battle of Brandywine—11 September 1777
General George Washington deploys his divisions on the east bank of Brandywine Creek, as he assumes that General Sir William Howe's army of British and Hessian soldiers will attack at Chad's Ford. However, Howe directs General Lord Cornwallis' troops in a wide envelopment of the American position and feints toward Chad's Ford with General Knyphausen's Hessians.

enemy under observation. At about 11:00 A.M. Lieutenant Colonel James Ross of the 8th Pennsylvania Regiment observed "a large body of the enemy, from every account five thousand with sixteen or eighteen field pieces" marching on the Great Valley Road. Astounded, Washington could not believe that Howe had divided his army, and Washington decided to exploit the British "blunder" by attacking both divisions—Sullivan to cross the

Brandywine and strike Cornwallis in the rear and Greene and Wayne to attack Knyphausen. Greene began to carry out his maneuver when Washington received another dispatch from Sullivan. He reported that Major James Spears of the militia who had reconnoitered the Great Valley Road had "heard nothing of the enemy about the fork of the Brandywine, and is confident they are not in that quarter; so that Colonel Hazen's information must be wrong." Spears report directly contradicted the two previous reports. Yet, Washington chose to accept the Spears report as true, and the general canceled his orders to Sullivan and Greene. He would wait for further developments.[17]

In the afternoon of 11 September, Colonel Bland's party of cavalry discovered the British about a half mile to the right of the Birmingham Meeting House. Bland at once notified General Sullivan who, in turn, dispatched Bland's note with his own, datelined "Two o'clock, P.M.," to Washington. Sullivan informed him "that the enemy are in the rear of my right about two miles, coming down. There are, he [Bland] says, about two brigades of them. He also says he saw a dust back in the country for above an hour." The wide envelopment of the American right hit Washington like a thunderbolt. Notwithstanding, he reacted promptly and decisively. He ordered Sullivan to pull his three divisions from positions along Brandywine Creek and march them rapidly to the vicinity of the Birmingham Meeting House. Washington also ordered Greene's division to back up Sullivan, having evaluated the movement of Cornwallis as the greater threat. Thus, Washington kept only Wayne's and Brigadier General William Maxwell's brigades at Chad's Ford.[18]

At about 2 P.M. General Howe halted Cornwallis' grand division for a much-needed rest near Sconneltown (now extinct). The troops had been marching steadily since daybreak. The pause of about one hour gave Sullivan a little more time to form two divisions across the road to Dilworth. At about four o'clock, Cornwallis ordered his soldiers, formed in three divisions, to attack the Americans with cold steel. The patriots had not learned, as yet, how to stand up to bayonets of disciplined regulars.

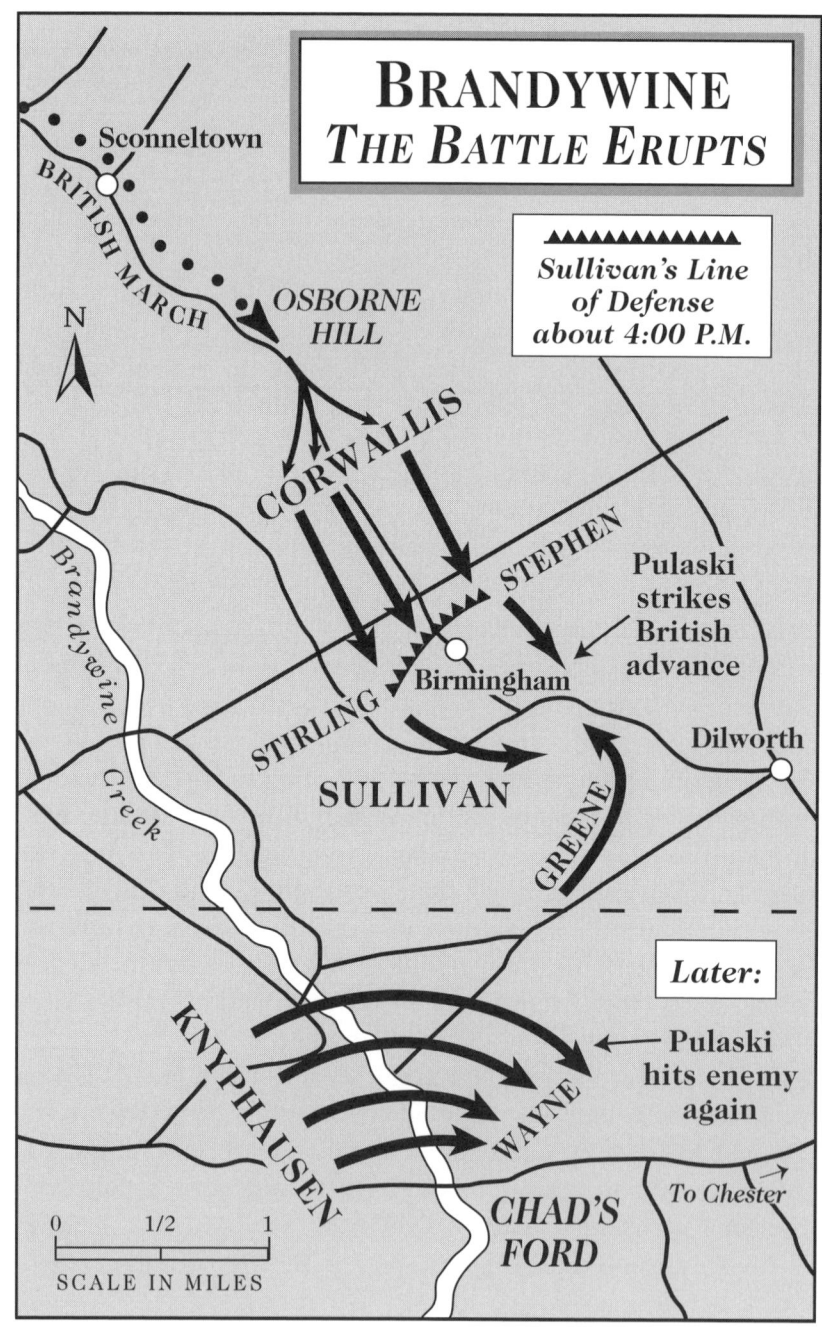

Consequently, Sullivan's troops broke and fled to the rear. Having traveled with Greene, Washington watched with dismay the rout of Sullivan's soldiers. But Greene's division, deployed behind Sullivan, opened up corridors for the fleeing men to pass through, and closing ranks again, Greene stalled the Britishers. Dusk brought the fighting to an end. Under the cover of darkness, the Americans retreated to Chester.[19]

Earlier at Chad's Ford, General Knyphausen heard the firing of artillery coming from the direction of the Birmingham Meeting House. The sound was his signal to attack, and an avalanche of Hessian and British soldiers overwhelmed Wayne's Pennsylvanians who fought their way south in the direction of the Chester Road. By the end of the day, the condition of the American Army had become chaotic, as described by Lafayette: "The rout became complete...In the midst of this horrible confusion and the darkness of the night, it was impossible to recognize one another."[20]

The defeat of the Americans became an unexpected opportunity for Pulaski to demonstrate his skill and bravery. He had been following the fighting closely as Washington's aide. The intense drama of the battle had aroused his passion for the fight. Although he had no rank or command, he pleaded with Washington to give him the thirty horsemen who formed the general's escort. Looking for help from any source, Washington agreed. With his small cavalry unit, Pulaski struck a leading element of the British advance. The surprise attack caused the British to stop and evaluate the threat. Even though the delay was relatively short, Pulaski gained some precious time for the retreating Americans to make good their escape. And before the British could sweep Pulaski's cavalry out of the way, he quickly withdrew. The Pole had executed his favorite tactic that he had used so successfully in Poland against superior Russian forces.

Bentalou recounts Pulaski's action at Brandywine:

> At the time when our right wing was turned by the victorious enemy pressing upon us, and the rapid retreat of the right and centre of our army became the consequence, Count Pulaski

proposed to Gen. Washington to give him the command of his body guard, consisting of about thirty horsemen. This was readily granted and Pulaski, with his usual intrepidity and judgment, led them to the charge and succeeded in retarding the advance of the enemy—a delay which was of the highest importance to our retreating army.[21]

Historian Rupert Hughes also lauds Pulaski's performance. He writes: "Among the distinguished warriors in this whirlpool battle was Count Pulaski, who borrowed some of Washigton's own Guard and led them in charges that drove back the British at dangerous crises."[22]

Pulaski had another opportunity on this same day of demonstrating his fighting ability—this time against Knyphausen. With Washington's approval, Pulaski rounded up a sizable number of scattered troops, mostly German Americans, and led them in an attack of the enemy's flank. Shouting encouragement in German, *Vorwarts, Bruden, Vorwarts!* (Forward, Brothers, Forward!), Pulaski charged the enemy and opened the only avenue of escape, the road to Chester.[23] Bentalou describes the action:

> The penetrating military *coup d'oeil* of Pulaski soon perceived that the enemy were maneuvering to take possession of the road leading to Chester, with the view of cutting off our retreat, or at least, the column of our baggage. He hastened to General Washington to communicate the information, and was immediately authorized by the commander in chief to collect as many of the scattered troops as he could find, and make the best of them. This was most fortunately executed by Pulaski, who, by an oblique advance upon the enemy's front and right flank, defeated their object, and effectually protected our baggage, and the retreat of our army.[24]

Although Bentalou does not say where on the battlefield Pulaski executed his second attack against the enemy, Historian Willard Sterne Randall places it in the area of Chad's Ford. He writes that when Knyphausen attacked Wayne's Pennsylvanians, "Wayne fought back marvelously with the aid of a half-mad Polish cavalryman named Casimir Pulaski. Their rear-guard tactics slowed the British drive across the ford until Washington arrived on the

Large stone monument in honor jointly of Casimir Pulaski for his valor at Brandywine and also of two young Americans killed by the British in the War of 1812. The light-colored marble tablet on the right gives a brief description of Pulaski's service. A gift of John G. Taylor in 1902, the monument is located on the Brandywine Battlefield in the Birmingham-Lafayette Cemetery. (Photo by the author, 21 September 1999)

scene and reorganized his men." Historian David Ramsay also lauds Pulaski's performance: "He was a thunderbolt of war, and always sought for the post of danger as the post of honor."[25]

The day after the Battle of Brandywine, Congress was aghast to learn of Washington's disastrous defeat. Tempers flared and many accusations were flung recklessly at the Commander-in-Chief and his generals, among them William Maxwell, Lord Stirling, Adam Stephen, and, particularly, John Sullivan in whose sector the British attack first occurred. In defending himself, Sullivan wrote Washington: "I had no orders to take any care above Buffenton's Ford, nor had I light troops or light horse for the purpose." Sullivan deplored the lack of cavalry for reconnaissance.

Marker in honor of General Casimir Pulaski. Located on U. S. Highway 1 near the entrance to Brandywine Battlefield Park. The Pennsylvania Historical and Museum Commission erected the marker in 1975. (Photo by the author, 21 September 1999)

"I have never had any light horse with me since I joined the army," he added. "I found four with Major Taylor, when I came to Brenton's Ford, two of whom I sent off with Colonel Hazen to Jones's Ford." Sullivan's complaint emphasized the crying need for an effective cavalry arm for the American Army. With regard to another general, Prudhomme de Borre, Congress accused the Frenchman of misconduct (he failed to rally his men and fled before them) and ordered that he stand trial by court martial. De Borre avoided the ordeal by resigning his commission and returning to France.[26]

In contrast to the denunciations hurled at many generals, Pulaski's daring exploits reverberated impressively among the members of Congress. Within three days of the Battle of Brandywine, Congress awarded Pulaski the rank of brigadier general and appointment as commander of the American Light Dragoons. On 15 September 1777, Congress resolved: "That a commander of the horse be appointed with the rank of brigadier; the ballots being counted, the Count Pulaski was elected." James Lovell, writing to General William Whipple, 17 September 1777, informed him: "Count Pulaski, who headed the Polanders, is now commander of our cavalry, having first signalized himself at the Battle of Brandywine." And General Washington announced the appointment in General Orders, 21 September 1777: "The Honorable Congress have been pleased to appoint the Count Pulaski to chief command of the American light dragoons, with the rank of Brigadier General."[27]

· 2 ·
Commander of the Horse

Casimir Pulaski undoubtedly was pleased to be appointed brigadier general and the first commander of cavalry of the Continental Army. However, the favorable action of Congress proved to be a dubious honor because the Pole faced almost unsurmountable problems. For one, General Washington, having relegated the cavalry to a secondary role, did not understand the proper employment of this arm. To him, the combat arms that won victories were the infantry and artillery. After one year following his defeat at the Battle of Long Island, 27 August 1776, Washington had not become convinced of the need for an effective cavalry arm. At that disastrous battle, Washington's army had been completely enveloped on the northern flank by the British without detection. Historian Charles Francis Adams questions why Washington did not realize, from an examination of his mistakes on Long Island, that he must have "an adequate mounted force of some kind, attached to his command, at once his army's eyes and ears, its safeguard against surprise and his most ready weapon of offense."[1]

Although Washington remained unimpressed with the cavalry, some voices spoke up in its favor. Major General Charles Lee was one. On 1 July 1776, he wrote Washington from Charleston,

Casimir Pulaski

South Carolina: "For God's sake, my dear General, urge the Congress to furnish me with a thousand cavalry. With a thousand cavalry I could insure the safety of these Southern Provinces; and without cavalry, I can answer for nothing." Lee, second in command of the Continental Army, possessed a good knowledge of cavalry operations. He had served as an aide to King Stanislaw August Poniatowski and a major general in the Polish Army, 1765-1769. Although Congress had authorized the mounting of four regiments of Continental dragoons, Washington and most of his generals lacked an appreciation of the cavalry's capability. Consequently, Washington frittered away the cavalry on ceremonial escorts and messenger service. Occasionally he employed the cavalry appropriately to gather intelligence on the enemy. Although most Americans were good horsemen, they did not understand the role of a powerful and mobile striking force as perfected in Europe and especially in Poland.[2]

With respect to his responsibilities as cavalry commander, Pulaski's ignorance of the English language proved to be a serious drawback. It restricted his opportunities to develop rapport with his officers through casual conversation. Only by demonstrating his leadership and bravery in battle could he gain the respect of the Americans. But this opportunity would come when the four regiments were consolidated into a brigade and trained in the tactics and cavalry operations on the European level. From the very start, his efforts were thwarted by the reluctance of Americans to serve under a foreign officer. Their feelings were exacerbated by the flood of foreign, and mostly incompetent, volunteers that Silas Deane had dumped on America. Three of Pulaski's regimental commanders exhibited different levels of hostility toward him. In particular, Colonel Stephen Moylan proved to be a thorn in the side of the Pole. In contrast, Colonel Theodorick Bland maintained a civil and respectful manner toward his cavalry chief. Tall and personable, he spoke French that he had acquired in the West Indies. Pulaski and Bland's ability to communicate directly with each other in a common language undoubtedly brought about a better understanding. Other leaders as well as Pulaski had formed favorable opinions of Bland. Timothy Pickering, militia colonel and soon to be a member of the Board of War of Congress, first met Bland at Morristown, New Jersey, on 20 February 1777. "Here was Major Bland, a Virginian, who commanded six troops of Virginia lighthorse," Pickering wrote. "The Major appeared to be a man of sense, knowledge, and stability."

Stephen Moylan's hostility toward Pulaski sprang in large measure from bitterness over Pulaski's promotion in 1777 to the position of brigadier general of cavalry that he had coveted for himself. Born in Cork, Ireland, in 1737 and educated in Paris, Moylan emigrated to America in 1768. In the American Revolution, he joined the Continental Army, but his service was undistinguished. For three months in 1776, he acted as secretary to General Washington. On 7 June 1776, Congress elected him Quartermaster General (QMG) of the Continental Army with the rank of colonel. He served only four months in this post. The vast logistical responsibilities for the newly-organized Continental Army were simply too demanding for a man of mediocre ability, and he resigned his office on 28 September 1776. Washington then requested him to raise a regiment of cavalry that became the 4th Continental Regiment of Dragoons. After continuing in grade of colonel for eight years, Moylan was finally promoted at the end of the war when Congress made a mass brevet promotion of all officers who had not been promoted since 1 January 1777. During the time Pulaski was Commander of the Horse, Moylan took advantage of his acquaintance with Washington to undermine Pulaski's standing with the Commander-in-Chief.[3]

Pulaski found almost no time to begin training his regiments, for in less than three weeks after his appointment, the Battle of Germantown was fought, 4 October 1777. Leading up to the battle, Pulaski performed a critical role of scouting the presence of the enemy as Washington marched his army north to Philadelphia. On 16 September 1777, Washington encamped the army near Warren and White Horse Taverns on the Lancaster

Road, south of the Schuykill River, where he decided he must oppose General Howe's march on the Quaker City. On the same day, Howe departed Chad's Ford in the direction of the same area. A collision of the two armies appeared imminent. Concerned about the security of the American position, Pulaski, on his own initiative, led a cavalry patrol in search of the enemy. At the time, Washington's army was "dispirited with defeat," suffering from fatigue, and needing rest. The soldiers were hungry, and happily they were served rations here. Bentalou writes that Pulaski "could not for a moment remain inactive." He "went out with a reconnaissance party of cavalry and did not proceed very far, before he discovered the whole British army in full march upon our camp." Pulaski sped back to headquarters to report the ominous intelligence to Washington "who, as can be imagined, received it with equal surprise and uneasiness for he had not the most distant idea of such a movement from the enemy," Bentalou stated. Washington's staff scoffed at Pulaski's report. Alexander Hamilton, who spoke French, asked Pulaski whether he may not have mistaken British troops for American. Pulaski, however, stuck to his report. Historian William W. Gordon writes that it was through Pulaski's intelligence and activity that further disaster was prevented.[4]

Pulaski recommended that Washington order a force of about 300 infantry, and his cavalry, to harass and delay the approach of the enemy long enough to give the Commander-in-Chief time to deploy his divisions for the expected British attack. Washington approved. He placed Brigadier General Charles Scott of Virginia in command. As Christopher Ward writes, "Washington sent Count Casimir Pulaski, newly appointed 'commander of the horse' ranking as a brigadier, with the cavalry and 300 infantry to retard the advance of the enemy; but the foot soldiers shamefully fled at the first fire and delayed the enemy not at all." Nevertheless, the Americans escaped a devastating defeat by an unpredictable nature. As the fighting was about to begin, a deluge of rain struck the area, beating down on both friend and foe. The driving rain forced the soldiers to abandon all thoughts of fighting and concentrate on saving themselves. The ground quickly became a quagmire, and ammunition was thoroughly soaked and rendered useless. Hessian officer Major Baurmeister reported: "I wish I could give a description of the downpour which began during the engagement and continued until the next morning. It came down so hard that in a few moments we were drenched and sank in mud up to our calves." Consequently, Washington marched away to obtain a fresh supply of ammunition, and the British maneuvered quickly to occupy Philadelphia.

Following the deluge, General Howe occupied Philadelphia and stationed Lord Cornwallis there with 3000 soldiers. He encamped the remaining 9000 at nearby Germantown. The British enjoyed the amenities of a large and pleasant town. Baurmeister describes the city:

> Philadelphia is rather a lovely city of considerable size and is laid out with parallel streets. The public squares are beautiful. For the most part, ordinary houses are moderately large and built of brick in the Dutch style. Classical architecture and its embellishments are met with only in the churches and in a few public buildings, of which the city hall, where Congress has been holding sessions, is one of the most noteworthy.[5] *

Smarting from his recent defeat, Washington determined to strike the British at Germantown. He had received reinforcements and felt strong. He developed a brilliant plan of marching four columns simultaneously that would envelop and defeat the British. Perhaps the plan was too ambitious for an inexperienced army, for the plan went awry, and the expected victory turned into defeat. On the day of the battle, Pulaski was greatly disappointed by his inactive role. He commanded only four under strength regiments of dragoons. Three of the four regiments were with the army. Nevertheless, on the day of battle, 4 October 1777, Bentalou explains that "Guards were furnished out of three regiments, to attend to the commander in chief, and on other generals

---

* See Note 5 for the author's analysis of two short essays on the internet placed there by Independence Hall Association which portray General Pulaski very negatively.

—or employed in other service so that Pulaski was left with so few men as not to have it in his power to undertake anything of importance." Bentalou adds that Pulaski's status in the battle—more as an observer than participant—was "a matter of deep regret and bitter chagrin." Historian Rupert Hughes reinforces Bentalou's complaint of dissipating the cavalry for trifling tasks: "And this was in keeping with Washington's unvarying failure to recognize the importance of properly handled cavalry."[6]

Pulaski did play a minor role in the Battle of Germantown. Historian Benson J. Lossing writes that in the retreat of the Americans, the divisions of Greene and Stephen were the last to leave the field, and these were covered by Count Pulaski's cavalry. Forty-five years after the battle, Pulaski was accused of dereliction of duty. Judge William Johnson of Charleston, South Carolina, wrote that Washington found Pulaski asleep in a farm house. This simple fact is no cause for alarm, inasmuch as generals like privates must sleep at times. Hughes explains that Washington's whole army was almost ruined with fatigue, and he understands how Pulaski could have fallen asleep. Hughes points to General Peter Muhlenberg who "fell asleep on his horse in the midst of the battle and was saved by an aide." Muhlenberg "had been two nights and a day in the saddle almost without relief." Nevertheless, Johnson insinuates that Pulaski should have been patrolling instead of sleeping. Thereby, Washington lost the Battle of Germantown due "chiefly to Pulaski's want of vigilance." Johnson repeats the allegation made by Charles Cotesworth Pinckney (whom Bentalou claims was a bitter opponent of Pulaski). At Germantown, Pinckney served as an aide to General Washington. In his report to Congress, Washington never attributes any failure to Pulaski. Yet, if true, the General was obligated as Commander-in-Chief to report the battle factually and honestly. General Adam Stephen, for example, was found drunk during the battle and was cashiered from the army. Johnson tries to explain Washington's silence to his alleged policy of conciliating foreigners. "Forbearance in such a case," Johnson writes, "became almost a duty." However, Johnson writes nonsense. The editor of *The North American Review* refutes Johnson: "Such a policy, indeed, would have been little else than betraying the high trust confided in him[Washington], and a most unjustifiable breach of right conduct, in suffering the odious consequences of the neglect of one officer to be borne by those who had faithfully done their duty." To repeat, Washington never reported any wrong doing by his cavalry commander. Indeed, he respected Pulaski's bravery and fighting ability. When Pulaski resigned his position as commander of the horse, Washington endorsed the Pole's plan for an independent legion and strongly supported Pulaski's successful recruiting program.[7]

In 1824, two years after Johnson's wild charge, Paul Bentalou, then a resident of Baltimore, Maryland, wrote a defense of Pulaski under the published title *Pulaski Vindicated from an Unsupported Charge*. For the historical record, Bentalou soundly rejects Johnson's accusation. The greater value of Bentalou's essay to historians, however, stems from the details of Pulaski's service that otherwise might have remained unknown. Bentalou's essay enhances Pulaski's significant contribution to American freedom. George Washington's adopted son, George Washington Parke Custis, defends and praises Pulaski in his *Recollections and Private Memories of Washington:*

> The celebrated Count Pulaski, who was charged with the services of watching the enemy and gaining intelligence, was said to have been found asleep in a farm house. But although the gallant Pole might have been overtaken by slumber from the great fatigue growing out of the duties of the advanced guard, yet no soldier was more wide awake in the moment of combat than the intrepid and chivalric Count Pulaski.[8]

Years later when the Marquis de Lafayette visited the United States in 1824-25, Americans everywhere greeted the esteemed guest with enthusiasm. General Washington had been very fond and solicitous of the "boy general," who was only nineteen when he arrived in America in 1777. On 7 October 1824, Lafayette arrived in Baltimore where he was welcomed by a committee of distinguished residents, including his countryman Paul Bentalou who had the honor of riding with Lafayette in his carriage. Troubled with Johnson's charge against Pulaski, Bentalou asked Lafayette a direct question "whether he had heard Washington or anyone else say that Pulaski had been found asleep by Washington, and that the ill success at Germantown was principally to be ascribed to that circumstance." Lafayette answered emphatically, "No! Never!" Or, to use his own expression, as the question was put in French, *"Non! Jamais!"* As Lafayette continued to tour the country, he came to Savannah, Georgia, where he dedicated the cornerstone of the Pulaski Monument in Chippewa Square on 21 March 1825. Bentalou rightfully states that the virtuous Lafayette could not have participated in a tribute to Pulaski if Lafayette knew that the Pole had been a careless soldier at Germantown. On his return to Baltimore, 30 July 1825, Bentalou entertained Lafayette. On a Sunday, the Marquis, his son George Washington Lafayette, secretary A. Levasseur, and Bentalou went together to the evening services at the Unitarian Church. On leaving, Lafayette proposed to spend the rest of the evening at Bentalou's home. John Barney, Representative to the U. S. Congress from Baltimore, also joined the group. Bentalou recorded the cordial atmosphere of the gathering: "On that social evening, in the bosom of my family, we conversed much on the men and the events of our revolution, and Pulaski was a favourite topick." During the evening Bentalou asked Lafayette the same question about Pulaski as he did on the former visit. Lafayette gave the same earnest reply, "No! Never!" Congressman Barney confirmed Lafayette's answer, and added: "My impressions were that the memory of Pulaski was cherished by Lafayette as a gallant soldier, who had devoted himself to the service of our country, and that he terminated his life without blemish or reproach." Jared Sparks scoffs at Johnson's charge against Pulaski: "It seems both idle and unjust to entertain for a moment such a suspicion, especially when it is not pretended to rest on any better foundation than conjecture and hearsay.[9] Perhaps Johnson looked for a scapegoat on whom to pin the blame for Washington's defeat at Germantown.

Commander of the Horse

• • •

AFTER THE BATTLE OF GERMANTOWN, the British settled down in Philadelphia, where they spent the winter of 1777 in fine style. Washington initially set up his headquarters at Whitemarsh, Pennsylvania, and then moved the army to Valley Forge where it suffered terribly all winter long. Taking advantage of the long pause in operations, Pulaski began vigorous training of his cavalry brigade and the provisioning of his under equipped troops. He was determined to build a cavalry corps that could fight effectively as a unit rather than be wasted on escorts for the generals. Pulaski organized a program of exercise and discipline with the help of a very capable French officer, the Marquis de Fleury, a veteran of the French Army since the age of seventeen. After Fleury arrived in America in 1776, Congress commissioned him a captain. He first distinguished himself in the Battle of Brandywine. On 3 October 1777, Congress promoted the 28-year-old officer to brigade major and assigned him to Pulaski's staff. The cavalry commander benefited from Fleury's experience only a short time, for, on 26 November 1777, Fleury was promoted to lieutenant colonel of engineers and assigned to Lafayette's division.[10]

Pulaski had the valuable service of another European officer, Jan Zielinski, who had fought in Pulaski's Army of the Confederation of Bar against the Russians in Poland. A proud and experienced cavalryman, Zielinski was somewhat disdainful of amateur American cavalrymen. That he and the provocative Moylan would tangle was almost foreordained. At the cavalry camp near Upper Dublin, Pennsylvania, Moylan and Zielinski got into a heated argument that quickly developed into a confrontation. Historian Burt Garfield Loescher writes that Zielinski, acting as Pulaski's aide, brought conflicting and apparently unintelligible orders to Colonel Moylan who made no effort to withhold his prejudice. The problem became exacerbated by their failure to communicate. Moylan struck the Pole with his glove and placed him under guard for his "uncivil" manner. When

Pulaski entered the controversy, Moylan turned his wrath on his commander.[11]

Historian Page Smith subtly takes Moylan's hostile position. Writing of the Zielinski-Moylan affair, he states that Pulaski "managed to be constantly embroiled with his officers." On the contrary, Pulaski sought to get along with his officers, but the prejudice of some Americans, especially that of Moylan, prevented amicable relations. Smith also impugns Pulaski's motive in joining the fight for independence and casts him into the sorry lot of foreign adventurers and glory seekers. The historian describes Zielinski as "another of those military acolytes that every foreign officer felt himself entitled to bring with him when he left for America." But Pulaski made a good choice to invite Zielinski. His fellow Pole possessed the cavalry expertise that the Continental Army desperately needed. Indeed, Pulaski was fortunate to have the capable Zielinski in his command. Both were dedicated to the Polish tradition as exemplified by the motto: "For Your Freedom and Ours." Pulaski had stated this noble tradition earlier to Benjamin Franklin in France: "Our nation loathes tyranny and especially foreign. Therefore, wherever on the globe people fight for freedom it is as if it were our own cause." Pulaski's noble purpose penetrated the consciousness of many Americans. In his speech at the laying of the cornerstone of the Pulaski Monument in Savannah, 11 October 1853, Henry Williams reminded his fellow citizens that Pulaski then in France became aroused by the shots fired at Concord and Lexington. "The sound stirred the heart of Pulaski like the voice of a battle-trumpet," Williams said. "It was a struggle for *Liberty*! It was *his* cause, whoever the people and wherever the scene of conflict."[12]

In the aftermath of the unfortunate confrontation between Zielinski and Moylan, Pulaski had only one option—prefer court martial charges against Moylan for "disobedience to the orders of General Pulaski, a cowardly and ungentlemanly action in striking Mr. Zielinski, a gentleman and officer in the Polish service when disarmed...and giving irritating language to General Pulaski." A court martial took place on 24 October 1777, presided over by Colonel Theodorick Bland. Although Moylan was clearly guilty of conduct unbecoming an officer, the board voted to acquit the accused. The members seemed unwilling to rule in favor of a foreigner against one of their own. In General Orders, 31 October 1777, General Washington approved the verdict of the court martial and ordered Moylan released from arrest.[13]

The verdict reverberated beyond Pulaski's cavalry brigade. The partiality of the American officers upset General Lafayette, who told Washington: "Count De Pulaski was much affronted by the decision of a court martial entirely acquitting Colonel Molens...as I know the English customs I am nothing else but surprised to see such partiality in a court martial." Even Colonel Thaddeus Kosciuszko in Albany, New York, learned of the court martial. In his own conduct, Kosciuszko went out of his way to maintain good relations with his fellow Americans. He now grew alarmed by the evident necessity of resorting to court martial to resolve problems. On 17 January 1778, he wrote General Washington to plead for protection and justice. "I begin my Letter," he wrote, "to beg your Protection for me and my Countryman, Mr. Zielinski, if his side is right as he informed me." But Kosciuszko was not ready to concede that Zielinski may have been entirely blameless. "But if it is not," Kosciuszko continued, "tell him Sir that he had better return to his Country than make confusion to me and others."[14]

Not long after Moylan's court martial, Zielinski took advantage of an opportunity to embarrass the arrogant Moylan. The Pole unhorsed Moylan with a lance during a cavalry exercise. The enraged Moylan protested directly to Washington. Pulaski also reported the affair to the Commander-in-Chief, sending his letter by the dragoon who had been present at the drill. Pulaski informed Washington that the affair was not as Moylan had complained; it was accidental. Zielinski had no other motivation than to reciprocate Moylan's prior attack on him. Zielinski had not drawn his sword nor threaten Moylan by other means. He was a proud individual who tolerated no mistreatment. Nevertheless, Washington reprimanded Zielinski and held up his appointment of captain of dragoons in Pulaski's Independent Legion until April 1778. Later, the brave Zielinski gave his life for American independence in a fight with British forces at Charleston, South Carolina, 11 May 1779.[15]

Not only did Colonel Moylan cause trouble for foreign officers, he also aggravated some of his own officers with his cavalier behavior. Henry Bedkin, adjutant of Moylan's Fourth Continental Cavalry Regiment, became disgusted with Moylan and planned to resign from the army. Bedkin brought his problem to Pulaski who told Washington that he would be glad to place the young Pennsylvanian on his staff and employ him in supervising cavalry instruction. Pulaski wrote, "It would be a loss to the Cavalry if he should quit the service." Bedkin left Moylan's regiment to become Pulaski's Brigade Major. A few months later he was made captain of dragoons in Pulaski's Independent Legion.[16]

The adverse verdict of the court martial of Moylan undermined Pulaski's authority. Discontent against the foreign commander increased, and Moylan played a major part in instigating the misunderstanding. The respected patriot Colonel John Laurens spoke up in support of Pulaski. Laurens wrote his father Henry Laurens, President of Congress: "The dislike of some of his officers to him as a stranger, the advantages which they have taken of him as such, and their constant contrivances to thwart him on every occasion, made it impossible for him to command." In the aftermath of the court martial, Pulaski undoubtedly began to consider the unhappy choice of resigning from the command of the horse. Nevertheless, for the present he would carry on and try to rise above the pettiness of some Americans and thereby fulfill his goal of fighting for American independence.[17]

Not only was Pulaski plagued with disciplinary problems but also by numerous complaints of civilians over the cavalry's seizure of horses and accoutrements. Confiscating the property of loyalists was accepted practice. However, Pulaski and his regimental commanders had difficulty in differentiating between lukewarm and true patriots, not to mention pseudo-patriots and neutral Quakers. The four cavalry regiments seized property, especially horses, and instigated strenuous protests of Pennsylvanians to Washington and Congress. Washington, forced to act, issued on 25 October 1777, a stern order to the cavalry chief and his four regimental commanders: Colonels Bland, Sheldon, Baylor, and Moylan. "I am sorry to find," Washington wrote, "that the Liberty I granted to the light dragoons of impressing horses near the Enemy's lines has been most horribly abused and perverted into a mere plundering scheme." He was angry that under the pretense of the authority granted, the cavalry plundered whomsoever they labeled Tories and converted what they got to their own private profit. "This is an abuse that cannot be tolerated," Washington emphasized. In strong language Washington ordered Pulaski: "You will therefore immediately make it known to your whole Corps, that they are not under any pretense whatever to meddle with the horses or other property of any inhabitant whatever, on pain of the severest punishment." In order to identify and dispose of illegally-seized horses, Washington ordered Pulaski that "all the horses in your Corps in the use of the Non-Commissioned Officers and privates, not already stamped with the Continental brand, are without loss of time to be brought to the Qr Master General to receive that brand." As a result of Washington's order and Pulaski's enforcement, there was an evident decrease of complaints.[18]

The problem of obtaining horses for the cavalry grew with time. General Nathanael Greene, who accepted the unwanted assignment of Quartermaster General, learned the problem first hand when horses could be procured only by impress warrants. He admitted that "some mistakes and several abuses appear to have happened." Nevertheless, the Quaker general came to a profound conclusion: "In war it was impossible to conform to all the ceremonies of law and equal justice, and to attempt it would be productive of great misfortune to the public from the delay that all the inconveniences which an individual may suffer." In June 1778, a confrontation occurred between none other than William Paca of Maryland, signer of the Declaration of Independence, and Captain Michael Rudolph of Major Henry Lee's Partisan Legion. Rudolph demanded horses from Paca and showed him a

MEMORIAL ARCH AT VALLEY FORGE
NATIONAL HISTORICAL PARK, PENNSYLVANIA

General Washington encamped his army at Valley Forge during the terrible winter of 1777-1778. Pulaski was the only one of twenty generals who recommended that Washington continue operations during the winter. (Photo by the author, 22 September 1999)

document containing a vague authorization to seize horses. Paca became incensed. As he wrote Maryland Governor William Johnson: "After reading his Authority, I told him if he attempted to seize any of my horses I would blow his brains out and if he did not leave this State or cease to exercise such power I would issue my warrants and commit him to Jail." Rudolph withdrew empty-handed.[19]

At times, when Pulaski rode to Washington's headquarters, he demonstrated his horsemanship for the many staff and visiting officers. All rode horses, probably since childhood, and they admired those that possessed more than usual capability. In Poland, Pulaski had acquired skill and experience when he served as military commander of the Confederation of Bar, 1768-1772.

Commander of the Horse

He led his dragoons over rough as well as level terrain. Striking the hated Russian units that occupied his country, he often approached the unsuspecting enemy over difficult ground that the Russians believed precluded attack from that quarter. Consequently, he honed his skill to a high degree. In America, he displayed his capability on suitable occasions. Lossing writes: "It is related that among other feats, that daring horseman would sometimes, while his steed was under full gallop, discharge his pistol, throw it in the air, catch it by the barrel and then hurl it as if at an enemy. Without checking the speed of his horse, he would take one foot from the stirrup, and bending over toward the ground, recover his pistol, and wheel into line with as much precision as if he had been engaged in nothing but the management of the animal." Some American historians have called Pulaski a showoff. The label appears to fit. However, Pulaski had a deeper purpose for his showmanship than vanity. He constantly stressed to Washington, his generals, and Congress the great value of cavalry as a combat arm. He wanted to demonstrate what an experienced cavalryman could do and thereby promote his goal. American officers, indeed, were impressed with his consummate horsemanship, and some tried to imitate his hazardous feat. While galloping on the field, many of them were unhorsed and injured. Trying to convince Washington, however, was an uphill battle.[20]

As the cold weather began to set in, Washington and his staff were faced with finding suitable winter quarters for the army. Washington called his generals into a council of war at Whitemarsh, 30 November 1777. He asked them to recommend whether the army should cease operations and retire to winter quarters. Of the twenty generals present, nineteen favored bedding down for the winter and suggested various locations. Only Pulaski advocated a winter campaign against the British. Having fought the Russians in Poland during four winters, he knew that quick strikes at the enemy could keep them confined to their bases. In America, winter campaigning even with small forces could limit British forays into the countryside for horses, cattle, and foodstuffs. Pulaski recommended that Washington continue military

NAMES OF GENERAL OFFICERS OF THE CONTINENTAL ARMY On the Memorial Arch at Valley Forge National Historical Park, Pennsylvania. Pulaski's name was omitted when the arch was built in 1917. Historian and journalist Ed Dybicz of Swedesburg, Pennsylvania, discovered the error in 1950. He called the omission to the attention of Pennsylvania Governor James Duff who, in cooperation with the State Legislature, promptly added Pulaski's name to the available space at the end.

operations, as he had done with striking results at Trenton and Princeton the year before. "Our continuing in a state of activity," Pulaski explained, "will give courage to our Friends, be an antidote to the effeminacy of young Soldiers, and enure them to the fatigues which Veterans undergo—keep them in the exercise of their profession and instruct them." Pulaski predicted that the inactivity of winter quarters would ruin the Army, discourage the Country, and leave an extent of Territory for the Enemy to ravage and depopulate. And he was right. The following spring the American Army emerged greatly decimated. However, that previous December 1777 Washington believed that the army was exhausted and needed rest. On 19 December the soldiers limped into Valley Forge. Dr. James Thacher wrote in his *Journal*: "It was not uncommon to track the march of the men over ice and frozen ground by the blood from their naked feet."[21]

The army suffered greatly during the winter. Writing about morale, historian Allen Bowman says: "At Valley Forge (1777-1778) the troops were brought literally to the verge of starvation. Only with the greatest difficulty was the army kept from mutiny." Inaction, against which Pulaski had cautioned, became an insidious enemy of soldiers and officers alike. Both ranks were greatly underpaid. Falling back on their own resources, officers kept sinking into poverty. "While friends in civilian life amassed fortunes," Bowman states, "they were compelled to implore, half naked, for consideration from Congress." In one day, more than fifty officers in General Greene's division at Valley Forge resigned because their families at home were suffering. Resignations of officers occurred at a steady rate of two to three a day. Instead of being engaged actively against the enemy, Washington's Army remained in camp brooding over the miserable conditions. Bowman stresses that "the discouraging effect of long periods of inactivity became a serious problem as the war progressed." And he points to the bleak winter at Valley Forge as a prime example. Fortunately, General Baron von Steuben converted some of the slack time into useful activity when he trained the soldiers in the use of the bayonet and coordinated maneuver.[22]

· 3 ·
Pulaski Attacks British at Haddonfield

✺

General Pulaski's cavalry took up winter quarters at Valley Forge along with General Washington's army. The horsemen faced the same severe hardships as the foot soldiers, perhaps more difficult than would have been encountered in winter operations. Washington quickly learned that the area at Valley Forge lacked food, clothing, and other basic necessities. He reported to Congress: "I am now convinced, beyond a doubt that unless some great and capital change suddenly takes place in that line [Commissary Department], the Army must inevitably be reduced to one or other of these three things: Starve, dissolve, or disperse in order to obtain subsistence in the best manner they can." There was no forage for horses, either. Major General Baron Johan De Kalb scathingly described the conditions at Valley Forge. He wrote to the Comte de Broglie in France, 25 December 1777: "The army reached this wooded wilderness, certainly one of the poorest districts of Pennsylvania; the soil thin, uncultivated, and almost uninhabited, without forage and without provisions!" He claimed that the idea of wintering at Valley Forge could only have been put into the head of Washington by a speculator or disaffected person. Although De Kalb believed that

Washington was a man of sound judgment, still he thought the Commander-in-Chief could be easily persuaded. "It is a pity that he is so weak," De Kalb said, "and has the worst of advisers in the men who enjoy his confidence." Furthermore, he termed these advisors to be "gross ignoramuses" if not "traitors." The lack of food for the soldiers exasperated the baron: "Now we have hardly been here six days and are already suffering from want of everything. The men have had neither meat nor bread for four days, and our horses are often left for days without fodder." Consequently, the absence of forage and the threat of starving the horses convinced Washington to order the cavalry out of Valley Forge after a stay of only three weeks.[1]

Meanwhile, Pulaski, quartered with Brigadier General Enoch Poor in the home of John Beaver, spent long hours on ways to organize, equip, and employ the cavalry. In two letters to Washington, he attempted to convince the Commander-in-Chief of the requirement for a cavalry force superior in number and capability to that of the British. When achieved, he predicted that "the enemy will not dare to extend their force, and, notwithstanding we are on the defensive, we shall have many Opportunitys of attacking and destroying the enemy by degrees." Even if Washington overlooked or failed to understand the ineffectual capability of the cavalry, the commander of the horse, nevertheless, sought to explain why some missions could not be carried out. "I must not omit to mention here the dissatisfaction you have expressed at my seemingly inattention to your orders," Pulaski wrote. "Your Excellency may be assured that the Good of the Service is my constant Study but the Weak State of the Corps I command render it impossible to perform every Service required."[2]

During the period of the American Revolution, the Prussian cavalry was considered a model combat arm in Europe. Pulaski, well acquainted with it, recommended to Washington that the regulations of the Prussian cavalry be printed in English and distributed to the regiments for the instruction of officers and enlisted men. As part of the augmentation of the cavalry, Pulaski proposed the organization of a special squadron of lancemen. They had been a favorite unit of Polish cavalry. As he recommended, the squadron would consist of one captain, two lieutenants, one cornet, four sergeants, eight corporals, and 128 privates. Pulaski said he would command the squadron in person. "With these means, I will undertake to perform every Service necessary and continue the Campaign throughout the winter."[3]

Although the winter quartering at Valley Forge was considered a time for rest and recuperation for the army, Washington tasked Pulaski to stop the flow of supplies to the British in Philadelphia. On 24 December 1777, Washington ordered one of Pulaski's officers, Major John Jameson: "You are hereby directed to repair to the East side of Schuykill and take command of the parties of Horse stationed upon the different Roads leading into the City of Philadelphia." Washington's order went directly to Jameson, probably in the interest of time and other circumstances. Nevertheless, Washington had no intention of bypassing the cavalry commander, and he ordered Jameson: "You are to inform Genl. Count Polaski [sic] of your being sent upon this command." Pulaski ordered out additional parties of cavalry against British foraging groups. But in their weakened condition, the American horsemen were ineffective. At Valley Forge, they were on the verge of losing their horses to starvation. Realizing this dire condition, Washington ordered Pulaski on 31 December 1777 to find winter quarters in Trenton, New Jersey. The Commander-in-Chief reminded Pulaski to take advantage of favorable weather for "perfecting the Cavalry in the most useful manoeuvres" and in bad weather to "perform the ordinary exercises of the Riding School." Washington also approved the organization of lancers as part of the cavalry. He wrote: "You will have sufficient time for training a Troop of Lancemen, and the Lances may be made according to your directions on the spot."[4]

At Trenton where the cavalry arrived on 9 January 1778, Pulaski found no housing for his men and no forage for the animals. The cavalry commander ran into the confusion that often existed between Congress, the state governments, and Washington's staff. Trenton was overflowing with sailors (galley men) who had been directed to spend the winter in this town. Pulaski informed Washington: "I arrived here yesterday with the Cavalry where I expected to have found forage sufficient to subsist the Cavalry, at least for a few days, my Brigade forage master had been informed by Col. Biddle that such provision was made and that he would have nothing more to do then Issue the same, but, so far to the contrary, there was not a Load of Hay in Town. With the greatest difficulty we have been enabled to put our heads under Cover." Pulaski added that the cavalry could not be quartered in Trenton unless the galley men were removed. However, they claimed prior possession by order of the Governor and the New Jersey Council.[5]

Even though he wrestled with new problems, Pulaski never lost sight of his goal of organizing and training an effective cavalry arm. He told Washington that "the Cavalry is in want of every article." At the same time, the inexperience of the troopers worried him immensely. He flatly informed Washington that the cavalry must be exercised and taught the rudiments of cavalry. He had the officer he needed for the position of Master of Exercise: Michael Kovatch, a Hungarian of merit and ability. Kovatch had served in the Royal Prussian Army where he had gained the rank of captain of hussars. Pulaski needed approval of Washington and a commission from Congress to have Kovatch take up his duties. Washington agreed to designate Kovatch Exercise Master of dragoons (as he had made Baron von Steuben the infantry drillmaster). Although Washington approved the assignment of Kovatch, he harbored reluctance to admit foreigners into the Continental Army. He told Pulaski: "I must caution you against a fondness for introducing foreigners into the Service; their ignorance of the Language of the Country and of the genius and manners of the people, frequently occasion difficulties and disgusts which we should not run the risque of." As he so often did, Washington allowed exceptions for meritorious officers, those of "extraordinary Talents and good Qualities." However, Washington had no reason to feel uneasy over Pulaski's selection of officers. They were veterans of wars in Europe. Pulaski knew most of them personally. A number had fought with him in the Army of the Confederation of Bar against the Russian occupiers of Poland.[6]

Trying to solve the acute problem of housing and subsistence for his soldiers, Pulaski appealed for help to the magistrates and residents of Trenton. In a printed circular of 12 January 1778, Pulaski promised them the protection of his cavalry against raids by the British. He requested their help in obtaining food and called on their patriotism to inspire them "with the diligence and activity requisite to give satisfaction to those men, who from motives of honour, sacrifice themselves to a cause so righteous as that of liberty." Unfortunately, Pulaski's appeal fell on deaf ears, and the merchants reacted by raising prices on all articles. Finally, Washington directed Pulaski to station his cavalry regiments outside Trenton. Moylan's and Baylor's regiments occupied the village of Flemington, some twenty-five miles north of Trenton, while Bland's and Sheldon's units were quartered closer at Pennington, eight miles away. Meanwhile, Pulaski maintained his headquarters in Trenton.[7]

On 20 January 1778, Pulaski informed Washington that he planned to remain in Trenton, where he would gather the most capable and equipped dragoons from the four regiments. "I hope in time to procure a sufficiency of forage to subsist 120 horse," he said. He planned to employ this select unit as a rapid-reaction force to counter British raids. He also informed Washington that he was composing a set of regulations for the cavalry: "I will have them printed and distributed among the Officers." Pulaski also mentioned some disciplinary problems. For example, two dragoons in Moylan's regiment showed disrespect to an officer who arrested them. When one of the dragoons attempted to see Pulaski, the officer seized a sentry's sword and struck the dragoon twice, maiming him. Pulaski arrested the officer for abusing his authority and imprisoned the two dragoons. Although Moylan and others opposed him, Pulaski disclosed that there were exceptions: "As I have reason to complain of the ill-will of the rest of the Officers, I cannot but praise those of Bland's Regiment who conduct themselves with the greatest propriety." In his letter Pulaski added a plea for rum for his men: "I hope my General that when you give orders for furnishing the infantry with means for making themselves merry, you will not leave the Cavalry in the dumps." Washington answered that the army was temporarily out of rum.[8]

Pulaski began training the squadron of 120 lancers under the watchful eye of his Master of Exercise, Michael Kovatch. The dragoons had been selected from each of the four regiments. Although the lance was expertly and routinely employed in Europe, Americans found the lance a strange weapon. They struggled to acquire a familiarity with its handling and sometimes lost their balance and fell from the horse to the ground. In fact, Americans never took to the lance. They preferred the sword. Lieutenant Colonel William Washington, an able cavalryman who served under General Nathanael Greene in the Southern Army, praised the sword as the "most destructive and almost the only necessary weapon a Dragoon carries."[9] Nevertheless, under Kovatch the steady training began to show results, and General Washington approved the appointment of Captain John Craig of the 4th Continental Cavalry Regiment to command the squadron of lancers. Feeling proud of his lancers, Pulaski sent a fully-equipped lanceman to Washington's headquarters for his and his staff's personal inspection, 10 February 1778. Washington's reaction is unknown. Undoubtedly, he was somewhat startled.[10]

Not only did Kovatch bear down on the lancemen, but Pulaski also conducted rigorous training for the entire brigade. He followed the regulations of drill and discipline that he introduced into the American cavalry for the first time. He stressed horsemanship and the use of the cavalryman's weapons. He strove to prepare his brigade for the opening campaign in the spring. But many of his officers found new grounds for complaint. They rebelled against his unrelenting training, and some complained directly to the Commander-in-Chief, forcing Washington to chide his commander of the horse. He wrote Pulaski:

Your Officers complain that the Cavalry undergo severer duty now, than they did while they were in Camp. As rest and refreshment are two of the principal objects of your removal from Camp, I hope you will by proper arrangement give your Men and Horses an opportunity of reaping these benefits from their Winter Quarters.[11]

Notwithstanding, Pulaski sought to make his command an effective cavalry brigade. He had taken over a ragged cavalry with no proper mission, little discipline, and negligible competence. The cavalry needed much training, and little time remained for it. It seems that Pulaski was years ahead of his time. In the American Army today, training is carried on vigorously and continually in order to maintain a combat-ready force.

In reply to Washington's admonition, Pulaski acknowledged the responsibility that Washington and Congress had placed in him as the commander of the horse. He passionately wanted the cavalry to play a greater and more effective role in the war for independence. "Our time is short," he wrote, "and I suppose the campaign is to be opened by the cavalry. It will not be for want of attention in me if they are not in a condition to do it."[12]

Pulaski repeatedly tried to convince the infantry-minded general that the cavalry could do more than perform as orderlies or reconnoiter the enemy lines. It could execute combat missions, as well. However, the standing of the cavalry and its role in combat differed markedly between Washington and Pulaski, who strongly believed in its employment in the European manner. He wrote Washington:

> The Cavalry in an Army Generally forms a separate division and has greater privileges than the Infantry, which the Honor of the service exacts, but here I find it is the Contrary, not that I aim at a Superiority over the rest of the Army, but am desirous of having Justice done the Corps I command.[13]

Clearly Pulaski was becoming frustrated. He revealed his inner feelings in a letter from Trenton to his sister in Poland, Anna Walewska, 24 February 1778. He wrote that he commanded the entire cavalry and participated in several battles with some success, but he does not intend to remain in America. He explained that the customs of the country did not agree with his temperament, and besides his service was a waste of time. "It is impossible to do anything good," he wrote. "The people here are too jealous; in the whole army everyone is against me, but I will have one more campaign." With only seven months in the country, he found the most profitable occupation, as he told his sister: "In the future, if it would be possible, I shall become a merchant, which here is the most useful." He also wrote to his friend in France Claude de Rulhiere, 24 February 1778, telling him that he planned to resign his commission. "Here I command the cavalry, but I am not very happy," he lamented. "I rack my brain to accomplish my duty and equip them, but it is hopeless." He also pointed to the hostility of many American officers. "Foreigners are not liked here and they are tolerated only so long as it is necessary." His most telling statement centered on his decision to resign: "I have decided to quit this army. I can find neither benefit nor pleasure here." He added that upon arriving in France, he would undertake new projects.[14]

Four days after writing Rulhiere, Pulaski drafted a letter of resignation to Washington:

> I shall try, My General, to diminish Your embarrassment on my Account by resigning from my charge, with which Congress has honored me by your recommendation. I repeat to Your Excellency the very great necessity of attending to the needs of the Cavalry. They lack everything.

Anticipating that Washington might give the command of the cavalry to Colonel Moylan, Pulaski cautioned Washington: "If after me the Command shall be given to Col. Moylan, all the Cavalry shall be in the same condition as his Regiment." Pulaski recommended the able Colonel Theodorick Bland as his replacement.[15]

Historian Jared Sparks explains Pulaski's reasons for resigning. He writes: "After five months' experience, however, at the head of the cavalry, he found it was not a post which answered his expectation or in which he could perform a part adequate to his hopes and his desires." Sparks points to the wasted method of employing the cavalry, where the regiments were constantly divided into small parties and subject to the command of the general officers of the different divisions. Consequently, the cavalry was not capable of acting as a unified force with telling effect at a critical point in battle. The chasm in the brigade between Pulaski and his senior officers, as Sparks explains, resulted from the changed circumstances upon Pulaski's assumption of command. Previously, the four regimental commanders were loosely supervised and enjoyed a measure of independence. Now they were not easily reconciled to the orders of a superior, "particularly of a foreigner, who did not understand their language, and whose ideas of discipline, arrangement, and maneuvers were different from those to which they had been accustomed."[16]

When Pulaski wrote his sister that he would resign "after the next campaign," he was about to help Brigadier General Anthony Wayne at Haddonfield, New Jersey, where a superior British force threatened Wayne's command. Earlier, Washington had ordered Wayne to search for food, supplies, horses, and forage around Philadelphia in order to prevent the British from seizing these critical items badly needed for the starving American Army at Valley Forge. Dr. Thacher recorded in his *Journal* that "more than once our general officers were alarmed by the fear of a total dissolution of the army from the want of provisions." From Pennsylvania, Wayne entered New Jersey with some 500 soldiers for another foraging expedition. This time, however, the British decided to stop Wayne. General Howe ordered a force of some 2000 redcoats, commanded by Colonel Stirling, to defeat Wayne and seize his supplies. At Haddonfield, Wayne received intelligence that a large enemy force was marching on him. Escaping north to Mount Holly, Wayne ordered Pulaski at Trenton to assist him with his cavalry. Pulaski reacted angrily that Wayne did not have command authority over him, and he protested to Washington. However, Washington's order for Pulaski to cooperate with Wayne arrived late after Wayne's. Unaware of Washington's directive, Pulaski wrote the Commander-in-Chief from Burlington, 28 February 1778: "I do not expect to be under his orders. Nevertheless, I shall serve to my own prejudice the Public interest." Undoubtedly, Pulaski would not stand on protocol and miss a good fight. Few of Pulaski's troopers were fit for combat. Assembling Bland's small regiment and the detachment maintained at Trenton, Pulaski inspected and selected only those dragoons suitable for the mission. He came up with forty-four dragoons and five officers. With this small unit, Pulaski reached Burlington and paused there for the night. He joined Wayne the next day at Mount Holly, and both forces advanced to Haddonfield where they found a strong British outpost located at a mill. Pulaski strained to attack the enemy, but Wayne held back. Biographer Harry Emerson Wildes writes: "For the first time, and last, in all his military career Wayne hesitated; the odds, he thought, were far too great." Pulaski did not wait for Wayne's decision. With his selected unit, Pulaski charged the superior British force in a surprise night attack, 1 March 1778, that precipitated a profound psychological effect. The British became alarmed that they faced a superior force and retreated hurriedly. As a bold commander, Pulaski wanted to continue the attack and cut down the retreating enemy, but Wayne restrained him. Historian Paul David Nelson brushes off Pulaski's attack as being "without much result." But he hastens to add, "except, as Wayne noted, to convince Stirling that the rebel force arrayed against him numbered in the thousands." Indeed, Pulaski forced Stirling to abandon the fight. The redcoats withdrew to Cooper's Ferry and the protection of their warships on the Delaware River. The *New Jersey Gazette* described Pulaski's bold charge more dramatically:

> Though they knew our inferiority of number, our attacking them with a few light horse at Haddonfield, under the command of Brigadier General Count Pulaski, made their fears get the better of their knowledge, as well as their courage, and happiest was the Briton who had the longest legs and the nimblest heads. Leaving bag and baggage, they retreated precipitately to Cooper's Ferry.[17]

The next day, 2 March 1778, Wayne and Pulaski advanced to Cooper's Ferry. They found the British troops still on the eastern shore of the Delaware, not able to cross in boats because of high

Pulaski Attacks British at Haddonfield

BRIGADIER GENERAL ANTHONY WAYNE
General Pulaski with his cavalry joined Wayne at Haddonfield, New Jersey, where Pulaski attacked a far superior British force in a surprise, nighttime attack and alarmed the enemy into retreating, 1 March 1778. The next day Pulaski and Wayne forced the British to give up the fight and withdraw across the Delaware River to the safety of Philadelphia. (Portrait of Wayne as a major general in 1795 by Sharples. Independence National Historical Park Collection)

Pulaski Strikes British at Haddonfield

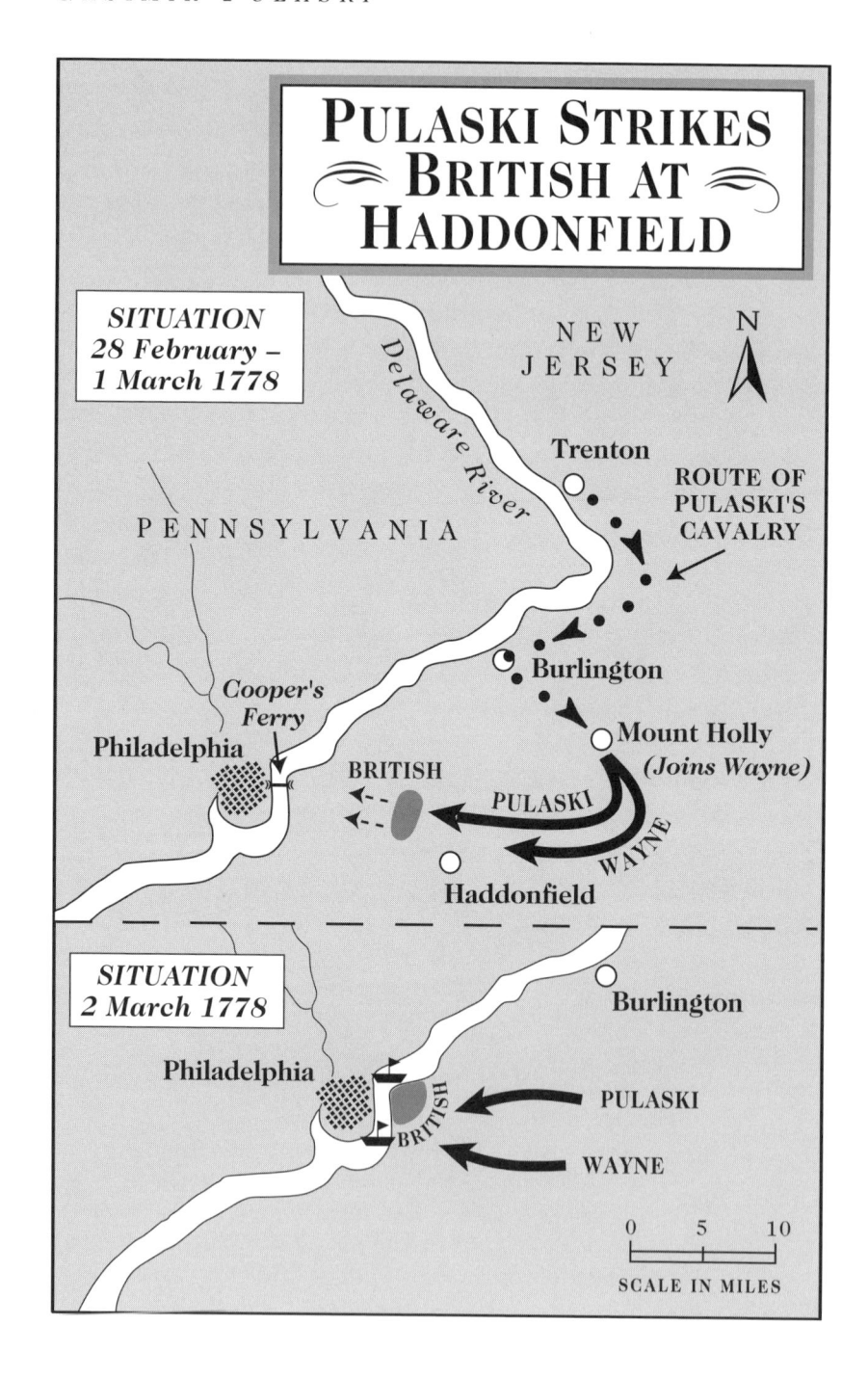

SITUATION 28 February – 1 March 1778

SITUATION 2 March 1778

winds. The enemy position was strong, due not only to their superior strength but also to the fire power of the warships that protected the flanks. Wayne waited. In mid-afternoon the wind subsided, and the British began crossing to Philadelphia. Pulaski was eager to charge, and Wayne ordered the available infantry and cavalry to attack. Stirling suspended the crossing, as he faced about to engage the bold Americans. Despite his strength, Stirling could not be persuaded to move out of his strong position. At the same time, the heavy fire of British warships, field cannon, and muskets held the Americans off until nightfall when the British completed their retreat to Philadelphia. The aggressive action of a small American force caused a superior British unit to retreat and abandon the supplies it had picked up. Most of all, the British failed to stop Wayne's foraging mission.[18] Thus, Pulaski not only saved Wayne from probable defeat but also helped the starving army at Valley Forge.[18]

Writing to Washington, Pulaski reported the loss of ten horses: four killed, three totally disabled, and three slightly wounded. He lost his own horse, a costly and magnificent animal that was shot in the leg and disabled. His dragoons escaped unscathed. Nevertheless, the loss of seven horses affected the capability of the small cavalry command, since suitable horses were difficult to obtain. During the engagement, Pulaski captured seven sailors, including a sea captain, who were trying to escape through woods. Pulaski praised his cavalry: "I have the honor to say to your Excellency that the Dragoons accomplished wonders. They are good Soldiers." General Wayne lauded Pulaski's performance. He told Washington: "Genl. Pulaski behaved with his usual bravery on the Occasion, having his own with four Other Horses Wounded." He also praised his infantry that had attacked with Pulaski: "The fifty Infantry being the only part that had an Opportunity of Engaging—behaved with a Degree of bravery that would have done Honor to the Oldest Veterans."[19]

As to the matter of seniority in the Continental Army, Washington rejected the cavalry commander's protest of 28 February. "In answer to your question respecting the right of command in

Officers of equal rank in the Infantry and Cavalry," Washington answered Pulaski, "I am to inform you that there is no other preeminence in our Service than what arises from Seniority. The Officer whose Commission is of prior date commands all those of the same grade indiscriminately whether Horse or foot." Pulaski believed that the commander of cavalry should serve directly under the Commander-in-Chief. Nevertheless, Pulaski did not anticipate any more problems over seniority. He resigned his post of commander of the horse. On 3 March 1778, General Washington acknowledged Pulaski's letter of 28 February in which he said he intended to resign. Although the differences between Washington and Pulaski over the chain of command caused misunderstanding, the Commander-in-Chief nevertheless recognized Pulaski's fighting ability. He wrote:

> Your intention to resign is founded on reasons which I presume make you think the measure necessary. I can only say therefore that it will always give me pleasure to bear testimony of the zeal and bravery which you displayed on every occasion.[20]

Governor William Livingston of New Jersey also praised Pulaski. He wrote Washington, who replied on 14 March 1778:

> I am pleased with the favourable account which you give of Count Pulaski's Conduct while at Trenton. He is a Gentleman of great activity and unquestionable bravery, and only wants a fuller knowledge of our language and Customs, to make him a valuable Officer.[21]

The fundamental difference between General Washington and Pulaski over the role of cavalry in battle undoubtedly became Pulaski's main reason for resigning. Washington's lack of understanding and appreciation of the capability of the cavalry as a powerful combat arm frustrated the commander of the horse. And he complained to Rulhiere: "Our cavalry is forever dispersed in small groups and when we must fight, we are reduced to nothing." Pulaski, however, was not alone in facing continual disappointment and thoughts of resignation. Major General Johan de Kalb found frustration with Washington's bumbling army and threatened to resign repeatedly. As De Kalb's biographer, Friederich Kapp, writes: "Almost every letter to his wife winds up with the expression of a wish, or with a definite plan for his immediate return home." The jealousy of the native against foreign officers was always irritating to De Kalb. He said that "the great majority of the French officers have returned home." [Undoubtedly due to American ill-will but more directly to an overcrowding in officer ranks.] Because he had obtained a two-year leave of absence from the French Army in order to serve voluntarily in America, De Kalb felt bound to fulfill his commitment. Notwithstanding, he made repeated requests to French authorities for his recall and promotion in the French Army, but his requests were ignored, and so he remained until the Battle of Camden, South Carolina, 16 August 1780, when the general fell gallantly fighting the British in hand-to-hand combat.[22]

Despite Pulaski's warning against naming Stephen Moylan the chief of cavalry, Washington did assign the command of the four small Continental cavalry regiments to the troublemaker. At Valley Forge, 20 March 1778, Washington informed Moylan: "As Count Pulaski has left the Command of the Horse never, I believe, to return to any general command in it again, I have to desire that you will repair to Trenton, and take upon yourself the comd. of that Corps till Congress shall determine further on this head." He urged Moylan to exert himself to the utmost in placing the cavalry in the best order possible so "that they may take the field with some degree of éclat." In his letter, Washington enclosed orders to the commanding officers of Bland's, Sheldon's, and Baylor's regiments to obey Moylan.[23]

The noticeable degree of éclat that Washington expected from Moylan never came about. In fact, the discipline and morale of the cavalry decayed rapidly. Moylan's insolence, disrespect, and cavalier behavior toward Pulaski boomeranged against him. Many of the officers displayed the same indifference and disrespect toward Moylan that he had constantly shown Pulaski. Officers left camp whenever they pleased and without proper authority. Thus, they neglected their duties and preparations for the summer campaign. Washington had cautioned Moylan: "Not a moments time should be lost in repairing the Saddles and other accoutrements; and in getting the Troopers Arms compleated and repaired." However, Washington quickly became disillusioned with Moylan's lack of leadership. On 11 April 1778, he severely criticized Moylan. "Your return of the Cavalry is really vexatious," he stated, and then exclaimed, "But what can be expected when Officers prefer their own ease and emoluments to the good of their Country or to the care and attention which they are in duty bound to pay to the particular Corps they command." Washington ordered Moylan to investigate the conduct of every officer present and determine whether those absent had gone upon furlough regularly obtained. If Moylan found that the officers neglected their duties or were absent without leave, Washington ordered him to "arrest and have them brought to trial." Washington was determined to make examples of those who shamefully neglected their duty and responsibility. The Commander-in-Chief also blamed Moylan for the loss of rank that Lieutenant John Craig suffered. Earlier, Pulaski had selected this able officer for the command of the squadron of lancers while it existed in the brigade. Washington bluntly told Moylan: "I am sorry that this Gentleman has lost his Rank, because you did not take care to procure him the Commission of eldest Lieutenant." By 1780, Moylan's own regiment had dwindled down to only eighteen effective dragoons. It bears repeating that Washington never recommended Moylan to the rank of brigadier general. But Moylan may have seized upon a rumor to prod Washington. This scheming individual wrote Washington on 23 April 1778 that he (Moylan) understood some members of Congress were dissatisfied with the determination of rank between Colonels Bland, Baylor, Sheldon and himself. Washington answered curtly: "If it is so, I have never heard any thing of it from any person but yourself." Although Washington refused to recommend Moylan to the rank of brigadier general, he still felt keenly the need for an effective cavalry chief. On 3 August 1778, he told the President of Congress that the cavalry branch "calls loudly for the appointment of a General Officer." He explained: "For want of a proper regulating head in this Corps, the whole has been in confusion, and of very little service." He blamed the four regimental commanders for their suspicions and distrust of each other, a condition that had largely been fostered by Moylan. Washington further commented; "The principal Officers in it do not harmonize, which circumstance with their disputes about rank would, were there no other Objections, effectually prevent the Corps from rendering the Public the service they have right to expect, and of which it should be capable." He said he could not recommend any officer in the brigade to a general. Not only would the other officers not acquiesce, but also such action would add to the misunderstanding and confusion. Washington suggested either John Cadwalader or Joseph Reed for the command of the cavalry (both declined). As far as the Commander-in-Chief was concerned, Moylan remained unqualified. Moylan finally obtained a brevet promotion in the mass advancement of officers that Congress made at the end of the war in 1783.[24]

Clearly Washington was dissatisfied with Moylan, the acting chief of cavalry. He also had a low opinion of the other regimental commanders of the brigade. When Washington received Colonel Sheldon's status report, he exclaimed: "I scarce know which is greater, my astonishment or vexation, at hearing of the present low condition of your horse." Washington pointed out that the cavalry, like the army as a whole, was exempted from the rigors of a winter campaign so that the regiments could prepare themselves for the summer campaign. In doing so, Washington deprived himself of cavalry for security patrols of the camp at Valley Forge and for stopping the flow of supplies from the countryside to the British in Philadelphia. "But for what purpose did I do this?" an exasperated Washington wrote on 14 April 1778, and continued mockingly, "Why, to furnish the Officers and Men it seems with opportunities of galloping about the Country and by neglect of the Horses, reducing them to a worse condition than those which have been kept upon constant and severe duty the whole Winter"! Washington intimated that Sheldon had failed to carry out his responsibilities as an officer and had thus committed a disservice to his country.[25]

The Continental cavalry continued marginally effective. As usual, the four under strength regiments were dispersed on various and sundry duties. Colonel George Baylor's regiment, in fact, was destroyed by the British at Old Tappan, New Jersey, 28 September 1778. On this occasion, Baylor served under the command of General Wayne, who was charged with harassing a large British foraging expedition along the Hudson River. Baylor occupied the site of Old Tappan. Leading a night attack against Baylor, British General Charles Grey surprised and captured Baylor's twelve-man security guard and then encircled three barns in which about 100 dragoons were sleeping. The British attacked with the bayonet, killing some thirty Americans and capturing fifty, including Baylor. Major Alexander Clough received a mortal wound. Some forty other dragoons escaped. Grey was again accused of showing no mercy for the sleeping troopers. Earlier, he had massacred Wayne's soldiers at Paoli, Pennsylvania. For all practical purposes, Baylor's regiment was wiped out.[26]

About a week after the massacre of Baylor's regiment, Washington was angered again by another surprise attack, this time on Colonel Sheldon's cavalry. One of his patrols was attacked unexpectedly on the Clap Tavern Road in New Jersey on the morning of 7 October 1778. The British killed nine men and eleven horses. Washington called it a "new disgrace which has happened to Sheldon's horse." Washington charged that "these surprises can only be attributed to the unpardonable inattention of Officers, and their scandalous sacrifice of every other consideration to the indulgences of good Quarters." He told Brigadier General Charles Scott that the frequency of the surprise British attacks "becomes intolerable and demands some exemplary punishment." He threatened retaliation: "If any Officer regardless of his own reputation and the important duty he owes the public, suffers himself to be surprised, he cannot expect if taken, that interest should be made for his exchange, or if he saves his person, to escape the Sentence of a Court Martial." Thus, the

Commander-in-Chief became totally disappointed by the poor performance of his regimental cavalry commanders. Ironically, when Pulaski was the commander of the horse, Washington chided him for being too hard on his dragoons! By 1779, Washington had no further use for the cavalry. He ordered the remnants of the regiments to the South.[27]

·4·
The Pulaski Legion

Although Pulaski, gripped with frustration, resigned from the command of cavalry of the Continental Army, he did not abandon the cause of American independence despite his statements about returning to France. In his many letters to Washington and Congress, he kept repeating his passion for freedom. On 19 August 1779, having been hounded by the Treasury Board about expenditures for his Legion, Pulaski bared his soul to Congress:

> …know that as I could not submit to stoop before the sovereigns of Europe, so I came to hazard all for the freedom of America, and desirous of passing the rest of my life in a country truly free, and, before settling as a citizen, to fight for liberty.[1]

Pulaski now fell back on his original plan of raising an independent legion and operating directly under the command of General Washington or another separate army commander. Following the clash at Haddonfield, Pulaski left for Valley Forge to see Washington about organizing the legion. He proposed a corps of 68 cavalrymen and 200 foot soldiers equipped as light infantry. The cavalry would be armed with the lance. Pulaski believed he could fill the ranks of the cavalry quite easily with Americans of good character. However, recruiting the larger number of infantry would prove more challenging due to the expected competition with the states in attracting able-bodied men for the regular Continental Army. Therefore, he sought to persuade Washington to allow more latitude by permitting him to sign up prisoners and deserters from the enemy. Pulaski was thinking of Hessian deserters and prisoners of war who had been forced to come to America and unwillingly fight for British Royalty. On the matter of enlisting the cavalry, Washington advised him to seek the Continental bounty. However, on the subject of deserters and prisoners, Washington pointed out that Congress forbade this practice. In his letter on Pulaski's plan to Henry Laurens, President of Congress, 14 March 1778, Washington wrote: "How far Congress might be inclined to make an exception and license the engaging of prisoners in a particular detached corps, in which such characters may be admitted with less danger than promiscuously in the line, I could not undertake to pronounce." Washington told Laurens that Pulaski expected to retain his rank of brigadier general, and he declared that Pulaski is entitled to it from his general character. Clearly Washington supported Pulaski's continued service. The Commander-in-Chief also praised Pulaski. "I have only to add," Washington concluded, "that the Count's valour and active zeal on all occasions have done him great honor; and...he will render great Services with such a Command as he asks for; I wish him to succeed in his application." At Valley Forge, Colonel John Laurens, aide to Washington, gave Pulaski a letter addressed to his father, Henry Laurens. The son strongly supported Pulaski's proposal and urged his father to approve it. After explaining the purpose and composition of the legion, Colonel Laurens ended with praise for Pulaski. "His zeal for our cause and courage, proof against every danger will cover him with glory, and I hope promote the general interest."[2]

Pulaski traveled to York, Pennsylvania, where Congress had relocated to and presented his plan for an independent legion.

HENRY LAURENS OF SOUTH CAROLINA
He served as President of Congress from 1 November 1777 to 9 December 1778. Of French Huguenot ancestry, he spoke French fluently, as did his son Colonel John Laurens. (Portrait by Charles Willson Peale, 1784. Independence National Historical Park Collection)

CASIMIR PULASKI

COLONEL JOHN LAURENS
Colonel John Laurens served as aide-de-camp to General Washington at Valley Forge. Pulaski and Laurens became staunch friends. When Pulaski asked Congress for approval of an independent legion, Laurens wrote a strong letter of support to his father, President of Congress: "His zeal for our cause and courage, proof against every danger, will cover him with glory, and I hope promote the general interest." (Portrait by Charles Fraser. Courtesy of Gibbes Art Gallery/ Carolina Art Association, Charleston, South Carolina)

The Pulaski Legion

President Laurens referred the plan to the Board of War for its review and recommendation. At the time, General Horatio Gates served as president of the Board. He was favorably disposed toward Pulaski, undoubtedly influenced by his admiration for Pulaski's compatriot Colonel Thaddeus Kosciuszko, whose engineering skill insured the defeat of General John Burgoyne's British Army at Saratoga in October 1777.

Gates discussed the plan with General Charles Lee, on parole while waiting to be exchanged from his prisoner-status. Lee enthusiastically endorsed Pulaski's plan and praised him: "He is a Polander whose genius is adapted to the light or expedite war—in the second place he has had much practice in the best schools—is undoubtedly brave and enterprising." Lee recommended expanding the legion to 1200 soldiers—400 cavalry and 800 light infantry drafted with young men from the Continental regiments. Lee also favored incorporating the cavalry of Major Henry Lee, Jr. into Pulaski's legion, promoting Lee to lieutenant colonel, and placing him in charge of the legion's cavalry. He predicted that his proposed corps, led by Pulaski and Lee, "will render more effectual service than any ten Regiments on the Continent." General Lee's organizational idea was bold, indeed, and sounded very promising. However, the Board of War stuck to Pulaski's original proposal of 68 horse and 200 foot.[3]

The members of the Board of War, Gates, Timothy Pickering, and Richard Peters, submitted a very favorable report to Congress, 19 March 1778. Just eight days later, Congress, after considering the report, resolved:

> That the Count Pulaski retain his Brigadier in the army of the United States and that he raise and have command of an independent corps to consist of sixty-eight horse and two hundred foot, the horse to be armed with lances, and the foot equipped in the manner of light infantry....

The resolution gave Washington the oversight for enlistments in the Legion in the manner that the Commander-in-Chief thought "expedient and proper." As to the sticky point of recruiting deserters from the enemy, Congress also authorized Washington to "dispense, in this particular instance, with the resolve of Congress against enlisting deserters."[4]

Pulaski set up his recruiting headquarters at the home of Mrs. Ross in Baltimore, perhaps determining in advance that his organizational effort would have more success in Maryland. He was right. The legislature placed his Legion on the same footing as those of Maryland units and facilitated his work in other ways. Thus, Pulaski could offer the Maryland bounty of $40 in addition to the Continental bounty of $20. Besides Baltimore, Pulaski recruited in Easton, Pennsylvania, with Colonel Michael Kovatch in charge, and at Trenton under Captain Henry Bedkin. Major Count de Montfort directed the recruiting operation in Baltimore. General Washington positively assisted Pulaski to achieve his goal. He gave him the opportunity to select his cadre from the four cavalry regiments. Washington gave the following order to Moylan on 9 April 1778: "Brigadier General Count Pulaski is hereby authorized to draught from each Regiment of horse, two Privates of his own choice with their horses, Arms and Accoutrements, and one Serjeant belonging to Sheldon's Regiment." Being familiar with the more capable troopers in the four regiments, Pulaski had his pick of personnel.[5]

Congress, too, eased the way for Pulaski. It gave persons enlisting in the Legion the Continental bounty and allowed the one promised by the states. To eliminate rivalry between the Legion and the states, Congress authorized the states to credit persons recruited for the Legion to their own quotas of Continental soldiers. At Trenton, Bedkin recruited vigorously with an attractive notice in *The New Jersey Gazette* of 23 April 1778, in which he promised the members of the Legion an exciting life of close engagement with the enemy. He compared Pulaski's Legion to the legions of history. "All those who desire to distinguish themselves in the service of their Country," the notice read, "are invited to enlist in that corps, which is established on the same principles as the Roman legions were." In Baltimore, Major Count de Montfort managed to snare from Maryland units twelve soldiers who

The Pulaski Legion

already had enlisted in those units. General William Smallwood became outraged and protested to Washington that some of Pulaski's officers enlisted several men out of the drafts and recruits belonging to Maryland. Washington ordered Pulaski, "That every man so inlisted be immediately returned and delivered to General Smallwood or any officer of the Maryland troops."[6]

General Pulaski eagerly sought to complete the enlistment of his Legion and enter the field of battle. His recruiting officers began to take some British prisoners in addition to Hessian prisoners of war. When Washington learned of the practice, he put a stop to it. On 1 May 1778, he called Pulaski's attention to his earlier permission to enlist one-third deserters for the infantry, being induced to believe that Pulaski would enlist mainly Germans in whom a greater confidence could be placed. As for the British, Washington explained: "The British prisoners will cheerfully inlist, as a ready means of escaping; the Continental bounty will be lost and your Corps as far as ever from being complete." Nevertheless, the American Revolution was a fight among Englishmen. American "patriots" turned unreliable, too. The record shows many instances when they deserted to the British side, and some with vital intelligence just prior to important battles. Historian Edward J. Lowell asserts: "Neither among the English nor among the Germans was desertion so prevalent as among the Americans." Lowell, however, brings out one big difference: "The British or German soldier could only desert to the enemy," while "The American militiaman generally returned to his home." With regard to the British prisoners of war, Washington ordered Pulaski to return them to confinement and in the future to adhere to the restrictions that the Commander-in-Chief had laid down. Washington also reminded Pulaski that his cavalry were to be, without exception, Americans with ties to property and family. On 5 June 1778, the Board of War revoked Pulaski's authority to enlist prisoners.[7]

Although Pulaski had obtained two troopers from each of the four cavalry regiments and one sergeant, he asked Washington to transfer sixteen more, four from each regiment. Washington refused this time because, he said, the transfers would simply redistribute military personnel without increasing their number. Washington undoubtedly realized that further stripping of troopers from the Continental cavalry would appear to be favoritism for Pulaski's Legion and lead to dissatisfaction and resentment in the four Continental cavalry regiments. The addition of sixteen cavalrymen could have been a financial gain for Pulaski because of the high cost of horses, saddles, weapons, and other items of equipment. The resultant loss in manpower, however, was quickly made up by vigorous recruiting.[8]

Pulaski had no difficulty in selecting experienced officers for the Legion. Washington assisted him greatly by granting him the privilege of choosing his own officers. On 9 April 1778, the Commander-in-Chief informed the Committee of Congress for the Affairs of the Army: "As I know the superior confidence which a Commandant places in officers of his own choice, I have given him my approbation of the Gentlemen whom he has nominated." Washington's wise policy became the standard practice in the United States. During the massive expansion of the army during World War II, for example, newly-designated division commanders had the privilege of selecting the key officers of their divisions, consistent with other requirements of the army.[9]

Although the Legion had a few American officers, the majority were European. Many of them had languished in America because they were not welcome in the Continental Army. General Pulaski, however, gave them a chance to fight. He had the very capable Michael Kovatch whom Pulaski named Colonel Commandant of the Legion, a position of authority next to Pulaski's. Baron Carl August von Bose became commander of the infantry with the rank of lieutenant colonel. He was a scion of a prominent Saxon family in Europe. Jan Zielinski, long delayed a commission because of his altercation with Colonel Moylan, was finally commissioned captain and assigned the commander of the first company of lancers. Waiting expectantly for more than a year for Congress to appoint him to a cavalry unit, Count Julius de Montfort got his chance when Pulaski selected

> Head Quarters 9th April 1778.
>
> Gentlemen
>
> By a Resolve of Congress, the appointment of officers to the Corps which Brigadier General Count Pulaski is authorised to raise, has been refered to your decision in conjunction with me as I know the superior confidence a Commandant places in officers of his own choice, I have given him my approbation of the Gentlemen whom he has nominated; it remains with you to decide in their favor, or have others substituted.
>
> I have the honor to be with the greatest respect
>
> Gentlemen
>
> Your most obedt Servt
>
> G Washington

Writing to the Committee of Congress for the Affairs of the Army, 9 April 1778, General George Washington established a wise policy that the United States Army has followed. Washington wrote: "...as I know the superior confidence which a Commandant places in his officers of his own choice, I have given him my approbation of the Gentlemen whom he has nominated." (Papers of the Continental Congress)

him for Brigade-Major. De Montfort, an experienced officer, had served as a first lieutenant in Colonel Thomas Hartley's Continental Regiment. Kovatch, Zielinski, and De Montfort were the first officers in the Legion to be nominated and approved by Congress, 18 April 1778. Other officers joined the Legion in quick succession. As captain, Paul Bentalou took command of the second company of dragoons. He, too. was an experienced officer. Bentalou came to America from France before the end of 1776. He sought a commission in one of the four Continental regiments of dragoons, but there were no vacancies. To fulfill his desire of fighting for American independence, he entered the infantry as a private and was assigned to the German battalion commanded by Colonel Nicholas Haussegger. Bentalou fought in the Battles of Brandywine and Germantown and rose to the rank of second lieutenant, but he became dissatisfied with the troubles in the battalion (his reasons included Haussegger's desertion from the unit) and resigned in November 1777. He joined Pulaski's Legion on 20 April 1778 and was commissioned captain. The Pennsylvanian, Henry Bedkin, who quit Moylan's regiment in disgust, assumed command of the third company of dragoons. The Frenchman Jerome Le Brun de Bellecour, Pulaski's aide-de-camp, was promoted to captain and the command of the first company of infantry. Another French officer was the young Le Chevalier Maria Blaise Jacques de Segond de Sederon. He first served as lieutenant in the Regiment de la Martinique in the Caribbean Sea. At age twenty, he volunteered for the Continental Army, taking part in the battles of Brandywine, Germantown, and Whitemarsh. He was with Washington's Army at Valley Forge during the winter of 1777-78. Eager for active field duty, he asked Lafayette to help him gain an assignment in Pulaski's Legion. On 10 April 1778, Lafayette wrote President Henry Laurens:

> I take also the Liberty of recommending to Congress a gentleman Mr de second who has been introduced to me by the desire of my father in law the duke of dayen, and I beg you would mention my desire of seeing him employed—Count de pulaski has told me he would make him a Captain in his Legion which if

The Pulaski Legion

Congress approves of it will suit that gentleman very well.

I have no doubt but that Count de pulaski will obtain what he desires—if ever a good, active, indefatigable officer, a brave and honest man as far as these expressions can be extended, and a man of notice and reputation in the world, is entitled to the Consideration of Congress the count deserves it on every respect.

Lafayette's letter clearly shows that the Marquis not only endorsed and supported the organization of Pulaski's Independent Legion but also urged the Pole to select French officers for his unit. Historian Louis Gottschalk calls Lafayette the self-appointed spokesman for Frenchmen in America. As usual, Lafayette was persuasive with Congress, and De Segond was commissioned captain on 22 April 1778. Pulaski placed him in command of the second company of infantry of the Legion. Pulaski's Polish comrade, Frederick Paschke from the Confederation of Bar, was also commissioned captain and assigned command of the third infantry company. Paschke was an experienced officer, having joined Colonel Thomas Proctor's Pennsylvania Artillery Regiment as a lieutenant since 14 March 1777. When Congress gave Pulaski his Independent Legion, Paschke turned to his former commander in Poland. Pulaski made the Italian, Joseph Baldesqui, paymaster and captain of the supernumerary company. Additional company grade officers entered the Legion: Lieutenants William Palmer, John Seydelin, James de Bronville, Francois de Roth, William Welch, John Stey, Francois Antoine de Troye, and Joseph de la Borderie, with George Elton and Adam Melchior as officer cornets of the cavalry. Nicholas Jacques Emanuel de Belleville served as surgeon. Dr. Belleville was Pulaski's former schoolmate. At the time of Pulaski's arrival in Paris in 1775, Belleville was an intern at a military hospital where his father served as resident physician. Pulaski had entered France quietly, uncertain how the authorities would receive him. He was sick and destitute, worn out with fatigue and exposure. He turned to Belleville who welcomed the old friend to his apartment, cared for him, and contacted Pulaski's other friends in France. By 1 May 1778, Pulaski told Congress that he expected the recruiting

THE PULASKI LEGION

Brigadier General Casimir Pulaski

Commander

Col. Michael Kovatch *(Hungarian)*

Legion Commandant

Maj. Count Julius De Montfort *(French)*

Lt. Col. Baron Carl Von Bose *(Saxon)*

Cavalry   **Brigade Major**   **Infantry**

Nicholas Jacque Emauel de Bellville *(French)*

Capt. Samuel Sullivan *(American)*

Surgeon   **Quartermaster**

Capt. Jan Zielinski *(Polish)*

Capt. Jerome Le Brun de Bellecour *(French)*

1st Lancers   **1st Company**

Capt. Paul Bentalou *(French)*

Capt. Maria Blaise Jacques de Segond *(French)*

2nd Dragoons   **2nd Company**

Capt. Henry Bedkin *(American)*

Capt. Frederick Paschke *(Polish)*

3rd Dragoons   **3rd Company**

Capt. Joseph Baldesqui *(Italian)*

Supernumerary Company

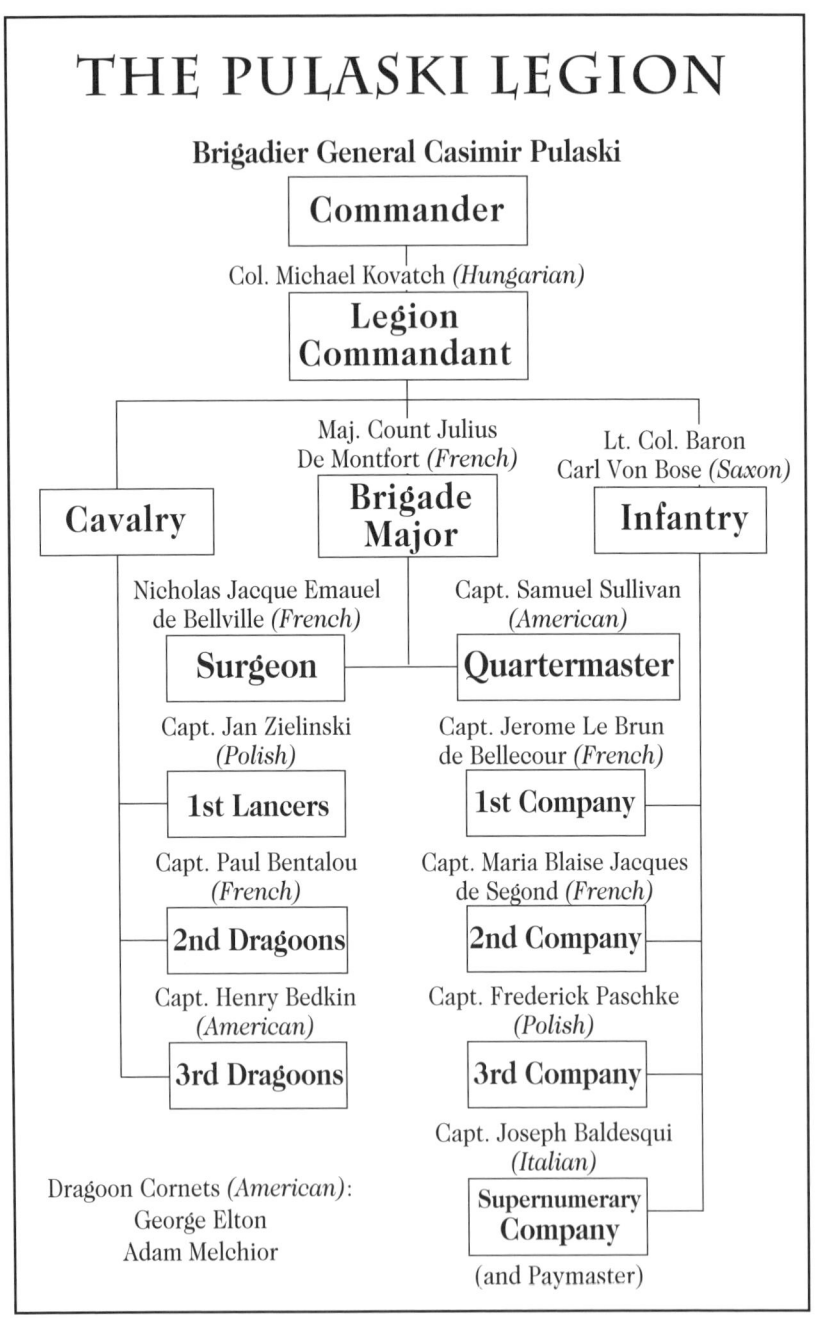

Dragoon Cornets *(American)*:
George Elton
Adam Melchior

(and Paymaster)

Figure 1. Officers of the Pulaski Legion, September 1778

for the Legion to be completed in four weeks. In numbers, he did better than he had hoped, gaining a total of 330 men.[10]

Recruiting the manpower for his Legion was one goal, but equipping the cavalry and infantry was more challenging. The Legion must have horses, weapons, uniforms, camp equipment, and many other items essential to a combat unit. Pulaski needed money immediately to pay the $20 Continental bounty for each enlistment. Congress voted him $10,000 for purchasing horses and recruiting his corps, 1 April 1778. Five days later, Congress resolved that General Pulaski receive "for every man inlisted and mustered in his legion and who shall be furnished by the said brigadier with the following articles of clothing and accoutrements [Enumerated in Note 11] one hundred and thirty dollars, including the Continental bounty money." To permit Pulaski "to raise and equip his legion with the utmost despatch," the Board of War authorized the Treasury to advance from time to time sums of money not to exceed $50,000. However, Pulaski had to wait a month before he received the first sum of $10,000 on 7 May 1778, followed by $16,000 more on May 11th, and the balance of $24,000 on May 27th (the money was depreciated Continental currency). The same resolution of Congress authorized Pulaski to grant the additional state bounty to anyone signed up in a given state and that enlistment "shall be credited to the quota of the State in which they shall be inlisted."[11]

Prices during the war escalated sharply, as merchants increased them on practically all items. When Congress failed to provide the funds promptly, Pulaski reached into his own pocket for more than $16,000. Horses were especially costly. On one occasion, Captain Bentalou had to pay $400 for a horse. Even General Washington rebelled at the price of horses, including old nags and the sickly. An exasperated Washington remarked: "A Rat in the shape of a horse is not to be bought at this time for less than £200." To safeguard his costly investment in horses, Pulaski had them branded with the initials "I.L." (Independent Legion).[12]

The sum of $50,000 voted by Congress for Pulaski was expended before the Legion was fully equipped. So on 11 May 1778,

Pulaski asked for $10,000 more. Writing the President of Congress, he explained: "You know that the sum of 50,000 Dollars is not sufficient enough to buy the horses whom thei ask the foolish price everywhere." The value of the Continental currency was falling rapidly daily. Washington complained that "a waggon load of money will scarcely purchase a waggon load of provisions." Congress, therefore, responded favorably to Pulaski's request for more money. On 20 August 1778, it resolved that "a warrant issue on Thomas Smith, Esq. commissioner of the continental loan office in the State of Pennsylvania, on the application of the Board of War and Ordnance, for 17,786 dollars, to be paid to Joseph Nourse, their paymaster, and to be by him forwarded to Brigadier General Count Pulaski, for the equipping of his legion."[13]

Having granted equal status to Pulaski's recruits and those enlisting in Maryland units, the Maryland Council authorized the issue of quartermaster and camp equipment for the personnel of the Legion who were credited to the state's quota of Continentals. The Council's help was of substantial financial worth, as Pulaski concentrated his recruiting effort in Maryland. *Military Collector & Historian* suggests that "at least 100 Marylanders succumbed to the lure of a 'martial appearance' and the implied possibility of a double bounty (state and Continental)." During a six-week period, Captain De Segond received from Maryland supply bases such sundry items as shoes, overalls, linen for shirts, cloth for officers' cloaks, canteens, camp kettles, some rifles and pistols. Soon the legionnaires began to make a presentable appearance, and Pulaski bent every effort to complete the organization and equipping of his Independent Legion.[14]

Historian Harold L. Peterson writes that the exact style of the uniform for the Pulaski Legion is unknown, as yet. However, the basic elements have been recorded:

> Both horse and foot had blue coats, and helmets with black turbans, a star, white feathers, and horsehair crests. The cavalry wore leather breeches and sleeve waistcoats, boots, and blue and gray cloaks. Trumpeters had green lace trimmings and sergeants

wore silver lace. The infantry had gaiters and white smallcoats and all ranks had white buttons marked "USA."

Pulaski replaced the white buttons with silver buttons stamped "P. L." for the Pulaski Legion. As to arms, the light infantry carried muskets, bayonets, and tomahawks; the cavalry was armed with sabres, pistols, rifled carbines, and lances.[15]

The Legion commander traveled to his recruiting stations in Pennsylvania, New Jersey, and Maryland, personally engaging with the recruits. He visited Bethlehem, Pennsylvania, as well, hoping to find saddlers, glovers, and founders, who could be hired to do work for the Legion. He also wanted to visit his friend Marquis de Lafayette who was recovering there from wounds he had suffered at the Battle of Brandywine. Pulaski arrived in Bethlehem on 16 April 1778 in the company of Colonel Kovatch. The visit is noted in the Moravian Records:

> On Maundy Thursday, they assembled in the Old Chapel for the reading of the tragedy of Gethsemane, and were astonished to see two distinguished officers enter the chapel. The bearing of the officers at once denoted they were men of high position. They reverently seated themselves and followed the service with close attention. After the service it was found they were Count Casimir Pulaski and Colonel Kobatsch. This was the first visit of Pulaski to Bethlehem but not the last.[16]

Pulaski remained in the vicinity of Bethlehem for the next month. Historian John Hill Martin writes that Pulaski detailed members of his staff to protect the Sisters' House, "surrounded as they were by rough and uncouth soldiery." In appreciation of his thoughtfulness, Eldress Susan von Gersdorf proposed that the Sisters sew a banner for the Legion and present it to Pulaski as a compliment for his chivalry. Rebecca and Erdmuth Langley, English women, embroidered the silken banner. They were assisted by Julia Bader, Anna Blum, Anna Hussey, Maria Rosina Schultz, and Anna Maria Weiss. Pulaski returned to Bethlehem on Sunday May 17 with a small unit of legionnaires. He held a dress parade and marched the Legionnaires to the Moravian service, which Samuel Adams and a Dr. Foster also attended. At the service, the Sisters presented the General with the beautiful banner. In 1825, American poet Henry Wadsworth Longfellow captured the joyful occasion with the poem "Hymn of the Moravian Nuns of Bethlehem at the Consecration of Pulaski's Banner."[17]

Lossing writes that after the American Revolution the banner was displayed in the procession that welcomed the Marquis de Lafayette to Baltimore in 1824. It was then placed in Peale's Museum. In 1844, Edmund Peale presented the banner to the Maryland Historical Society where it is preserved to this day. In 1937, artist George Gray created a painting of Pulaski receiving the banner from the Moravian Sisters. The attractive painting forms one scene of a mural at the Hotel Bethlehem in Bethlehem, Pennsylvania.[18]

While Pulaski worked tirelessly to organize and ready his Legion for combat in the shortest time, he closely followed and studied the evolving war between the British and the Americans. Invariably, he compared his four-year-long battle against the hated Russians in Poland to military operations in America. He expressed his observations to Henry Laurens on 5 July 1778: "I believe that this campaign [summer of 1778] will be very instructive," he wrote. Concluding that the British wanted to draw the Americans into general battles, Pulaski advised against such strategy and cautioned that Americans must avoid losing the gains they already made. He understood the British objective of suppressing the rebellion as quickly as possible and stressed that "the English must risk every thing for the present, or entirely

---

OPPOSITE PHOTO: *PULASKI LEGIONNAIRE (INFANTRY). The smartly-dressed Legionnaire drew praise from Admiral D'Estaing's French troops at Savannah, Georgia, in 1779. Historian Alexander A. Lawrence wrote: "Among the American regulars only Pulaski's outfit was to impress the French." (Drawn by artist Anna Hornkohl and based on descriptive historical data. From* Pulaski, A Portrait of Freedom (1979), *with the permission of author R. D. Jamro.)*

The Pulaski Legion

Casimir Pulaski

Hymn of the Moravian Nuns of Bethlehem
At the Consecration of Pulaski's Banner

When the dying flame of day
Through the chancel shot its ray,
Far the glimmering tapers shed
Faint light on the cowled head;
And the censer burning swung,
Where, before the altar, hung
The crimson banner, that with prayer
Had been consecrated there.
And the nuns' sweet hymn was heard the while,
Swung low, in the dim, mysterious aisle.

"Take thy banner! May it wave
Proudly o'er the good and brave;
When the battle's distant wail
Breaks the sabbath of our vale,
When the clarion's music thrills
To the hearts of these lone hills,
When the spear in conflict shakes,
And the strong lance shivering breaks.

"Take thy banner! and, beneath
The battle-cloud's encircling wreath,
Guard it, till out homes are free!
Guard it! God will prosper thee!
In the dark and trying hour,
In the breaking forth of power
In the rush of steeds and men,
His right hand will shield thee then.

"Take thy banner! But when night
Closes round the ghastly fight,
If the vanquished warrior bow,
Spare him! By our holy vow,
By our prayers and many tears,
By the mercy that endears,
Spare him! he our love hath shared!
Spare him! as thou wouldst be spared!

"Take thy banner! and if e'er
Thou shouldst press the soldier's bier.
And the muffled drum should beat,
To the tread of mournful feet,
Then this crimson flag shall be
Martial cloak and shroud for thee."

The warrior took that banner proud,
And it was his martial cloak and shroud!

—Henry Wadsworth Longfellow (1825)

74

Created by George Gray in 1937, the painting is one of seven historical events forming a mural at Hotel Bethlehem in Bethlehem, Pennsylvania. (Photo courtesy of The Moravian Museum of Bethlehem)

THE HISTORIC BANNER OF THE PULASKI LEGION

The size of the banner is twenty inches square made of double crimson silk. The designs are embroidered with yellow silk. The letters are shaded green. A deep green buillon fringe ornaments the edges.

On one side of the banner are the letters U. S. and in a circle around them the Latin words UNITA VIRTUS FORTIOR (United Valor Is Stronger). Historian Benson J. Lossing wrote in 1851 that the letter c in Forcior of the orginal banner is incorrect; it should be a t. The replica shown above spells Fortior correctly.

The letters U. S. (United States) are believed to be the first time (1778) that U. S. was displayed on a banner or flag.

(Banner photos are the gift of Michael Ciesielski Photography of Baltimore, Maryland)

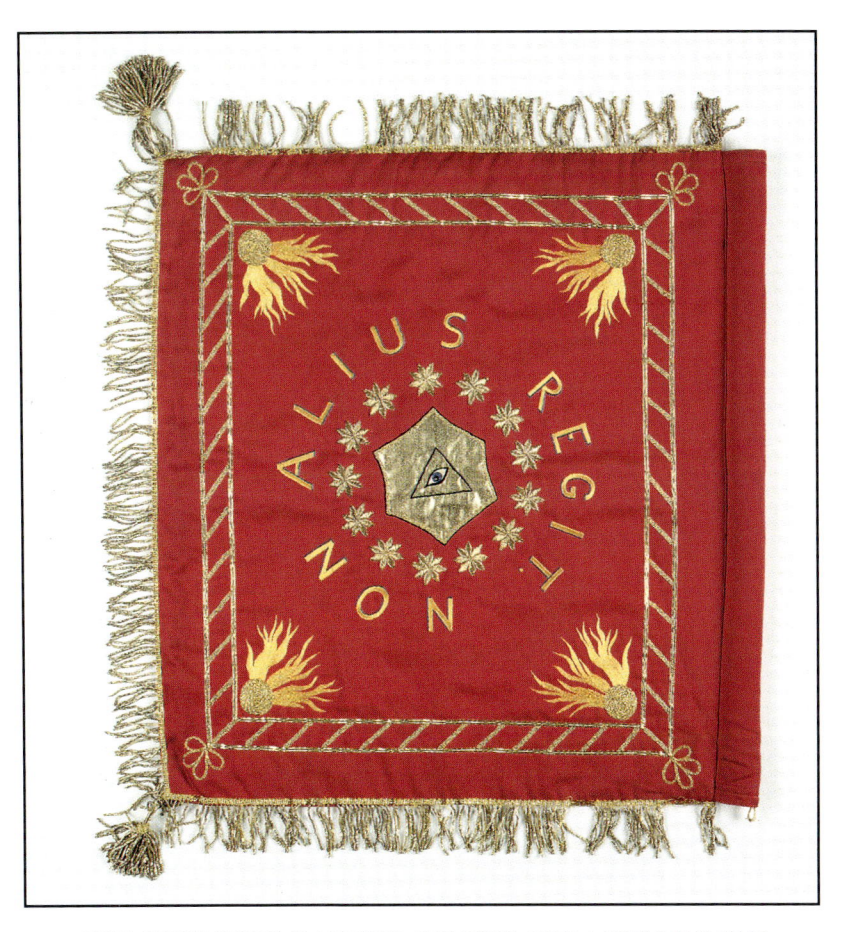

THE HISTORIC BANNER OF THE PULASKI LEGION

(Obverse Side): In the center is the All-Seeing Eye and the words NON ALIUS REGIT (No Other Governs). The banner was attached to a lance when carried into the field. After more than 200 years of exposure to the environment, the original banner at the Maryland Historical Society faded to a dull brownish red. In 1976, the Polish Heritage Association of Maryland commissioned Sister Irene Olkowska of the Sister Servants of Mary Immaculate to sew two replicas of the Pulaski Banner. The Association presented one replica to the Maryland Historical Society and the second to the Sons of the American Revolution, Maryland Chapter, who display it with the Color Guard at patriotic observances. (Sources: Benson J. Lossing, The Pictorial Field-Book of the American Revolution, *I: 392-93; and Stanley A. Ciesielski, President of the Polish Heritage Association of Maryland, to the author)*

PULASKI BANNER MARKER
In Bethlehem, Pennsylvania, the marker calls attention to the historic deed of the Moravian Single Sisters who made the banner for Pulaski's Legion and presented it to the General in Bethlehem on Sunday, May 17, 1778. (Erected by the Pennsylvania Historical and Museum Commission. Photo by the author, 25 September 1999)

abandon America." He posed the best strategy for Americans: "I believe it then necessary that our great object should be not to risk every thing on the fate of one general engagement, and by many detachments, observe the movements of the enemy, disconcert them whenever possible, cut off their divisions at favorable opportunities, rather than to attack them with our whole army." Pulaski's strategy was sound, and General Washington learned it himself the hard way. In the early phases of the rebellion, Washington engaged the British in general battles. As a result, he got trounced at the Battles of Long Island, Brandywine, and Germantown. To revive America's resultant sagging spirit, he executed during the Christmas Season of 1777-78 two surprise attacks on Hessian mercenaries at Trenton and Princeton. These successful attacks for limited objectives fell into Pulaski's strategy of "cutting off their divisions at favorable opportunities."

General Washington opened the summer campaign of 1778 with the great Battle of Monmouth, New Jersey, 28 June 1778. He won it by a display of decisive leadership. Subsequently, he preferred to follow a waiting game. He disposed of his divisions around the British in New York, always interposing strong forces between New York and the Highlands of the Hudson, so as to protect the construction of Fortress West Point under the Polish engineer, Colonel Thaddeus Kosciuszko. Washington waited nearly two years for an opportunity to strike a decisive blow. That opportunity presented itself when General Lord Cornwallis marched his army into Virginia and reached Yorktown.

While Washington waited and watched British General Sir Henry Clinton in New York, General Nathanael Greene conducted a brilliant mobile campaign against Cornwallis in the South. Greene's rapid movements were assisted materially by his engineer, Kosciuszko. Greene did not hesitate to attack Cornwallis, even though he possessed inferior numbers. His guiding principle, however, was not to lose his army, as General Horatio Gates had done at Camden, South Carolina, 16 August 1780. At times, Greene might have won a battle, had he committed his Continentals at a critical point of the battle. However, he practiced caution, preferring to withdraw rather than risk the destruction of his regular units, the core of his army. He expressed his tactics: "We fight, get beat, rise and fight again." General Cornwallis, after defeating Greene at the Battle of Guilford Court House, North Carolina, 15 March 1781, marched his army into Virginia and Yorktown. There General Washington, French General Rochambeau, and French Admiral De Grasse bagged Cornwallis' whole army. The British government now stopped the fighting and began negotiations for peace.[19]

By August 1778, Pulaski had organized his Legion with a total strength of 330 men, exceeding the authorized strength of 268. Knowing how quickly units became under strength in Washington's Army, he added a reserve for the expected losses, due to sickness, combat casualties, desertions, and other reasons. Once the Legion entered the field of operations, there would be little time for recruiting. In the matter of equipment, Pulaski had managed to clothe and equip his legionnaires to a respectable degree. He was eager to lead the Legion into battle, and he became impatient when he learned of Washington's opening his summer campaign with a major attack on the British at Monmouth, New Jersey, 28 June 1778. Pulaski first introduced the Legion with a public review for Maryland authorities and civilians of Baltimore. *The Maryland Journal and Baltimore Advertiser* reported the event:

> On Wednesday last [July 29], the Hon. General Count Pulaski reviewed his independent Legion in this Town. They made a martial appearance and performed many Manoeuvres in a manner that reflected the highest Honour on both officers and privates.[20]

Pulaski had one remaining goal to realize before he could enter the fighting: The final acceptance of his Legion by Congress. He marched his legionnaires to Wilmington, Delaware, and wrote Richard Henry Lee, Virginia delegate to Congress. Pulaski's purpose was to gain Lee's support and the attention of Congress for a planned review and inspection in Philadelphia. Writing on 13 August 1778, he informed Lee:

> I have arrived here two days ago with all the cavalry, and expecting the infantry in four, will present myself with my corps to Congress, to pass the review in the end of this month, and pursue the enemy immediately after. I should have been very glad to be ready sooner, but I hope everybody shall be persuaded, that it is not the business of one day to raise and form a Corps.[21]

When Colonel Kovatch and his infantry joined Pulaski, the entire Legion spruced up their uniforms, arms, accoutrements, and groomed their horses, as well. On 25 August 1778, Pulaski's Legion proudly entered Philadelphia to the sound of the cavalry's trumpets. Meanwhile, the delegates to Congress gathered outside the doors of Independence Hall to watch the military procession. As the companies of lancers approached the delegates, the lancers saluted them. The colorful Legionnaires followed on foot, carrying the crimson banner of the Legion. A crowd of spectators around Independence Square loudly cheered the splendid-looking Legionnaires. Congress was favorably impressed. The French minister to America, Conrad Alexandre Gerard, was also present at the review. Two weeks earlier he singled out and praised Pulaski's horsemen and Major Henry Lee's as the best and most useful cavalry in the Continental Army.[22]

Pulaski and his Independent Legion were ready to join Washington's Army. Trouble for Pulaski, however, was brewing in the Treasury Board of Congress. Paymaster Baldesqui could not provide detailed paperwork for all the purchases and expenditures of the recruiting officers scattered over three states. Pulaski experienced a new frustration as Congress threatened to withhold his employment in the field until all accounts were cleared up. (They finally were settled in November 1779). This author believes the auditors' action was petty and relegates this episode to an appendix. The auditors placed administration above operations in importance: a classic case of the administrative tail wagging the operational dog.

· 5 ·
Betrayal at Little egg Harbor

General Pulaski was eager to take his Legion into battle against the British. Congress, however, delayed him with its insistence that he first account for the expenditures of his Legion. Pulaski was not an administrative general, and he detested paperwork. As Polish historian Wladyslaw Konopczynski aptly observes: "It was desired that Pulaski wave the sword with one hand and do bookkeeping with the other." Pulaski assigned Paymaster Baldesqui the task of overseeing the expenditures of the Legion. A conscientious officer, Baldesqui had acquired hundreds of receipts of small sums to substantial ones from the recruiting and purchasing officers. These receipts were accumulated quickly because of the rapid organization of the Legion. Baldesqui needed time to sort out and prepare the paperwork in the manner demanded by the auditors. As the Legion languished in Philadelphia, Pulaski tried to prod Congress into action. On 17 September 1778, he protested to Congress that, having come to America to fight for independence, he was full of desire to carry out this goal. "The revue is passed," he wrote; "there remains but for me to ask payment of the Soldiers, and commissions for the officers, with permission to march for the enemy."[1]

Two incidents in Congress at this time caused further indecision on ordering Pulaski's Legion into battle. One was instigated by Joseph Reed, a delegate hostile to Pulaski. As Chairman of the Committee of Arrangements, he posed several questions to George Washington about the recruiting of deserters and prisoners of war. Reed was adamantly opposed to the policy. Previously, Washington had forbidden Pulaski to enlist British prisoners of war, except Hessian soldiers. Reed was guessing when he claimed that "one-half of which [the Legion] is composed of Deserters and Prisoners," and he predicted "that upon strict Scrutiny there will be found a much greater Proportion." Nevertheless, Pulaski's recruiting officers had signed up these deserters and prisoners and, undoubtedly, had examined their loyalty and usefulness. Evidently Reed knew better than the Legion commander the kind of soldiers needed. Having recruited them, Pulaski would have to fight with them. Reed also told Washington that, if the undesirable soldiers are purged, a sufficient number should remain to compose the original strength of 68 horse and 200 foot. On this score, Reed again was objecting to Pulaski exceeding the authorized number of 268. Assuming that one-half were released, the strength of the Legion would fall from the high of 330 to 165 and be decimated as a consequence. Washington answered Reed on 6 October 1778. The Commander-in-Chief, always respectful of Congress, had some difficulty in answering Reed's sticky questions. After all, Congress itself was ambivalent on the question of enlisting deserters and prisoners of war. Congress encouraged the desertion of Hessian soldiers of the British Army and felt obliged to integrate them into the Continental Army. With respect to Pulaski's Legion, Washington explained that the special circumstances of its organization prompted him to make an exception and permit the enlistment of deserters, up to one-third of the Legion's infantry. He pointed to the resolve of Congress of 28 March 1778 in which Congress empowered him to make the decision, provided "I should deem it not injurious to the service." In the matter of Pulaski exceeding the authorized strength of 268, Washington said he had not given the matter any thought.

Betrayal at Little Egg Harbor

He admitted that there would be no injustice in reducing the extra number. However, he added: "But whether as the men are raised and clad and the expence already incurred, it may not be as well to risk the additional disadvantage which may attend bringing them into the field is a question which Congress will decide." As far as it is known, Pulaski's Legion, composed as it was for the review that passed Congress on 25 August 1778, remained intact. In a short while at Little Egg Harbor, the Legion's number dropped to about 250. Reed's criticism appears to have been mere sniping.[2] (A curious connection seems to have existed between Reed and Colonel Stephen Moylan, enemy of Pulaski. Reed and Moylan knew and corresponded with each other. Because Moylan took advantage of his acquaintance with Washington to vent his spleen against Pulaski directly to the Commander-in-Chief, it appears reasonable to assume that Moylan also denigrated Pulaski in correspondence with Reed. Thus, in some degree, Moylan may have prejudiced Reed toward Pulaski).

The second incident that kept the Legion languishing in Philadelphia was provoked by Thomas McKean, delegate to Congress and Chief Justice of Pennsylvania. The incident began when a member(s) of Pulaski's Legion refused to pay for property from a civilian in Philadelphia County. The citizen complained to the sheriff who then attempted to serve General Pulaski an arrest warrant. The General loyally defended his men and resisted the sheriff. Justice McKean then took the complaint formally to Congress on 2 October 1778. Congress was aghast at Pulaski's resistance to civil authority and ordered him to appear at the War Office for questioning the next morning. Writing to James Warren about the incident, Samuel Adams revealed some details. He said: "The count acted upon the principle of honor. The debt was for the support of his Legion, and he thought the charge unreasonable, as it probably was." After the Board adjusted the price, it paid the debt, and the creditor was satisfied. For Pulaski, the incident was a humiliating experience.[3]

The problem of Pulaski's soldiers with merchants and shopkeepers was not unique. The Legionnaires undoubtedly showed resentment when civilians demanded high prices and profits, despite the fact that soldiers were willing to endure the hardships of military life while fighting for the freedom of all. Another case of military versus civilian authority, like that of Pulaski and the sheriff, involved an officer of Major Henry Lee's Legion. Lieutenant Patrick Carnes was charged by Governor George Clinton of New York for illegally seizing forage, and Major Lee was accused of preventing the sheriff from arresting Carnes. The Governor complained to Washington, 25 November 1778, who chastised Lee. "This complaint I confess gives me extreme pain," Washington wrote, "as there is nothing I wish so much as a perfect good understanding and Harmony between the Inhabitants and every part of the Army." He insisted that Carnes must be amenable to civil authority and that Lee must permit law officers to carry out their duties. Although Washington upheld the authority of civilian government over the military, he undoubtedly understood the frustrations of his soldiers with the constant lack of support.[4]

It is no wonder that Pulaski was anxious to get out of Philadelphia. Fortunately, Washington himself prodded Congress to order Pulaski's Legion into the field. On 19 September 1778, he urged the Board of War to employ Pulaski's Legion without delay. "I think it will be best for them to join the Army," Washington said, "if Congress should concur with me in sentiment." Anticipating that Congress would agree, Washington instructed Pulaski on the same day to be prepared to join the Army. Washington followed up his contingent order with a positive one on 29 September 1778. "You are to proceed immediately upon receipt of this, with your whole Corps both Horse and Foot and put yourself under the command of Major General Lord Stirling, who will be in the Neighborhood of Paramus." Washington had composed a force in Northern New Jersey, consisting of the brigades of Generals William Woodford and William Maxwell, Pulaski's Legion, and militia, all under the command of Stirling, whose mission was to stop British foraging in the area and maintain contact with the forts in the Highlands.[5]

Betrayal at Little Egg Harbor

Persuaded by the Commander-in-Chief and temporarily putting aside its preoccupation with the Legion's accounts, Congress resolved that "Count Pulaski, with his legion and continental soldiers fit for service in and near Philadelphia" join the army. Reaching Princeton, Pulaski received new emergency orders— On 5 October 1778, Congress directed Pulaski to "assist in the defence of Little Egg Harbor" in order to counter the British attack on the American privateer base there. Having committed Pulaski to combat, Congress moved briskly to commission the officers of the Legion whose appointments had been left pending. On the same day, 5 October, the delegates commissioned the officers and rushed the appointments to Pulaski by express courier.[6] Evidently the unexpected danger to the American base at Little Egg Harbor alarmed and spurred Congress into action.

Little Egg Harbor, lying on the east coast of New Jersey, is separated from the Atlantic Ocean by a narrow sand dune. American privateers used the harbor as a base of operations against British shipping between New York and southern ports. The privateers darted out from the harbor to surprise British merchant ships and take the prizes into Little Egg Harbor. Along the Mullica River, the patriots built shipyards and warehouses at Chestnut Neck and the Village of the Forks, just thirty-five miles from Philadelphia. Fourteen miles up the Mullica, the Americans operated the important logistical base of Batsto. The iron works there produced cannon balls, camp kettles, and other war goods for the American Army. So successful were the privateers that the British termed their base a "nest of rebel pirates."[7]

The effective work of the privateers provoked George Germain, Secretary of State for the Colonies, to direct General Sir William Howe in New York to organize an expedition of ships and men "with Orders to attack the ports on the Coast from New York to Nova Scotia, and destroy all ships and other property along shore whenever practicable." Howe was replaced by General Sir Henry Clinton as Commander-in-Chief of British forces in North America on 8 May 1778. When in the summer of 1778, privateers captured the very valuable *Venus of London,* Clinton decided to act. He planned a dual action: Deploy two divisions on the east and west banks of the Hudson River for the protection of foraging parties in New Jersey, and send an expedition to strike the privateers at Little Egg Harbor. The purpose for the soldiers along the Hudson, as Clinton explained his plan, was to draw Washington into a general battle. "This position was also intended to serve the double purpose of covering a general forage," Clinton said, "and favoring the operation of a corps I had detached, under Captain Ferguson, to destroy a nest of privateers at Egg Harbor, which had done us a great deal of mischief."[8]

Washington refused to be drawn out of his secure positions around New York, but he ordered detachments to thwart the British foragers. One unit, the 3d Continental Cavalry Regiment of Colonel George Baylor, was practically annihilated at Old Tappan, New Jersey, when General Charles Grey surprised the American troopers in a vicious, nighttime attack, 28 September 1778. Meanwhile, General Clinton organized a small squadron of ships, consisting of the sloops *Zebra* (flag ship), *Nautilus*, *Greenwich*, and *Granby*, a few gallies and small armed vessels, and transports, under Commander Henry Colins of the ship *Zebra*. The landing force was composed of 300 disciplined soldiers of the Fifth Regiment of Foot and 100 Loyalists of the Third Battalion of New Jersey Volunteers. The Loyalists also were organized and trained. To command the 400 soldiers, Clinton chose Captain Patrick Ferguson of the 70th Regiment of Foot. He was a thoroughly professional soldier and inventor of a breech-loading rifle that could fire five or six rounds in one minute. The Scotsman introduced his rifle to the British high command in 1776 and demonstrated its effectiveness. On 4 December 1776, Ferguson received approval of his patent. Despite the advantages of the Ferguson Rifle over the smooth-bore "Brown Bess" musket, the British generals preferred the musket, and it remained their standard weapon. During the Revolutionary War only some 200 Ferguson rifles were used.[9]

Departing New York on 30 September 1778, Colins' squadron sailed for Little Egg Harbor, arriving there in the evening of

Betrayal at Little Egg Harbor

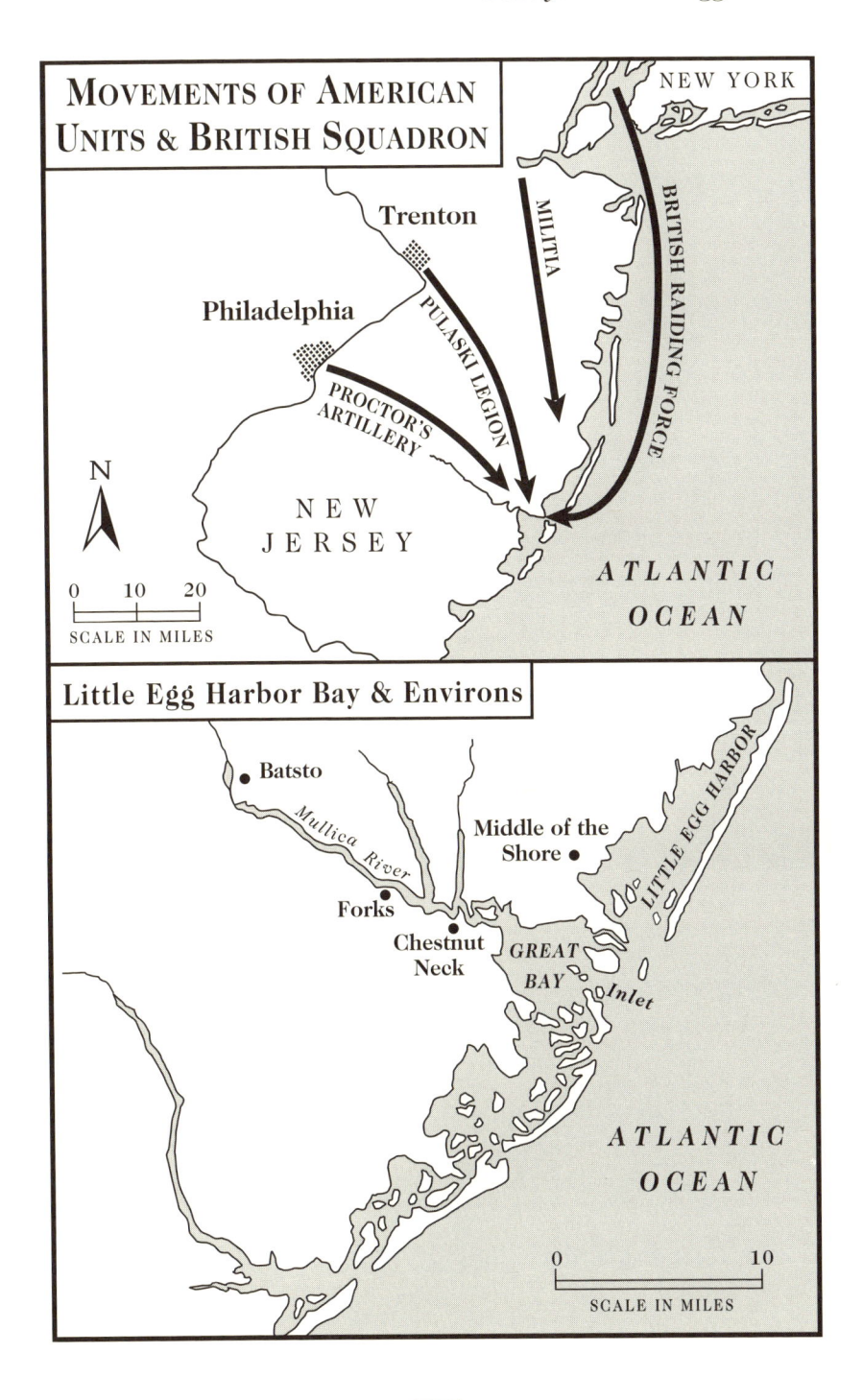

MOVEMENTS OF AMERICAN UNITS & BRITISH SQUADRON

Trenton
Philadelphia
MILITIA
PULASKI LEGION
PROCTOR'S ARTILLERY
BRITISH RAIDING FORCE
NEW YORK
NEW JERSEY
ATLANTIC OCEAN

N

0 10 20
SCALE IN MILES

Little Egg Harbor Bay & Environs

Batsto
Mullica River
Middle of the Shore
Forks
Chestnut Neck
GREAT BAY
Inlet
LITTLE EGG HARBOR
ATLANTIC OCEAN

0 10
SCALE IN MILES

5 October. Meanwhile, Americans learned of the sailing of the British squadron. New Jersey Governor William Livingston dispatched fast riders to alert the privateers. Alarmed by the news, four privateers sailed out to sea and escaped. Other vessels were pulled up the Mullica River as far as the depth of the water would permit. Colins wasted no time. The next morning, although unfavorable winds prevented the ships from entering the harbor, Colins off-loaded the soldiers onto smaller vessels that proceeded up the river for about ten miles to Chestnut Neck. The patriots had erected two battery positions to ward off enemy attacks, but no cannon had been installed, as yet. They took cover behind the battery positions and additional breast works. Nonetheless, as soon as the British troops landed under the cover of the ships' cannon, the patriots fled. The landing party destroyed the batteries and the store houses laden with British goods. The British seamen burned ten large prize ships, although the patriots already had scuttled them upon the first alarm. Ferguson's plan called for him to march next to Batsto and destroy that important base. However, the row galleys with their firepower were prevented by the shallow water to move up the river. Ferguson could have marched his raiders the fourteen miles to Batsto, but he received the alarming news that Americans were rushing relief forces to Little Egg Harbor, consisting of Pulaski's Legion, Colonel Thomas Proctor's Pennsylvania Artillery Regiment, and New Jersey militia. Ferguson thought it prudent to abandon the planned attack on Batsto. He reembarked the troops on the vessels, which sailed down to the harbor. Along the way, however, the troops landed twice to destroy three salt works and some houses and stores belonging to patriot families. The galleys and small vessels joined the squadron in the harbor in the evening of 7 October. Commander Colins planned to sail away at once, but unfavorable winds kept him at anchor for several days. On 14 October 1778, Colins received a message from Admiral James Gambier, his immediate superior in New York, to break off the expedition and return to New York immediately, as the British were preparing to evacuate New Jersey.[10]

Meanwhile, marching rapidly from Trenton, Pulaski's Legion reached the small Quaker community of Middle of the Shore (present day Tuckerton) on the evening of 8 October 1778. The Legion continued south along Island Road a few miles and encamped on the farm of James Willets, about a mile north of Osborn's Island. Pulaski set up his headquarters at Willets' farm house. A few hundred yards from the house in the direction of Osborn's Island, Pulaski selected a position for his cavalry, artillery, and a portion of the infantry. This campsite was screened from view of the British ships by a thick growth of timber. Along Island Road and nearer Osborn's Island, Lieutenant Colonel Von Bose established a picket post of about fifty infantrymen. Von Bose was assisted by Lieutenant Joseph de la Borderie. The vacant farm house of Jeremiah Ridgway served as the site of the post. Von Bose depended on a single sentry posted further down the road to provide an advance warning against the enemy, but he neglected to place a guard on the bridge that crossed Big Creek to the island. He never suspected the British would leave their ships again and conduct further raids. The British squadron, anchored in the harbor, could be seen from the American camp. Pulaski kept the squadron under observation, but his officers could watch for movement only during hours of daylight. Pulaski's mission was to defend the area around Little Egg Harbor.[11]

The situation remained quiet for several days. Pulaski's soldiers were resting after their forced march from Trenton. In Von Bose's picket post, however, an explosive exchange of words with tragic consequences occurred between Von Bose and Lieutenant Carl Wilhelm Juliat. Von Bose castigated Juliat for deserting the Hessian forces of King George III. The Saxon showed utter contempt for the Hessian, and the injured Juliat secretly vowed revenge. In 1826, Captain Paul Bentalou recalled the incident: "This man, treated with such severity by De Bosen, whose high sense of honour led him to despise one who, though a commissioned officer, could be guilty of deserting his colours, that he determined to revenge himself in a manner that could not have been foreseen or imagined."[12]

Casimir Pulaski

How had Lieutenant Juliat become an officer of The Pulaski Legion? It appears that Congress forced Juliat on Pulaski. Juliat was one of three Hessian officers who deserted their units and came over to the American side. They were undoubtedly influenced by a propaganda campaign of Congress in the spring of 1778 to foster a spirit of desertion and discontent among British foreign mercenaries. Having deserted, Juliat petitioned Congress to join the Continental Army, and General Baron De Kalb assisted him with a recommendation. In its report to Congress, the Board of War (William Duer, Richards Peters, and Timothy Pickering) reported that they had "conversed with Mr. Juliat, and find that Genl. Pulaski would receive him as a volunteer in the infantry of his corps." The Board also considered Juliat for appointment in a new corps of German volunteers. However, Congress commissioned him a sub-lieutenant and assigned him to the Legion as a volunteer infantry officer, 2 September 1778. Before Pulaski departed Trenton for Little Egg Harbor, Juliat had joined the Legion.[13]

Juliat exacted a monstrous revenge. He betrayed the Legion, causing the deaths of Von Bose, De la Borderie, and some thirty to forty Legionnaires. Shortly after the confrontation with Von Bose, Juliat pretended to go fishing, taking along four other soldiers (two joined Juliat's plot; the other two went fishing innocently). They rowed out to the British ships in the harbor and boarded the *Nautilus,* where Juliat disclosed to Commander Colins and Captain Ferguson the strength and the exact locations of Pulaski's infantry and cavalry. As Stedman recounts the incident: "An officer and some privates, deserters from Pulaski's American legion, having come on board, gave such an account of the positions of that corps, lying only at the distance of twelve

---

Opposite page: *GENERAL PULASKI'S CAMP AT LITTLE EGG HARBOR. Marching rapidly from Trenton, New Jersey, General Pulaski's Legion reached Little Egg Harbor on the evening of 8 October 1778 and encamped on the James Willetts farm (today the town of Mystic Island).*

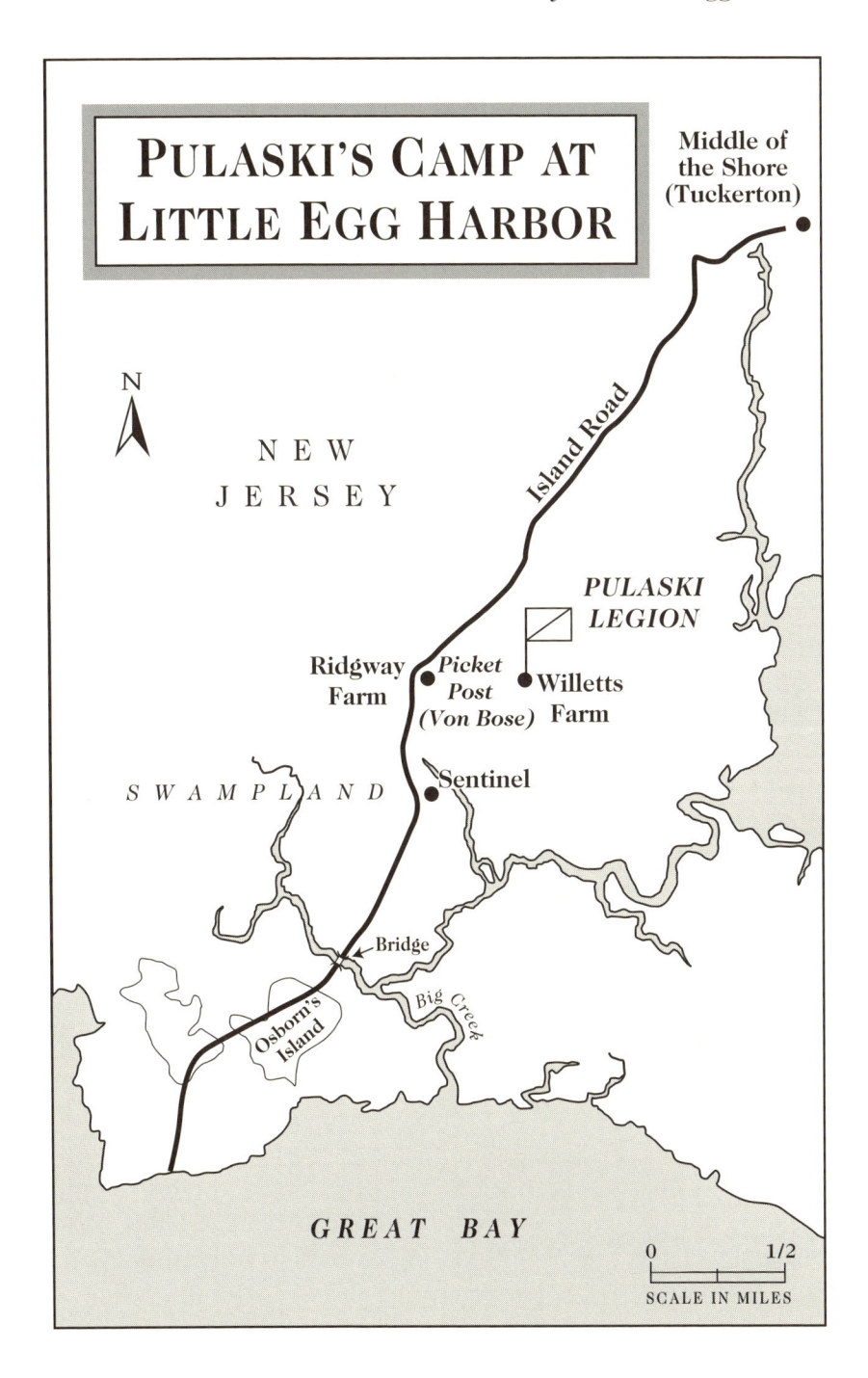

Betrayal at Little Egg Harbor

PULASKI'S CAMP AT LITTLE EGG HARBOR

miles up the river, as suggested to the active and enterprising mind of captain Ferguson the possibility of surprising it." Juliat revealed that the Legion consisted of three companies of foot, three troops of horse, and a detachment of artillery with one brass field, and that it was encamped about one mile beyond the bridge to Osborn's Island. The bridge figured prominently in Ferguson's planning; he would seize it for the purpose of insuring the safety of his retreat. He discussed Juliat's information and his plan of attack with Colins, who agreed to the venture.[14]

At eleven at night, 14 October, Colins embarked Ferguson's party of 250 selected soldiers on small boats. They rowed up river and landed on Osborn's Island at about 3 A.M. the next day. The British quietly approached Richard Osborn's farm house and seized his son Thomas to serve as guide. Crossing the island to the bridge spanning Big Creek, they found the bridge unguarded. Ferguson placed a group of fifty men to hold the bridge in case the attacking group had to beat a hasty retreat. Before continuing, he instructed the bridge detail to loosen the planking. Ferguson continued stealthily toward the picket post with the remaining two hundred soldiers. His advance guard surprised the lone sentry of the Legion and silenced him before he could sound the alarm. Moving quietly to the Ridgway farm, the British fell on the sleeping Legionnaires with drawn bayonets and complete surprise. "On the first alarm the Lieut. Colonel rushed out, armed with his sword and pistols," Bentalou said, "but though he was a remarkably stout man, and fought like a lion, he was overpowered by numbers and killed." Ferguson's men bayoneted and killed the Legionnaires without mercy. Meanwhile, the sound of fire of the defenders reached Pulaski's headquarters who at once rounded up the cavalry and galloped at breakneck speed to the picket post. Ferguson did not tarry. Having quickly accomplished his mission, he hurried his men back to the bridge and escaped. Pulaski pursued them to the bridge but was unable to cross; the planks had been removed. Some thirty British soldiers, cut off from the main party, saved themselves by disappearing into the woods and the darkness of night. Loyalist families are

Betrayal at Little Egg Harbor

believed to have sheltered these men, until they were able to make their way to British-held areas. Bentalou writes that Colonel Von Bose seemed to have been the primary object of attack. He says that the voice of the traitor Juliat was distinctly heard exclaiming, "This is the Colonel, kill him!" The body of Von Bose was found pierced with bayonets many times. Bentalou gives his opinion that Baron Von Bose did not adequately provide for the security of the picket post. "What mighty disgrace attaches to Pulaski or his legion from this surprise," Bentalou states, "is not so obvious. The fault belongs, if anywhere, to the Board of War, who sent the traitorous Hessian to Pulaski."[15]

In his report to General Henry Clinton, 15 October 1778, Captain Ferguson justified the massacre of Pulaski's men. "It being a night attack, little quarter could, of course, be given," he wrote, "so that there are only five prisoners." Ferguson's military reasoning is understandable. However, he added a retaliatory one: "The Captain who has come over to us is a Frenchman named Bromville [alias Juliat]. He and his deserters inform us that Mr. Pulaski has in public orders lately directed no quarter to be given; and it was therefore with particular satisfaction that the detachment marched against a man capable of issuing an order so unworthy of a gentleman and a soldier." Pulaski, of course, issued no such order, and, shortly after the massacre, the British had to admit that Juliat had lied. The British suffered few losses. Commander Colins had to scuttle his flagship *Zebra,* which got stuck on a sand bar in the harbor. Ferguson reported one officer and two soldiers wounded and three missing. He also said his soldiers destroyed part of the baggage and equipage of Pulaski's Legion by burning their quarters. As a final note, Major Ferguson was killed at the Battle of King's Mountain, South Carolina, 7 October 1780.[16]

General Pulaski reported the British attack immediately to Congress. He blamed Lieutenant Juliat as the instigator of the attack. Sadly he reported the loss of twenty-five to thirty Legionnaires, killed, wounded, and missing, as well as the deaths of Colonel Von Bose and Lieutenant Joseph de la Borderie. Pulaski said that "this slaughter would not have ceased so soon if on the first Alarm I had not hastened with my Cavalry to protect the infantry which then kept a good countenance." He reported taking some prisoners and should have captured many more, except that the horses could move only with difficulty through the swamp. Nevertheless, Pulaski continued to pursue until his cavalry reached the dismembered bridge. Still some of his infantry managed to cross on the framework of the bridge and fire on the retreating British who fired back. Pulaski then halted the pursuit, and he recalled the infantrymen, realizing they were heavily outnumbered and could not be reinforced. He told Congress that only the Legion was engaged in the fight. Proctor's artillery and the militia were not involved. He added that he dispatched Major Montford to the Forks to gather and bring the militia. But Montford found that half the militia had gone home, and the remainder resisted him and almost mutinied. He returned empty-handed. In a postscript, Pulaski expressed the usual contempt of the Continental regulars toward the militia. "I beg you would order the Militia to be obedient, or take them away intirely," he wrote. "For they are so ill inclined that they will only spoil our affairs, besides they disperse and retire when they please, and particularly when they are wanted to face the Ennemy."[17]

Pulaski was not alone in his low opinion of the American militia. Many generals, including Washington, felt likewise. After his loss of the Battle of Long Island in 1776, Washington saw his militia army practically disintegrate. The defeat dismayed the militia and filled them with fear. Washington reported to Congress: "Great numbers of them have gone off; in some instances, almost by whole regiments." Lowell also describes the militia's unpredictable conduct: "They came or went, as patriotism or selfishness, enthusiasm or discouragement succeeded each other in their breast." Washington's experience on Long Island shook him into realizing that, if he were to fight the British with some assurance of success, he would need a regular army of soldiers enlisted for an extended period of time. Despite its fear of standing armies, Congress carried out Washington's recommendation.

Betrayal at Little Egg Harbor

The Continental Army, however, was not large enough to do the job by itself, and militia were called into service for short periods of times, usually ninety days, and sometimes they performed well. But the militia were concerned more with a rigid adherence to the ninety-day enlistment than the need to repel any danger of the enemy. Brigadier General John Stark and his New Hampshire brigade offer a startling case. Stark first performed magnificently at Bennington, Vermont, 16 August 1777, when he decisively defeated a Hessian force ordered out on a foraging expedition by British General John Burgoyne. Despite the British setback, Burgoyne's invasion army from Canada threatened to capture Albany and sever the colonies along the Hudson River line. General Horatio Gates, American commander at Saratoga, desperately needed reinforcements. Stark and his 800-strong militia brigade arrived at Gates' headquarters on the morning of 18 September 1777, one day before the critical Battle of Freeman's Farm. Unbelievably, the New Hampshire militia immediately turned about, and at noon of the same day, Stark and his soldiers departed for home. Their enlistment had expired.[18]

During Pulaski's determined pursuit of Ferguson's raiders, Lieutenant Gerard de St. Elme attacked the escaping British with reckless abandon. Charging on horseback into a group of the enemy, he found himself surrounded by bayonet-wielding soldiers who knifed his horse to death. St. Elme miraculously escaped unhurt. St. Elme had served as a cavalry officer in the French Army. When he volunteered to come to America, the French Army promoted him to captain. Twice British warships intercepted his vessel and delayed his arrival in the United States. Pulaski welcomed him into the Legion as a volunteer officer, and he performed bravely at Little Egg Harbor. Unable to obtain a commission in the Continental Army, St. Elme decided to return to France. But first he asked Congress to grant him the brevet rank of major. Pulaski recommended him for the promotion in recognition of his role and bravery in battle, and Congress made the appointment "as a testimony of the approbation of Congress of his zeal and service."[19]

CASIMIR PULASKI

GENERAL CASIMIR PULASKI MONUMENT
In Mystic Island, New Jersey, the monument marks the site where Pulaski's Legion clashed with the British, 15 October 1778. The Society of the Cincinnati of New Jersey erected the monument in 1894 to commemorate the massacre. The current bronze tablet is an identical replacement for the one stolen by vandals in 1913. (Photo by the author, 23 September 1999)

Pulaski's report of the slaughter at Little Egg Harbor profoundly affected President Laurens and Congress. They concluded that committing massacres seemed to be a pattern of the British. In 1777, General Charles ("No-flint") Grey pounced upon General Wayne's unsuspecting troops and massacred them at Paoli, Pennsylvania. On 28 September 1778, Grey again made a surprise attack on Colonel George Baylor's cavalry at Old Tappan, New Jersey, and killed the Americans without mercy. Shortly thereafter, Ferguson viciously attacked Pulaski's Legionnaires at Little Egg Harbor. Congress had Pulaski's letter published in Dunlap's *Pennsylvania Packet* of 20 October 1778, and the delegates followed up the release to the newspaper with a unanimous manifesto, in which they warned the British:

We, therefore, the Congress of the United States of America,

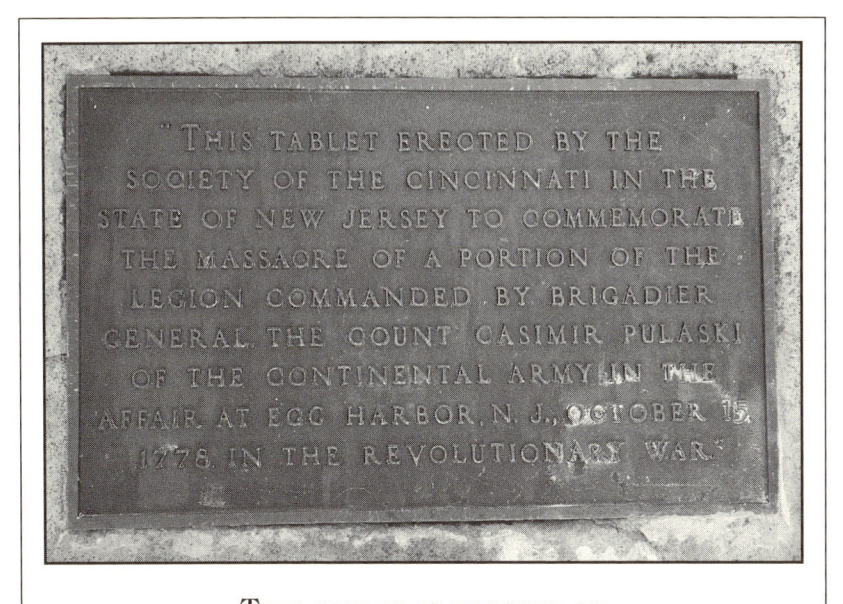

THIS TABLET IS ERECTED BY
THE SOCIETY OF THE CINCINNATI IN THE
STATE OF NEW JERSEY
TO COMMEMORATE THE MASSACRE
OF A PORTION OF THE LEGION COMMANDED
BY BRIGADIER GENERAL THE COUNT
CASIMER PULASKI OF THE CONTINENTAL ARMY
IN THE AFFAIR AT EGG HARBOR
NEW JERSEY OCTOBER 15 1778
IN THE REVOLUTIONARY WAR

Inscription on the Pulaski Monument, Mystic Island, New Jersey. Erected and Dedicated in 1894.

do solemnly declare and proclaim, that if our enemies presume to execute their threats, or persist in their present career of barbarity, we will take such exemplary vengeance as shall deter others from a like conduct.[20]

Pulaski buried Von Bose, De la Borderie, and the slain soldiers in a common grave on the Ridgway farm. The monument now stands near the site. The sudden loss of so many Legionnaires tore at Pulaski's heart. He knew the officers well, and they were close to him. During several months of recruiting, equipping, training, and marching, he undoubtedly met every Legionnaire. As he told Congress: "I went from one place to another to Look at Everything, to Get all the Recruits together, get them Dressed, and Exercise them."[21] Pulaski was proud of his Legion. He held high hopes that the Legion would perform magnificently in combat and cover itself with glory, only to suffer a tragic beginning. However, his rush to the defense of Little Egg Harbor was not in vain. Loyalist warnings of Pulaski's rapid march to the Atlantic Ocean caused Captain Ferguson to abandon his goal of destroying the important iron works at Batsto. Indeed, Pulaski is credited with saving Batsto.

THE AUTHOR WISHES to comment on the report of Little Egg Harbor by Colonel Mark Mayo Boatner III in his *Encyclopedia of the American Revolution* (1966). Unfortunately Boatner writes carelessly and his chronology is wrong. Here are his opening statements:

> To raid this privateers' nest, a few miles north of modern Atlantic City, Capt. Patrick Ferguson marched [?] with 300 men of the 70th Regt. and the 3d N. J. (Tory) Regt., while a sizable naval force approached from the opposite direction to support him. Pulaski's Legion was sent to oppose the British, but the latter destroyed 10 large vessels (among them prizes) and moved up the Mullica river destroying storehouses, shipyards, and houses of prominent patriots.

Boatner's account implies, as the reader can conclude, that Pulaski did nothing to stop the destructive work of Ferguson, even though Boatner assumes the Legion was in the vicinity of the British. To review the actual chronology of events: The British squadron arrived at Little Egg Harbor on 5 October 1778. Ferguson's troops attacked and destroyed the installations of

Street sign "South Pulaski Boulevard." The town of Mystic Island, New Jersey, named the street that bounds the Pulaski Monument Park on the north "SO PULASKI BLVD." When vandals bent the metal sign out of shape, the town officials had the sign straightened out sufficiently to be readable. (Photo by the author, 23 September 1999)

Street sign "Kosciusko Way." The street facing the Pulaski Monument was named "Kosciusko Way" in honor of Pulaski's compatriot Colonel Thaddeus Kosciuszko. Both South Pulaski Boulevard and Kosciusko Way lie along the former Island Road of Revolutionary War days. (Photo by the author, 23 September 1999)

the privateers on 6 and 7 October. By the evening of 7 October, Ferguson's soldiers had returned to their ships, and Commander Colins was ready to sail away. Pulaski reached Little Egg Harbor on the evening of 8 October. Captain Bentalou, riding with the Pulaski Legion, recalls the march to Little Egg Harbor: "On our arrival, the enemy reembarked, and the ships remained at anchor near the shore." John Frederick Lewis, President of the Historical Society of Pennsylvania, stated in 1929, "Pulaski was ordered to march from Trenton with his legion, but before he could arrive, the British had effected their mission and returned to their vessels."[22] If nothing else, Boatner is very careless as he is in his criticism of Colonel Thaddeus Kosciuszko, too, for the failure to capture Ninety-Six, South Carolina, in June 1781.

· 6 ·

Mis-Assignment to Minisink

❧

THE BRITISH SQUADRON of Commandant Colins and Ferguson's raiders did not sail away from Little Egg Harbor until 19 October 1778, almost two weeks after their destructive raid. Meanwhile, Pulaski placed the Legion on heightened alert. He guarded against another night time landing. His officers were well aware of that possibility. Lieutenant Gerard de St. Elme believed that the British might attempt it. "We shall be again under Arms this Night," he said, and "we are extremely fatigued." St. Elme was bitter toward the many Loyalists in the area. "We are betray'd on all sides," he wrote. "We can't take a step but an hour after the Enemy is informed of it, and knows where we go." He believed that the British understood Pulaski's passion for American independence and that they singled him out for retaliation. "I think they aim at our General," he said, "because he opposes them much."[1]

Pulaski prepared to march his Legion to Trenton and from there to continue and join General Lord Stirling. Signs pointed to British preparations to sail away as Colins attempted to refloat the *Zebra* caught on a sand bar, but he soon gave up. Pulaski wrote President Laurens, "This moment the Frigate run on shore

Casimir Pulaski

In CONGRESS.

The DELEGATES of the UNITED STATES of *New-Hampshire, Massachusetts-Bay, Rhode-Island, Connecticut, New-York, New-Jersey, Pennsylvania, Delaware, Maryland, Virginia, North-Carolina, South-Carolina and Georgia,* TO *James de Bromville Esqr.*

WE, reposing especial Trust and Confidence in your Patriotism, Valour, Conduct and Fidelity, DO, by these Presents, constitute and appoint you to be *Lieutenant of Infantry in the corps called the Legion, now under the command of Brigadier General Pulaski, to rank as such from the twenty-fifth day of April 1778.*

in the Army of the United States, raised for the Defence of American Liberty, and for repelling every hostile Invasion thereof. You are therefore carefully and diligently to discharge the Duty of *Lieutenant,* by doing and performing all manner of Things thereunto belonging. And we do strictly charge and require all Officers and Soldiers under your Command, to be obedient to your Orders as *Lieutenant.* — And you are to observe and follow such Orders and Directions from Time to Time, as you shall receive from this or a future Congress of the United States, or Committee of Congress, for that Purpose appointed, or Commander in Chief for the Time being of the Army of the United States, or any other your superior Officer, according to the Rules and Discipline of War, in Pursuance of the Trust reposed in you. This Commission to continue in Force until revoked by this or a future Congress. Dated at *Philadelphia the fifth day of October 1778.*

By Order of the CONGRESS,

Henry Laurens PRESIDENT.

ATTEST. *Cha Thomson secy*

is burning and all the rest will Sail immediately in my opinion." Not needing Colonel Procter's artillery any longer, Pulaski directed him to return to Philadelphia. Pulaski remained suspicious that the British expedition could land further north on the New Jersey coast. He, therefore, marched his Legion north to Barnegat, pausing there until he made certain the British did not land. After a hectic week at Little Egg Harbor, the Legion was exhausted and looked forward to some days of rest. Because of Ferguson's destruction of equipage, the Legion needed blankets, and Pulaski asked Congress for 100. Shortly after the clash of the 15th, Lieutenant James de Bronville told Pulaski that he wished to resign from the army (reason unknown) and surrendered his commission document that Pulaski forwarded to Congress. On 23 October 1778, Congress accepted De Bronville's resignation.[2]

Reaching Trenton, Pulaski asked Congress for commissions for several volunteer officers in the Legion. He requested that his quartermaster, William Sullivan, be granted a captaincy. Pulaski preferred an American for this post because of his general knowledge of the commerce of the country. As Pulaski said, it "is absolutely necessary that a place of so much detail be filled by a person of the Country." He also requested lieutenancies for three volunteers "who behaved extremely well in the last affair:" Andrew Kerlevan, Henry La Close, and Louis de Beaulieu. Congress did not commission the three until 1 March 1779.[3]

OPPOSITE PHOTO: *DOCUMENT OF CONGRESS APPOINTING JAMES DE BRONVILLE LIEUTENANT IN THE PULASKI LEGION. President Henry Laurens signs and Secretary Charles Thomson attests to the document appointing Bronville lieutenant in The Pulaski Legion, 25 April 1778. This document is believed to be only one of a very few surviving such documents. After the tragedy of Little Egg Harbor, New Jersey, 15 October 1778, Bronville decided to resign his commission. He turned it over to Pulaski who forwarded it to Congress. Thus, the document became a part of The Papers of the Continental Congress. (Courtesy of the National Archives)*

CASIMIR PULASKI

In addition to the matter of the three lieutenants, Pulaski had to replace the slain Baron Von Bose with another commander of the infantry. He found an excellent candidate in Charles Frederick Bedaulx, a Swiss soldier of fortune and scion of an old European family. Bedaulx had served in the Dutch army for twelve years and rose to be captain. Deciding to fight for the American cause, he contacted Franklin and Deane in Paris to obtain their recommendations. In March 1777, he sailed from Bordeaux in the company of the Marquis de Lafayette and Baron De Kalb. When Congress offered him a lowly officer's commission, he refused it as being less than he believed he deserved. However, in November 1778, Pulaski petitioned Congress to appoint Bedaulx a lieutenant colonel in his Legion. The Board of War approved Pulaski's request. On 10 December 1778, Congress resolved "That Mr. Charles Frederick Bedaulx be appointed Lieut. Colonel of the Legion commanded by General Pulaski, agreeable to recommendation of Count Pulaski." At this time, Pulaski lost Major Julius de Montford who returned to France to attend to personal affairs. Pulaski's selection to fill the key post of brigade major vacated by De Montford was Peter Verney. However, the Board of War selected Count De Mauleon, a German officer, whom Pulaski had recommended for a captaincy in his Legion four months earlier. But for his brigade major, Pulaski insisted on Verney. The Board's report to Congress of 22 January 1779 indicates the battle of wills between Pulaski and members of the Board (Timothy Pickering, Richard Peters, and Jesse Root). In part, the report reads:

> That they know of no way of providing for Captain Mauleon but by promoting him to the majority of General Pulaski's legion, which place they have no doubt of his filling with much reputation, as he is recommended to the Board and appears to be an Officer of great merit.
> But General Pulaski has made choice of a Monsieur Verney, who is an Officer of merit, and (both having come over with the Marquis de Brittannie) are in similar circumstances as to their sufferings by imprisonment with the enemy.... The Board would

choose to recommend Mon. De Mauleon. General Pulaski is desirous of having Monsieur Verney. Therefore the matter is stated specially for Congress to determine. They beg leave to submit the following imperfect resolve, that Congress may direct the filling it up with the name most agreeable to them. [De Mauleon or Verney].

The following month, Congress resolved on 23 February 1779: "That Mons. Verne[y] be appointed major in Brigadier General Pulaski's legion."[4]

Pulaski always nurtured the concept of an independent corps of cavalry striking the enemy whenever an opportunity presented itself. He had four years of experience of successfully carrying out this tactic against the Russians in Poland. The Pulaski Legion was a step forward. But, many in Congress opposed it. When his recruiting for the Legion went past the authorized strength of 268 soldiers, some members of Congress suspected that Pulaski secretly planned to establish a large and independent cavalry corps under the Commander-in-Chief (for one, Joseph Reed was a strong opponent). The Legion, however, could not grow by simple recruiting. At Little Egg Harbor, Pulaski's initial strength of 330 had fallen to about 250 Legionnaires. On 26 October 1778, he proposed to Congress that he command "a flying corps placed near Kings Bridge," located north of New York. Kings Bridge was important to the British for the defense of New York. It lay on the Post Road at Spuyten Duyvil Creek that divides Manhattan from the Bronx. Pulaski prefaced his proposal to Congress with an expression of obedience: "My duty is to perform whatever orders you give me." Nevertheless, he went ahead with his own plan of active operations against the enemy. He estimated that he would need to be reinforced with 300 infantry that would permit him to strike with confidence. He believed that General Lord Stirling's division to be more than sufficient to defend Northern New Jersey and to occupy Staten Island upon its evacuation by the British. When Pulaski's letter reached Philadelphia, Congress ignored it. The *Journals of Congress* of 27 October 1778 notes the reaction: "A letter, of 26, from Count Pulaski was read. Ordered, To lie on the table."[5]

Casimir Pulaski

On the day that Pulaski proposed to Congress that his Legion, augmented with 300 infantry, take post at Kings Bridge, Congress resolved "That Count Pulaski's Legion and all the cavalry at or near Trenton, be ordered forthwith to repair to Sussex court house, there to wait the orders of General Washington." Sussex County in northwestern New Jersey was probably meant to be a place of rest and recuperation. President Laurens informed Washington of the directive to Pulaski and asked Washington to select a location where Pulaski's cavalry would have easy access to forage. On reaching Sussex Court House, 6 November 1778, Pulaski reported his arrival to General Washington via his personal courier, Lieutenant St. Elme. He apologized that he could not see the Commander-in-Chief in person because of illness. He was worried to find little forage in Sussex Court House. "I am here without forage," he wrote, " if that is to last long the horses will suffer a great deal." The intended period of rest turned into a nightmare for Pulaski because the upcoming assignment threatened the destruction of his cavalry. Washington ordered him to march his Legion to the Minisink area on the Delaware River and there take a position near Cole's Fort. On 10 November 1778, Washington wrote Pulaski: "Upon consulting Govr. Clinton of the State of New York, upon a position in which your Corps can be employed to advantage, and at the same time be plentifully subsisted in the Article of Forage, he advises the Minisink settlement upon Delaware." Washington suggested that once there he keep his cavalry and infantry quartered together as near as possible, so that in case of Indian attacks, his Legion could be marshaled for action quickly. Perhaps sensing that food and forage may not be as plentiful as he had been led to believe, Washington added a note of caution, "I must beg you to make use of all means to keep your Corps from marauding or in any way distressing the Inhabitants."[6]

Minisink lay in a heavily forested, frontier area on the Delaware River between New York and Pennsylvania. The settlers feared Indian attacks of the kind that devastated the Wyoming Valley of Pennsylvania (Wilkes-Barre area). In July 1778, a well-organized

Tory force of 400 white men and 500 Indians, led by Sir Guy Johnson and Colonel John Butler, struck the settlers of the valley. The Indian allies were the Senecas, the most warlike Indians of the Six Nations of the Iroquois. Historian Page Smith writes: "It was a time of settlers murdered in their beds, of frontier cabins and lean-tos put to the torch, of children abducted, and of reprisals as savage as the raids that provoked them." The frontier needed to be safeguarded, and Washington attempted to provide some degree of military protection. But, cavalry could not be employed effectively against some skulking Indians in the brush. If they had been available, Daniel Morgan's sharpshooters would have been ideal. Nevertheless, Pulaski carried out Washington's order. He reached Rosencrantz on the south side of the Delaware and not far from Minisink on 15 November 1778. He reported to Washington that Cole's Fort had no forage because Indians had burned the place down. Rosencrantz, however, had a supply of forage, and he preferred to remain at this location, pending Washington's further orders. Besides, he said that Rosencrantz was near enough to Minisink for his Legion to defend the settlers there. He realized that he must gain information of the locations and movements of hostile Indians, if he was to ward off their attacks. In turn, Washington approved Pulaski remaining at Rosencrantz "or choose for yourself such other position in the neighborhood as appears to you best adapted to the accommodation of your Corps." In addition to Pulaski's Legion of 250 soldiers, Washington augmented him with Colonel Charles Armand's Legion and Colonel Oliver Spencer's small regiment of infantry from General Lord Stirling's division, both units totaling about 250 soldiers. Pulaski appreciated Washington's decision to provide him with the soldiers of Armand and Spencer. He needed them. The screened approaches through the forests had to be guarded more closely, especially against Indians who excelled in such an environment. Writing from Minisink on 3 December 1778, Pulaski told Congress: "It has pleased the commanding General to reinforce my corps and thereby to enable me to do some thing for the publick." He said he would conduct a reconnaissance of areas suspected of harboring Indians, because he had received reports that the Indians "prepare themselves to some new mischief upon our frontiers." Pulaski understood his mission at Minisink when he added: "I will try to prevent them, and if the Circumstances will allow, to make them less dangerous to the Inhabitants of this Country."[7]

Despite his resolve to carry out his mission, Pulaski keenly felt his assignment at Minisink to be wrong—a mis-assignment. He had conceived and organized an independent legion as a special force of the Commander-in-Chief—to be employed in battle at critical times. However, he could never convince Washington who continued to regard cavalry a secondary combat arm that could be employed wherever soldiers were needed. Pulaski's role at Minisink discouraged him greatly. Cole's Fort and the surrounding area had been ravaged and destroyed by Indians and Loyalist rangers; there was no forage for the horses, and the few inhabitants could barely support themselves. An exasperated Pulaski protested strongly to the President of Congress:

> I demand to be employed near the Ennemies Lines, and it is thought proper to place me in an Exile which even the Savages shun, and nothing remains but the Bears to fight with. I should have less grief—however, if the Earth produced a sufficiency to feed my Horses, but they will starve and it will be said it is my fault.[8]

In the fall of 1778, Count Stanislaw Kotkowski came to America as a volunteer to join the American cause. He had served as a lieutenant colonel in Pulaski's Army of the Confederation of Bar. He escaped from Poland when the resistance against the Russians collapsed. Before departing France, he obtained recommendations from Franklin and Deane. Undoubtedly Kotkowski's first contact in America was his former commander. Kotkowski brought the latest news from Poland and Europe where monarchs continued to wage war against each other. Kotkowski's name first appears in Pulaski's letter to Washington on 15 November 1778, in which he recommends Kotkowski for appointment in the Continental Army. Reaching Philadelphia next, Kotkowski applied for a commission, bearing the recommendations of Franklin, Deane, and Pulaski. The Board of War responded favorably, and the Pole was made captain in General Pulaski's Legion, 10 December 1778, "with the pay of a lieutenant, in which latter capacity he is willing to do duty in the corps."[9]

Captain Kotkowski joined the Pulaski Legion at Minisink, but not for long. He soon became involved in an unpleasant incident that led to his court martial. According to the abused resident, David Westfall, Kotkowski on 9 January 1779 rode through his house with drawn sword, cursing and knocking down chairs and other items. He ordered soldiers to open the cellar from which he took provisions and other items. Westfall and his wife ran to the quarters of Captain Baron De Fry of Pulaski's Legion and told De Fry that Lieutenant Kotkowski had threatened to kill them. De Fry hurried to the Westfall home to confront Kotkowski. During the encounter an aroused Kotkowski struck De Fry in the face. Brigadier General Edward Hand ordered a court martial that found the accused guilty of abusing Westfall and damaging his property. In his letter to Washington, forwarding the proceedings of the general court martial, Hand said that Kotkowski on January 11th tried to hand the general his captain's commission, but the general thought it improper for him to accept it. That night Kotkowski disappeared. During the trial Kotkowski pleaded not guilty; and the court martial board never established the reason for Kotkowski's wild search of Westfall's house. Washington answered Hand on 7 February 1779, telling him that before he received the results of the court martial, Kotkowski arrived in Philadelphia. Washington informed Hand: "He has, I believe, returned or is about to return to Europe, and consequently you will have no more trouble with him."[10]

Pulaski's contact with Kotkowski was an opportunity for the latest news from Europe. The information undoubtedly fired up Pulaski's imagination on how he could again fight the Russians and expel them from his homeland. At this time, Pulaski was frustrated with his assignment in the wilds of Minisink. In his mind, the Indians and the Tories were not the real enemy, but rather the British Army that attempted to suppress American independence. With his spirits sagging, Pulaski decided to resign from the Continental Army and return to Europe, where he believed he could do more good. On 15 November 1778, Pulaski told Washington of his intention to resign, but first he would deploy his Legion properly in the Minisink area and place it in the best condition of combat readiness. Washington granted Pulaski permission to go to Philadelphia for the purpose of resigning, "once you have arranged the affairs of your Corps." He informed Pulaski that he ordered Brigadier General Edward Hand to replace him in command at Minisink. Washington also said he understood Pulaski's motives that would cause him to return to Europe and called them "laudable." Washington took the occasion to praise Pulaski again:

> I assure you, Sir, I have a high sense of your Merit and services and the principles that influenced the part you have taken in the affairs of this country. The disinterested and unremitted zeal you have manifested in the service gives you a title to the esteem of the citizens of America and have assured you mine.[11]

PULASKI, HOWEVER, did not resign. He had a change of heart. Just as he did not quit after resigning his post of Commander of the Horse, he again decided to continue fighting for American independence. He got wind of a planned military action (General Sullivan's expedition to punish Indian raiders), and the distinct possibility of participating lifted up his spirits. He took advantage of Washington's permission to visit Philadelphia, not to resign but to try again to settle the pay accounts of his Legion. In his letter from Minisink, 3 December 1778, Pulaski said he would not demand reimbursement of $16,000 that he had expended from his own pocket during the organization of the Legion.[12]

Unable to find sufficient forage for his horses at Minisink and fearing that he would lose them to starvation, Pulaski ordered the cavalry of his Legion and that of Armand's Corps to Easton, Pennsylvania. He knew there was forage at Easton. Washington was surprised, although he had granted Pulaski some leeway in keeping the horses where they could be fed. James McHenry of Washington's staff wrote to General Greene, Quartermaster General: "His Excellency is not a little surprised to hear that Count Pulaski's legion has got back to Easton from whence he will remove them the moment he knows where to send them." McHenry said that Washington would order the horses back to Minisink if there were a possibility of subsisting them there. McHenry added that Washington "thinks their coming down is only a pretence to get into more comfortable quarters." Washington became adamant about Pulaski's horses subsisting in Easton. He wrote Pulaski: "It will not be possible for you to remain at Easton, without the greatest inconvenience to the service, as you must consume that Forage which is necessary for the Teams upon the communication and a great deal of that which is intended for this Camp." Pulaski's horses in Easton threatened to consume forage needed for Washington's headquarters in Middle Brook, New Jersey. Washington told Pulaski that Colonel Robert Hooper, Deputy Quartermaster, would direct him to a location where the horses could be cared for without interfering with the allocation of supplies at Easton. Washington's suspicion that Pulaski displaced to Easton in search of more comfortable quarters was put to rest by General Hand when he reached Minisink and saw the lack of forage for himself. He confirmed Pulaski's reason, and Washington accepted the reality at Minisink. On 1 January 1779, he told Hand, "I am sorry the Country about Minisincks or within supporting distance could not afford forage sufficient to subsist Count Pulaski's Horse. Matters respecting them and their Quarters are arranged before this." As an experienced cavalryman, Pulaski was always concerned with the health of his horses, keeping them groomed, fed, and fit for combat, rather than seeking his own comfort. Habitually, after every maneuver or training exercise, the cavalryman first tended to the needs of his horse.[13]

The unexpected presence of Pulaski's and Armand's cavalry at Easton (some 100 horses) angered Joseph Reed. General Nathanael Greene informed Colonel Clement Biddle, his Deputy and Commissary of Forage, "The Governor and Council of Pennsylvania complain that the State is overborne with cavalry and wagon horses." From Philadelphia on 20 January 1779, Greene told Biddle: "I have got an order for Pulaski's legion to go down into Kent and Sussex in the Delaware State." Greene had wrestled with the problem of finding suitable locations for the horses of the army, including those of Major Lee's Corps. He confessed to Biddle, "There is nobody willing to receive the horses and everybody desirous of getting rid of them."[14]

Once out of the gloomy forests of Minisink, Pulaski's outlook became cheerful. He had been aware of the departure of a large number of French officers to Europe. With the intervention and active support of France in the Revolutionary War, these officers now believed that the fighting was about over. French Minister Gerard reported the attitude of French officers to the Foreign Minister, Comte de Vergennes: "Almost all the French officers who have come to offer their services to the United States, even those who were well employed, are looking for the means to return to France, convinced that the campaign is finished." If true, there would be little opportunity for Pulaski to fight the British. Pulaski met with Gerard (probably during the month of September while awaiting an order of Congress to join the army). Gerard disclosed the nature of his visit: "Mr. de Pulawski feels the same [about returning] but I was able to persuade him not to ask to return to the French service, nevertheless he seems determined to solicit a position with the King of Prussia." Notwithstanding the mood of the French officers, Pulaski decided to remain in the Continental Army. On 4 December 1778, he wrote to Congress:

> I have given my reasons to the General of the Army for which I had a mind to depart for Europe, but this is not at this time, when I am in some activity. I love my profession and I can not employ this better as in the Cause of freedom.[15]

General Washington searched for a place to locate Pulaski's cavalry. Because the army had bedded down for the winter, all suitable locations were occupied by various units. Washington chose a location at some distance from the Continental Army—Kent and Sussex Counties in southern Delaware. He conferred with Delaware's President, Caesar Rodney, and received his concurrence. On 19 January 1779, Washington directed Pulaski to march his cavalry to Delaware, halting in Wilmington, where Quartermaster Frank Wade would guide him to a specific encampment. Meanwhile, Pulaski's infantry remained on duty at Minisink under the command of General Hand. The current arrangement, however, lasted a short time because of the decision of Great Britain to make the South a major battle zone. King George III developed a new strategy of conquering the southern colonies and then rolling up north. He counted on a large Tory population in the South to support the campaign. As historians George F. Scheer and Hugh F. Rankin write: "Perhaps, his Majesty reasoned, enough loyal inhabitants in Georgia would join the regulars to drive up the center of South Carolina to separate the seacoast from the back settlements and open communication with the loyalists of North Carolina."[16]

On 2 February 1779, Congress "Resolved: That Count Pulaski be ordered to march his Legion to South Carolina and put himself under the command of General Lincoln, as the commanding officer of the Southern Department."[17] Congress gave Pulaski a splendid assignment, and service directly under General Benjamin Lincoln was the kind of command relationship he had always advocated. Pulaski looked forward to an opportunity of active campaigning. Undoubtedly, he felt no regret over leaving the North where he had encountered many frustrations, much of which could be attributed to a Congress unable to provide adequately for its military forces. Other frustrations were provoked by Washington's failure to understand and appreciate the effective role of a separate and powerful cavalry corps. Pulaski would soon shake the mud of Pennsylvania off his boots and leave behind his tormentor, Joseph Reed.

· 7 ·

The Long March to Savannah

The decision of Congress to assign the Legion to the Southern Theater of Operations poised an unprecedented challenge for Pulaski. The scheduled march from York, Pennsylvania, to Savannah, a distance of some 700 miles, undoubtedly was the first long journey for an American unit in the Revolutionary War. Later, long-distance movements took place, like that of Washington's Army from near New York to Yorktown, Virginia, in the late summer of 1781 and General Arthur St. Clair's march of some 500 miles from Yorktown to South Carolina with a reinforcement of 2000 Pennsylvanians for General Greene's Southern Army. Pulaski's challenge involved extensive planning, coordination with the states, and logistical support along the march, not to mention financial planning and recruiting of soldiers. Pulaski faced the challenge resolutely and confidently. Inaction always devastated and depressed him. But the new assignment stimulated him into an exciting belief that he now could contribute to American independence in the manner he always dreamed of.

In Philadelphia, 4 February 1779, Pulaski expressed his appreciation to Congress for the new assignment, and he proposed several conditions for the delegates to consider and presumably approve. First, "he desires to be commanded by nobody, but by the Commander-in-Chief of the Southern Department." His second concern dealt with the care and replacement of horses along the march. He asked that the Board of War instruct the Quartermaster to provide forage from one destination to another, as well as to replace horses that became unfit for service from fatigue, sickness, or other causes. Because his Legion was under strength, he requested the authority to recruit soldiers on the march. He specifically asked that Captain John Schott's unit be joined to his Legion, according to the intent of General Washington. Schott commanded an independent company of some 100 infantrymen who originally were the corps of Baron Ottendorf. The Board recommended the addition of Schott's unit to Pulaski's Legion. However, Washington now ruled against the transfer, telling Pulaski "the detached corps under Captain Schott cannot be spared at this time." With regard to the unsettled accounts of the Legion, Pulaski said he would try to resolve this problem before departing for the South. He volunteered to meet with the auditors personally, since Paymaster Captain Baldesqui was ailing and unable to travel. The fifth point of his letter pertained to the appointment of officers to fill vacancies in the following grades: Peter Verney, major, Alexander O'Neil, captain, Baptiste Verdier, Louis de Beaulieu, Andrew Kerlevan, and Henry La Close, lieutenants. The Board of War found Pulaski's conditions reasonable and executed them promptly. The key condition of command-relationship was communicated to General Benjamin Lincoln, Southern Department Commander, on 6 February 1779. Timothy Pickering wrote Lincoln: "By a late resolution of Congress, General Pulaski is ordered to the Southern department with his Legion. We would request that the General and his Corps may be so employed that he will not be subject to the direction of any other officer inferior in rank to the Commander-in-Chief of the department."[1]

Among the new officers Pulaski requested for his Legion, all except O'Neil have already been mentioned. An Irish-Frenchman, O'Neil had served as a major under Pulaski in Poland. He possessed extensive military experience, having participated in two campaigns in Flanders, six in Germany, and, finally, in Pulaski's Army of the Confederation of Bar. After arriving in America at New Bern, North Carolina, he became a captain in the regiment of Colonel Chariot. Wishing to join Pulaski, he saw his chance when the regiment was reorganized. He then petitioned Congress for an appointment in Pulaski's Independent Legion. He received the endorsements of both Pulaski and Chariot. His regimental commander certified that O'Neil had served as captain with distinction and possessed distinguished merits. Pulaski said in O'Neil's favor: "I know that, in all the terms of service and duties that Col. O'Neil has fulfilled, he has conducted himself with fortitude, bravery, and distinguished merit. I have the honor to recommend him to everyone." Congress appointed O'Neil captain in Pulaski's Legion, 1 March 1779. In addition to the six officers whom Pulaski recommended for appointment, he asked Congress for the twelve soldiers recruited by Lieutenant Colonel Klein, who was unable to organize a unit of German deserters. The Board of War delayed its decision about Klein's stalled project. Meanwhile, the Pulaski Legion departed for the South. On 21 June 1779, the Board concluded that "there is no prospect of employing Lieutenant Colonel Klein with advantage to the United States, and that the men of that corps are now reduced to a serjeant and four privates." The five men were transferred to Colonel Armand's corps.[2] The incident shows Pulaski's vigilance and determination in searching for replacements for his own corps and perhaps helps to explain his success in organizing the Legion.

Prior to departing for the Southern Department, Pulaski gained another experienced officer, Captain Lewis Celeron, a Canadian. Celeron had served as captain in the Continental Army for two years. He was stationed at Fort Ticonderoga, when General John Burgoyne invaded New York State from Canada and approached the fort. Upon General Arthur St. Clair's hasty evacuation of the fort, Celeron lost all his clothes save those on his back. He told the Board of War on 16 February 1779 that he wished to serve in

General Pulaski's corps, even as a volunteer. Celeron was one of several capable officers who admired Pulaski's fighting ability, and he specifically asked to be assigned to his Legion. The Board recommended that Celeron be granted one thousand dollars as reimbursement for his losses in the service, and "That Captain Lewis Celeron, who has served near two years in the army of these states and distinguished himself as an active, brave and good officer, be promoted to the rank of major by brevet." Congress confirmed the Board's recommendation on 20 February 1779.[3]

Another foreign volunteer, Baron George Gustave d'Gugglaa, specifically asked the Board of War to be assigned to Pulaski's Legion. Like other Europeans, this Swedish nobleman knew of and admired Pulaski's reputation as a cavalry commander. D'Ugglaa first served as lieutenant in the army of the Empress of Russia (Catherine II) and next in the Dutch Army. He quit European service because he said he was "animated with the spirit of Liberty and desire of serving the oppressed." While sailing for America, his ship was intercepted by a British man-of-war about 200 miles from Boston and forcibly taken to New York. There he was confined as a prisoner for fourteen months. Finally, the Baron was exchanged at Elizabeth Town, New Jersey. Proceeding to Philadelphia, he applied to the Board of War for an appointment in the army. He wrote: "I humbly conceive myself skilled in the art of War and am desirous to be employed a Lieutenant in General Pulaskey's Legion." The Board acted favorably on his request and that of Pulaski who recommended D'Ugglaa for appointment as adjutant of the Legion. The Board reported to Congress: "That Mr. George Gustave D'Ugglaa be appointed a lieutenant in the legion commanded by General Count Pulaski." Surprisingly, Congress rejected the Board's recommendation. The *Journals of Congress* for 2 March 1779 read: "On the question to agree to the said report, the states were equally divided, and the question lost." John Jay, President of Congress, informed D'Ugglaa of the unfavorable decision by letter of 5 March 1779. Jay tried to soften D'Ugglaa's expected disappointment: "I have therefore to believe, Sir, that the objections to your appointment arise from the number of Supernumerary Officers in the American Service, & were by no means of a personal nature." This author suspects Jay's explanation to be a white lie. After all, the Board of War, most knowledgeable and responsible for army matters, did not object to the number of supernumerary officers, and neither did the delegates of half the states. Perhaps there remained in Congress a residual resentment with regard to the relatively large number of foreign officers in the Continental Army, especially in Pulaski's Legion. Undoubtedly some delegates harbored hostility toward Pulaski. As for Baron D'Ugglaa, he already had joined the Legion at Lancaster and was swept up in the final preparations for the march. He did not receive Jay's letter; therefore, Pulaski did not know of the denial.[4] Nevertheless, the incident shows again the reputation of Casimir Pulaski as an accomplished soldier under whom foreign officers were proud to serve.

Opposition to foreign officers in the Continental Army still simmered not only in Congress but also, and more so, in General Washington's army. At the time that John Jay informed D'Ugglaa of the refusal of Congress for an appointment, Washington rejected the plea of Baron de Knoblauch for an opportunity to serve the American cause. He was an experienced officer, having served in the Prussian army as well of those of other countries. He had acquired some knowledge in devising new infantry organizations. He told Congress that he gave General Von Steuben a concept of an infantry regiment after which Von Steuben modeled his own proposal. Perhaps what kept the baron unemployed was his radical scheme for recruiting a corps of 4000 Negroes with himself as commanding general. Congress would not touch the plan and procrastinated. Finally, Knoblauch sought help from Washington, who turned him down flatly. On 7 March 1779, Washington answered the baron:

> The introduction of a number of foreign officers, especially in the higher posts of the army, is considered by our own officers, as such a breach of their privileges, and occasions so much dissatis-

faction, that the practice cannot be continued without great injury to the service. And as upon this principle, I cannot with propriety recommend the appointment you now solicit.[5]

The enlistments for one year of the Legionnaires were about to expire, and Pulaski's Legion could not march south and be combat-ready at destination unless the losses in the unit, especially the infantry, were replaced. Colonel Armand's corps was also seriously depleted. Therefore, Congress resolved "That the Commander-in-Chief be directed to give the necessary orders for recruiting the corps commanded by General Count Pulaski and Colonel Armand respectively, to their full complement of infantry, to be inlisted for the war, and to receive the continental bounty granted to the rest of the infantry." Washington acknowledged the action of Congress to Pulaski on 8 February 1779. The Commander-in-Chief advised Pulaski that the required funds would have to come from Congress. He informed Pulaski of the current bounty: $200 to every man enlisting for the war, in addition to clothing and a grant of land. And every officer recruiting a soldier would be rewarded with a bounty of $20 and $3 per day as compensation for extra expenses. To hasten the preparations for the long march, Washington ordered the Legion's infantry, still stationed at Minisink, to march immediately to Lancaster, Pennsylvania. Pulaski courteously acknowledged and thanked General Hand at Minisink for his solicitous care of his Legion's infantry. "I return my heartful thanks for all the kindness you have treated my corps with during the time they have been under your command," he wrote. The bearer of the letter, Lieutenant Colonel Charles Bedaulx, carried money to reimburse Hand for advancing the pay of the Legion's infantry and for other expenditures on their behalf. Pulaski ended the letter warmly: "I would be very glad to find any opportunity to show and convince you of the regard and esteem, with which I am." By 18 February 1779, the infantry of the Legion approached Nazareth, Pennsylvania.[6]

When the infantry reached Lancaster, Pulaski was in Philadelphia, attending to the matter of the Legion's financial accounts and the planning for the march. The senior infantry officer in

Lancaster, of relatively low rank, was unable to provide his men with the necessities of bare subsistence, and the Legionnaires were not willing to wait for the slow administrative process of Pennsylvania officials to respond to their needs. In desperation, some of them roamed the countryside, intimidating both Tories and patriots alike, and seizing food and goods. The Pennsylvanians protested loudly to Reed, who was quick to act anytime the charges were against Pulaski. As President of the Supreme Council of Pennsylvania, Reed angrily asked Congress, 8 March 1779: "Is Pennsylvania to be forever scoured by that undisciplined & irregular Corps without Redress? Or must we be drove to actual Violence & resistance." Reed charged that Pulaski's infantry indiscriminately foraged and took whatever they wanted "from the poor terrified Inhabitants, many of whom strongly impressed by the Terrors of military Violence in Europe, submit to the spoiling of their goods & Insult to their person without complaining." Reed added that the growing resentment of the inhabitants could break out into open fighting between civilians and soldiers. An alarmed Timothy Pickering of the Board of War reprimanded Pulaski for the undisciplined behavior of his infantry. "The complaints are of such a nature as to demand a strict enquiry," Pickering wrote, "at the same time they should lead you and your officers to maintain a stricter discipline in the Corps." He continued: "It must give you pain, as it does us, to find the Legion followed with the execrations of the People among whom they have been stationed." Pulaski naturally felt disappointment that his Legionnaires caused trouble for the people. Nevertheless, he understood their frustrations, due to the indifference of many Americans toward the military and the continued inability of Congress and the States to support them adequately. Pulaski would quickly restore discipline with the help of the six newly-appointed officers who filled the existing officer vacancies. He gave up his personal involvement with the auditors over the accounts of his Legion to rejoin his soldiers. Bringing his cavalry and infantry together at Lancaster, he took personal control and supervision of his Legion. He concentrated on his objective of marching to the Southern Theater. Pickering assured Pulaski that the recent troubles would not delay the deployment of the Legion. "Its services are wanted at the Southward," Pickering stated,"whither we desire it may be marched with all possible dispatch." Pickering echoed the conclusion of Henry Laurens who was eager to provide some support for the South against the new British danger. On 12 February 1779, Laurens wrote the President of South Carolina: "I have most earnestly urged in Congress the immediate dispatch of Count Pulaski and his Legion, but they are still delayed for adjusting old Accounts. I think the Paymaster might remain for that purpose and another appointed *pro tempore,* but we move no faster than we would if the Southern States were in perfect peace and safety. The Count is as anxious for his departure as I am."[7]

In response to the directive of Congress, General Washington ordered Pulaski to join General Benjamin Lincoln's Army in Georgia. He also informed the Legion Commander that on various matters, such as recruiting, money, and support of states, he should turn to Congress, and that body acted promptly. On 13 February 1779, the delegates resolved to authorize Pulaski to recruit replacements to the established level for the losses in infantry, and to re-enlist men of his corps for the duration of the war (those whose times were about to expire). For this purpose Congress authorized the sum of $50,000 to be paid to the General, or his order, from time to time. To remove any objections from the states for reaching assigned quotas of Continental soldiers, Congress ruled that those individuals recruited to serve under Pulaski (and Armand) "be credited to the quota of the State in which they shall be inlisted." Planning in advance of his arrival in South Carolina in the spring, Pulaski asked Congress to authorize him to draw summer uniforms for his Legionnaires from stores there. He also requested authority to draw from Continental stores in Pennsylvania a number of caps, rifles, and saddles to replace those that became defective during the long march. Although Pulaski was about to depart, he still kept requesting more infantry, a total of 600 soldiers. He did not ask that Congress provide the soldiers from existing units; he would recruit the soldiers. Nevertheless, Congress probably balked at the added cost of bounties, pay, equipage, and maintenance. The Legion remained at its original strength.[8]

To insure that Pulaski's Legion would experience a sustained march without undue difficulties, Congress properly assumed responsibility for the journey. In turn, however, Congress gave the execution of the task to the Quartermaster General of the Continental Army, General Nathanael Greene. John Penn, member of Congress from North Carolina, and Attorney General Avery also of North Carolina, advised Colonel Charles Pettit, Assistant Quartermaster General, who then planned a route from York, Pennsylvania, "through the back country," to Purrysburg, South Carolina. The terminus lay on the Savannah River, some thirty miles from the City of Savannah. Pettit told Greene that when Congress provided the money for the journey, he would send an agent to deliver it to Pulaski and have that person accompany the Legion. Pettit explained to Greene: "Considering the Route I find it necessary for Genl Pulaski to take, I think it expedient to send a Person to precede him as a Qur Master and Forager the whole of the Way." He added that the designated person, going through an entirely new country, must have a sufficient amount of money with him. Greene approved Pettit's plan on 14 February 1779, and he pointed out the importance of a properly planned journey: "I wish you may make a happy choice, as it is a trust of considerable consequence." Following the movements of Pulaski's Legion, Greene's Deputy, Colonel Biddle, reported that the Legion was at York, Pennsylvania. He told Greene that he would write the Deputy Quartermaster in Georgia about providing forage for the Legion.[9]

On 21 February 1779, Pettit informed Greene that he had directed his agent, a Mr. Faucet, to carry money and instructions for the journey to General Pulaski. He said, "I was at much Pains in settling the Route and Plan, and at length concluded on what I thought clear Conviction to send them by way of Winchester and between the Mountains." [Shenandoah Valley]. Pettit enclosed a copy of the route. [Apparently the map has not survived]. After delivering the money and map, Faucet met with an unexpected problem—the number of wagons for the Legion. Pulaski had asked for eighteen, but the Board of War cut the number to twelve. When Faucet showed Pulaski the Board's order, the General became angry. (Pettit described the reaction as "the Count became enraged.") A frightened Faucet left Pulaski's camp and vowed that he would not return to the Legion. Therefore, upon consulting with the Board of War, Pettit appointed Captain Frederick Paschke to be the Quartermaster and Forager on behalf of the Quartermaster Corps. Pettit prepared instructions for Paschke and letters of explanation to Pulaski and Colonel David Grier, Assistant Deputy Quartermaster at York. Undoubtedly Pulaski did not appreciate having an experienced officer of the Legion tasked by Congress to perform quartermaster duties. Paschke's primary duty called for him to command and lead his company of infantry. Another of Pulaski's officers, Captain Baldesqui, was already immobilized in Philadelphia, where he worked with Congressional auditors to put the Legion's accounts in order. Pettit proposed to pay Paschke $60 a month plus traveling expenses. Pulaski held out for $90 because the captain would perform double duty, quartermaster and forager. At this point, Deputy Quartermaster General, Cornelius Cox, stepped in with a compromise offer of $80. Both Pulaski and Pettit accepted this figure. Pettit was shaken with the difficult time he experienced and expressed his discouragement to Greene: "I wish this Corps were safely under the Care of Genl Lincoln. The Board of War as well as we, I believe, are heartily sick of them."[10]

 The decision of the Board of War to reduce Pulaski's request for eighteen wagons to twelve troubled Pulaski because a shortage of six wagons could cripple and delay the march. During the long and grueling drive, the wagons would be subjected to severe wear and tear. As some wagons became worn-out, they would be disassembled into serviceable parts used to repair the remaining wagons. In the eighteenth century, the Continental Army did not "march on its stomach" but, rather, moved with its wagons.

In February 1779, Greene had urged upon Washington "the necessity of enlisting a Corps of Waggoners for the War." Greene believed that experienced drivers could not be hired for less than thirty to forty pounds a month. "Wages are rising daily," Greene warned,"and the difficulty of engaging men for this business hourly increasing." Greene also submitted a list and allocation of some 1100 wagons to provide the necessary transportation to generals and staff, brigades, logistical support units, and cavalry. Comparing the adequacy of twelve wagons for Pulaski's Legion to other units of the army may not be valid because of the units' different missions. However, examining the allocation of wagons for the cavalry could provide a reasonable comparison. The four Continental Cavalry Regiments (Moylan, Baylor, Bland, and Sheldon) received twenty-four wagons (six each). These regiments were seriously under manned, emaciated, and ineffective. For all practical purposes, the four cavalry regiments were going nowhere. Pulaski's Legion, in contrast, was about to travel some 700 miles. Pulaski was justified to object to a cut of one-third of the wagons that he believed were needed. Perhaps Pettit did not consider Pulaski's point of view. Nevertheless, Pettit did select a good route for the Legion. The course lay along towns and communities that could provide food for the soldiers and forage for the horses. On 18 March 1779, Pulaski marched the Legion to York where he made a final inspection that totaled 336 soldiers, both officers and enlisted men, and some attached volunteers. Pulaski organized the Legion as shown in Figure 2.[11]

Because the infantry marched slower than the cavalry, it departed first. Pulaski delayed the cavalry for ten days while awaiting Colonel Pettit's agent with the money to pay the soldiers and provide cash for the purchase of food and forage. Pulaski prepared a set of orders and instructions for the Legion while on the march. He reminded his officers of their responsibility for maintaining discipline and for the soldiers to avoid confrontations with civilians. He forwarded a copy to the Board of War and told Congress on 28 March 1779 about his final preparations. He informed the delegates that he had sent out three captains to recruit

ORGANIZATION OF
THE PULASKI LEGION
York, Pennsylvania, 19 March 1778

Brigadier General Casimir Pulaski, COMMANDER

COMMAND ECHELON:
Colonel Michael Kovatch, Legion Commandant
Lieutenant Colonel Charles Bedaulx, Infantry Commander
Major Peter Verney, Brigade Major

STAFF:
Captain Joseph Baldesqui, Paymaster (absent)
Captain Samuel Sullivan, Quartermaster
Dr. Felix Tixier, Surgeon
Dr. Nicholas de Bellville, Surgeon (absent)
Frederick Sander, Surgeon's Mate
Frederick Sunn, Surgeon's Mate
Godfried Leopold, Riding Master

CAVALRY:
1st Lancers, Captain Jan Zielinski (42 lancers)
2nd Troop, Captain Paul Bentalou (48 dragoons)
3rd Troop, Captain Henry Bedkin (49 dragoons)

INFANTRY:
1st Grenadier Company, Captain Maria de Segond (40 soldiers)
2nd Company, Captain Jerome de Bellcour (38 soldiers)
3rd Company, Captain Frederick Paschke (36 soldiers)
4th Chasseur Company, Captain Alexander O'Neil (47 soldiers)
Supernumerary Company, Lieutenant John Seydelin (25 soldiers)
(commanding in Baldesqui's absence)

Figure 2.

more soldiers. Of the $50,000 authorized him by Congress, he received $35,000, but he already had spent the sum simply to re-enlist 168 one-year soldiers ($200 bounty each). He requested that the remaining $15,000 be given to Paymaster Baldesqui in Philadelphia. Feeling upbeat on the eve of the march, Pulaski said: "I ought to believe I will have the satisfaction of announcing to you Some Good News from the field I am going to, and I hope also, time will show if I deserve the confidence you have honoured me with"[12]

Reaching Annapolis on April 10th, Pulaski approached the Maryland State Council for help in enlisting Marylanders in the Legion. He needed ready replacements for those losses by sickness and desertion that normally occur on a long march. He informed the officials that Captain De Segond would remain in Baltimore temporarily to conduct the recruiting. He requested the Council to offer the captain "the same protection and support which the Council granted him last year." In response to their expected help and in honor of the State of Maryland, he would name his command the "Maryland Legion." He vowed "to have that name forever honoured by our friends and respected by our enemies." To Pulaski's great disappointment, the Council ignored his gallant gesture and forbade De Segond to conduct any recruiting in the State. The Council cited the resolution of the last session of the General Assembly that limited recruiting in the state to Continental regiments of Maryland. The Council informed De Segond by letter of 20 April 1779.[13]

Meanwhile, the infantry of the Legion continued its march to Winchester, Virginia, and then due south to Staunton and North Carolina, averaging about fifteen miles a day. The march was uneventful. At Winchester, however, an unfortunate encounter occurred between two officers, one of whom was Baron D'Ugglaa. He called it "a melancholy event," in which the Baron wounded his opponent. The cause of the fight is unknown, although it may have been a duel over a question of honor. Neither General Pulaski nor Colonel Kovatch were with the infantry at the time. The two senior officers had marched the cavalry to Annapolis to seek the help of the State. Commanding the infantry corps at Winchester, Major Verney turned D'Ugglaa over to the civilian magistrate for trial. The official investigated the charges and concluded that D'Ugglaa had acted in his own defense, and he acquitted the Baron. Meanwhile, Verney confiscated D'Ugglaa's horse, which the Baron said did not belong to the Legion. Verney continued the march while D'Ugglaa was still in civilian confinement. Upon his release and without his horse, the Baron walked to Baltimore. Despite his unhappy experience in the Legion, he determined to overtake and rejoin Pulaski's command. From Baltimore, he embarked on a ship bound for Portsmouth, Virginia. He arrived there at the time General Clinton in New York ordered a British force to ravage Virginia. Seizing the opportunity to serve the Americans, he joined Colonel Marshall's detachment of artillery as a simple volunteer at Fort Nelson in Gosport. As he later reported, he skirmished against the enemy every day during the period of the British raid. On one occasion he found himself surrounded by about thirty or forty British dragoons who cut his horse from under him and forced him to flee. As the British mounted an attack on Fort Nelson, the small garrison retreated to escape capture. D'Ugglaa lost all his clothes and other personal possessions in the hasty evacuation. When the British sailed away for New York, D'Ugglaa felt free to return to Philadelphia. He now learned for the first time that his request for appointment to a lieutenancy had been denied by Congress. He then traveled to New Windsor, New York, to the headquarters of General Washington. No sooner had he arrived in New Windsor than he fell ill and remained so for six months. Upon recovering,

---

OPPOSITE PAGE: *PLANNED ROUTE OF THE PULASKI LEGION.*
The Pulaski Legion did not reach Purrysburg. At Charleston, Pulaski joined the fight to save Charleston from imminent British capture. In the following Savannah campaign, Pulaski's Legion led General Benjamin Lincoln's Southern Army into Georgia, crossing the Savannah River above Purrysburg at Zubly's Ferry.

The Long March to Savannah

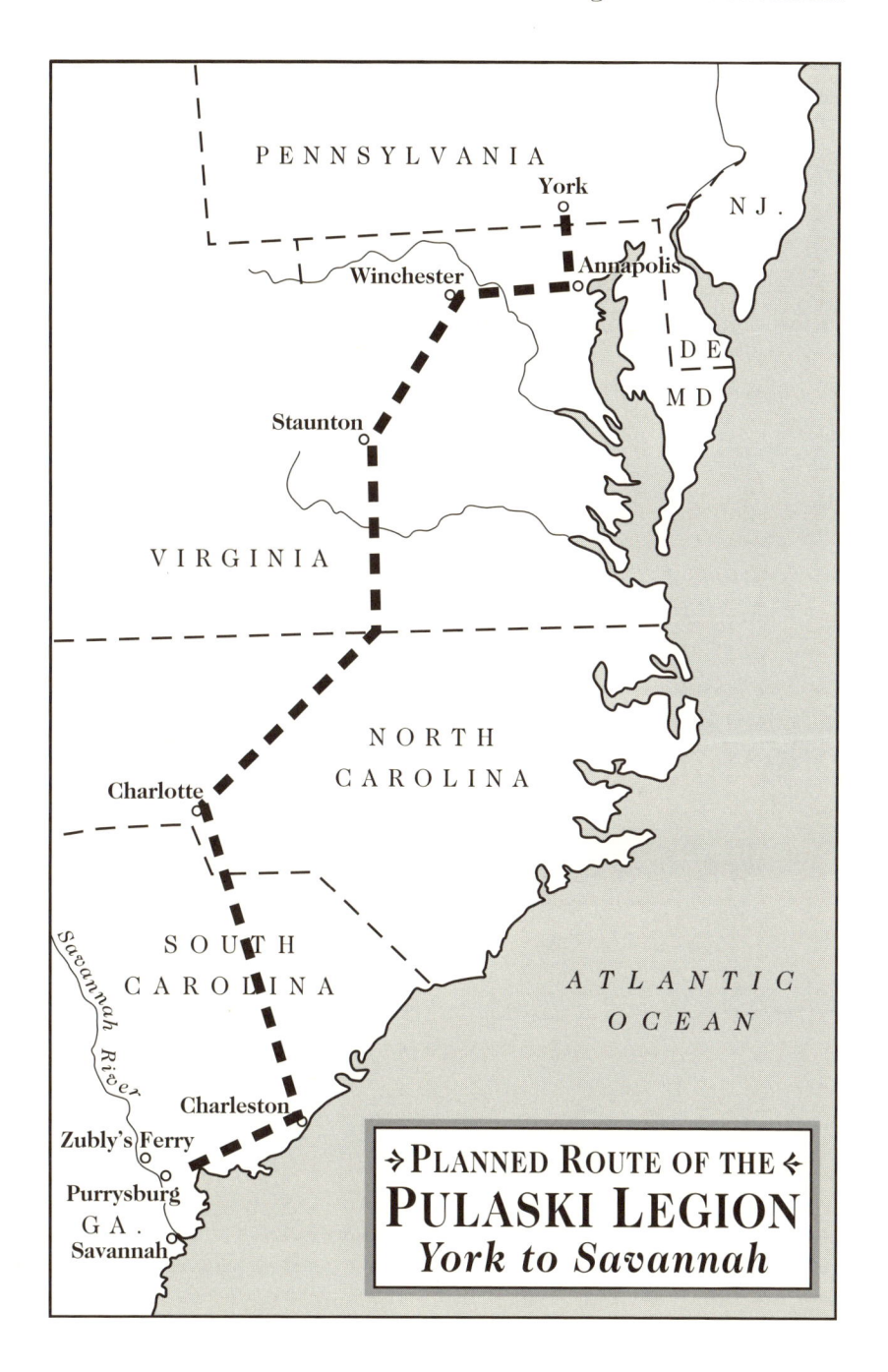

CASIMIR PULASKI

MAJOR GENERAL BENJAMIN LINCOLN
Commander of the Southern Army under whom General Pulaski served gallantly during the defense of Charleston, South Carolina, and the Battle of Savannah in 1779. Lincoln called Pulaski an intrepid general. (Portrait by Charles Willson Peale, 1781. Independence National Historical Park Collection)

he returned to Philadelphia. The Baron was destitute and devastated by his bad luck in America. He wanted to go home. On 2 June 1780, he asked Congress for financial help. He said a ship bound for Gothenbourg [Goteborg] was about to sail, and he could book passage. He pleaded with Congress "to grant him so much money as will enable him to go home, and, as he is an entire stranger in this Country, without any Friends or acquaintance, he humbly hopes his request will not be denied him." The Baron promised to repay Congress "as soon as he gets home." D'Ugglaa's request reached Congress on 5 June 1780, and the secretary routed the letter to the Treasury Board. What happened next is unknown, but it is believed that Congress granted the money for the journey.[14]

During the march of the Legion, the soldiers behaved properly. Evidently Pulaski's instructions and the presence of a full complement of experienced officers enforced discipline and prevented any problems with the people, many of whom saw military uniforms for the first time. The Legionnaires found the people friendly. The natives often greeted them with food and expressions of welcome, and Pulaski's soldiers could not help but notice the contrast between the warmth of the Southerners and hostility of many Pennsylvanians. In North Carolina, Governor Richard Caswell welcomed Pulaski and the Legion. Furthermore, he permitted Pulaski to recruit men from the state militia. The Legion Commander was buoyed by the unexpected friendly attitude of the Southerners. He felt that the people here appreciated his difficult service in the cause of American independence.[15]

At the beginning of May 1779, the Legion entered South Carolina. State officials knew that Pulaski was marching to their defense, but they were not overly enthusiastic. In fact, they were disappointed that Congress seemed to show little concern for the British threat in the South. However, Washington's undermanned army had no forces to spare. Recall that Washington initially agreed to assign Captain Schott's infantry company to the Legion but later reversed himself. On 29 March 1779, the *Secret Journals of Congress* noted "That the circumstances of the Army will not admit of the detaching of any forces for the defence of South Carolina and Georgia." Feeling abandoned, Lieutenant Governor Thomas Bee wrote Henry Drayton, member of Congress, on 5 April 1779. Bee painted a sharp contrast between the actions of the North and South. When the northern cities of Boston, New York, and Philadelphia were being attacked by the British in the earlier phases of the Rebellion, Bee said, military units as far south as North Carolina were rushed to defend them. "But now," he lamented, "not one Continental Battalion can be spared us in return, except Count Polaski's Horse, which I fear, if coming at all, will arrive too late or be too worn down...to be of any service." Despite Bee's fears, Pulaski's Legion arrived in the nick of time and became engaged in immediate fighting.[16]

Pulaski was now close enough to Charleston to receive reports of movements of British General Augustin Prevost. General Lincoln had been sparring with him in Georgia. Prevost, however, slipped away from Lincoln and marched his army north into South Carolina with the obvious intent of capturing the defenseless city of Charleston. The sudden danger threw South Carolinians into panic, for the loss of the major city in the South posed a great threat to American independence. Pulaski understood the danger and responded decisively. Although Pulaski was subordinate to Lincoln, the Southern Army Commander was out of reach in Georgia. Pulaski, therefore, took it upon himself to defend Charleston. Ordering his infantry to keep marching rapidly to Charleston, Pulaski led his cavalry at a fast pace toward the endangered city. Crossing the Cooper River, Pulaski's cavalry galloped into Charleston on 8 May 1779. The infantry arrived three days later. Pulaski could not have come at a more critical time, for the State officials were planning to surrender Charleston to General Prevost.[17]

· 8 ·

Pulaski Saves Charleston

Governor John Rutledge and members of the South Carolina Privy Council, gripped with fear for the safety of Charleston, spent long hours in heated debate of their difficult choice, fight or surrender. Rutledge was alarmed over the devastation the British could wreak on the people as well as their property. Even the slaves were at great risk. The British seized the slaves and shipped them to the West Indies, where they sold them for the financial benefit of the British Army. Historians Henry Steele Commager and Richard B. Morris explain the fears felt by South Carolinians: "The Prevost expedition [into South Carolina] was accompanied by enormous looting by the British troops. Many of the slaves who flocked to the British army were sold off to the West Indies." Counting up the number of his soldiers to oppose Prevost, Rutledge had only 400 militia commanded by Brigadier General William Moultrie and about a thousand more that the Governor himself had recently recruited. Rutledge was reinforced by the Pulaski Legion, albeit a small force, but commanded by a dynamic leader. The presence of Pulaski gave the residents an upsurge of morale. Historian Richard Barry writes that "Pulaski was not only a general of the Continental Army, by appointment of Congress, he was much more importantly... a person of authentic European title—Count Casimir Pulaski. For the moment this seems to be all that the city required."[1]

Questioning General Moultrie about the available military forces, Rutledge asked the General whether he knew the strength of a legion, since the designation was new to both. Moultrie believed a legion was composed of at least a thousand men (thinking of the strength of the ancient Roman legions). Next, Rutledge asked Moultrie whether he had visited the Pulaski Legion encamped on the neck of the peninsula just outside the city. Moultrie admitted he had not, but the Governor had been to Pulaski's camp that very day after breakfast. He said he found the strength to be 118 men, including Pulaski and two Polish aides. The remaining 115 Legionnaires were Americans brought down from Maryland, he said. Rutledge startled Moultrie with his next question, "Is not General Pulaski senior to you?" Moultrie did not know. He at once rode out to Pulaski's camp and returned with Pulaski. Moultrie was pleased. The two generals had compared dates of commission, and Moultrie was senior by eighteen days. Pulaski accepted Moultrie's seniority despite his insistence on taking orders only from the army commander, General Lincoln. In the face of danger, Pulaski again did not stand on rank or protocol. He wanted to fight and cooperate for the good of the American cause as he had done with Anthony Wayne at Haddonfield. Having resolved the question of rank amicably, Rutledge invited the two generals to dinner.[2]

On 11 May 1779, General Prevost's troops reached Ashley's Ferry, twelve miles north of Charleston, and continued to the outskirts of the city. Why Moultrie did not oppose him on the west bank of the Cooper River is not clear. Had he done so, the Americans could have taken advantage of water separating the British from their objective. Perhaps it was due to the vacillation of Rutledge. He still considered surrendering the city. With the concurrence of the Privy Council, by a vote of five to three in favor, Rutledge dispatched a message to Prevost, stating the terms of surrender:

That he [Prevost] be permitted to take possession of the Town provided the state and harbor be considered neutral during the state of war, the question of whether it belonged to the United States or Great Britain to be waived until the end of the war, and that whatever was granted to the other states it should enjoy.

The terms were advantageous to the British but disastrous to Americans. Pulaski and Moultrie protested vigorously. Supported by his friend Colonel John Laurens, Pulaski flatly told Rutledge that "as a continental officer he would defend the city for the United States." He strode out of the council chamber and galloped to his camp. Pulaski had a bold plan that he believed could revive the drooping spirit of the residents. He planned to strike Prevost in the expectation the British General would pause to assess the eruption of unexpected resistance. Perhaps he could stall the British for a day or two and also reinforce the spirit of resistance of those South Carolinians who wanted to fight the British. Pulaski set a trap, as he had done successfully many times against the Russians in Poland. He placed Lieutenant Colonel Bedaulx's infantry, some eighty of them, in a valley and screened by a simple breast work. He rode forward with his dragoons to meet the British advance. Then feinting a retreat, he would bait the redcoats to pursue his cavalry past the ambush from where a tremendous volley of fire would cut them down. On 11 May 1779, after placing the infantry in position, Pulaski rode forward with the cavalry to locate the British. About a mile north of the town, the Pulaski cavalry attacked a sizable force of British dragoons, led by Captain Tawes. Both sides engaged in a dramatic shock action, one of the few cavalry fights in the Revolutionary War. The scene turned chaotic—slashing sabers, piercing lances, and the cracking sounds of pistols. Disregarding his own safety, Pulaski boldly wheeled about the melee. Historian Joseph Johnson writes: "Attack on the British...without him [Pulaski] would certainly not have been made. In this very gallant attack on the British advance, he had personally several encounters with individuals of the enemy, and was always the victor." Meanwhile, Bedaulx waited patiently for a glimpse of the cavalry. Hearing the sounds of the clash and eager to get into the fight, Bedaulx abandoned the ambush. Unfortunately, he destroyed Pulaski's carefully laid plan. Quickly Bedaulx's infantry was engulfed by swarms of British regulars who inflicted severe casualties. Having lost the engagement, Pulaski ordered the survivors to retreat. With remnants of the dragoons and infantry, Pulaski and Bedaulx managed to extricate themselves and fight their way back to the American lines. Losses in the Legion were devastating. Colonel Kovatch was killed. He was mortally wounded in the fighting, and during the hectic retreat he fell from his horse and died on the ground. After the engagement, the British buried him at the site where he fell, on the west side of the road, at the corner of Huger Street. The brave Captain Jan Zielinski was seriously wounded while charging the British with his company of lancers. Kinsman of Pulaski, Zielinski survived the fight but lay struggling to live in a Charleston hospital for nearly five months. He died on 25 September 1779. The deaths of two very close companions, Kovatch and Zielinski, were especially heart wrenching for Pulaski. The Legion Commander may have reprimanded Bedaulx for the heavy loss of his soldiers, but he expressed his dismay within the confines of the Legion. In his *Memoirs,* Major Maciej [Matthew] Rogowski writes about Pulaski's failed entrapment of the British. Rogowski says that Pulaski, seeing the infantry had quit its screened position, cried out angrily, "May the geese trample down that Frenchman!" In camp, Pulaski rebuked his infantry commander, telling him bluntly that he had bungled the ambuscade. Nevertheless, Pulaski never criticized Bedaulx's failure to Governor Rutledge, General Moultrie, or Congress. Similarly, Pulaski earlier had not blamed Baron Von Bose for Captain Ferguson's attack at Little Egg Harbor. As the Legion Commander, Pulaski took the responsibility himself. He had selected his officers, they were his companions, and he would fight the enemy with them.[3]

The loss of Pulaski's infantry was drastic. Most of the eighty infantrymen were killed, wounded, or captured. Captain Celeron and Lieutenant De la Close were among the captured. But the British paroled and released the two officers the next day, perhaps

GENERAL AUGUSTIN PREVOST
General Pulaski's cavalry boldly attacked the vanguard of Prevost's army at Charleston, South Carolina, 11 May 1779, and stopped the capitulation of the city. Prevost subsequently successfully defended Savannah, Georgia, against the bloody assault by French and American armies, 9 October 1779. (Photo courtesy of Georgia Historical Society, Savannah)

in recognition of the Legion's gallant attack. Celeron informed Moultrie of his conversation with General Prevost, who remarked that General Lincoln's Southern Army did not exceed 1500 soldiers. As for the strength of the British Army, Celeron said he saw the whole army and estimated its number not to exceed 3500 including three to four hundred Indians. Moultrie passed this intelligence to Lincoln. Pulaski made up some losses in the cavalry with natives. Bentalou writes that "all the young men, who could procure horses, united to place themselves under his command." Undoubtedly, Pulaski was pleased to see young South Carolinians eager to join his Legion.[4]

Following Pulaski's attack on the British, General Moultrie recorded the event matter of factly, 11 May 1779:

> This day Count Pulaski's infantry came into town from Haddrell's Point, the cavalry of his Legion came in with himself on the 8th. We this morning had advice that the enemy were near our lines. Gen. Count Pulaski had paraded his Legion (about one hundred and twenty, and some militia) and attacked the advance of the British troops a little beyond the race ground in sight of our advance guard; but he was soon overpowered; in the skirmish he lost his Col. (Kovatch) killed and most of his infantry, killed and wounded and prisoners; and it was with difficulty the remainder got in with our advance guard.[5]

American Historian William Gordon, who experienced the Revolutionary War, wrote one of the earliest accounts of Pulaski's clash with the troops of General Prevost:

> Nine hundred of the British army, their main body and baggage left on the south side of the Ashley river, crossed the ferry and soon appeared before the town. The same day Count Pulaski's legionary corps of infantry crossed Cooper's river to Charlestown. They had scarcely arrived two hours, when he led 80 of them out of the lines and stationed them in a valley behind a small breast work, with the view of drawing the British into an ambuscade. He advanced a mile beyond his infantry, and joined a party of regular horse and mounted militia volunteers, and with that force engaged the British cavalry for a while, and then retreated to his infantry; who from an eagerness to engage, had quitted their breast work

and so rendered abortive the advantage of the intended ambuscade, and were by superior numbers compelled to retreat. Pulaski, however, by discovering the greatest intrepidity, and by successful personal recontres with individuals of the British cavalry, had a considerable influence in dispelling the general panic and in introducing military sentiments into the minds of the citizens.[6]

Brigade Major F. Skelly gives the British version of the fight with Pulaski's Legion, as he recorded in his *Journal:*

1779, May 12th. Polaskey (a great partisan) had advanced his Legion consisting of about a hundred foot and eighty Horse. The foot was posted behind a kind of Breast work thro which was a large entrance. Polaskey with his horse (the best Cavalry the rebels ever had) advanced towards our Dragoons. Capt. Tawes charged them [Tawes commanded about 200 dragoons], intirely routed them, pursued them thro' the Breast work, attacked their Foot and drove them to the woods. The Lt. Col. who comm[anded] the foot was killed and fifteen or sixteen of his men. A captain and a sub of the cavalry were taken and several of their privates killed and taken. In all, they loss'd between forty and fifty men. Our loss three dragoons Killed and three wounded.

Skelly's number of only six British casualties seems light. Nevertheless, the advance guard of Tawes dragoons was quickly reinforced by British infantry, part of the 900-man force of General Prevost's army that first arrived outside of Charleston.[7]

As a pure military action, Pulaski's attack against a vastly superior enemy seems foolhardy, as some American historians portray the event. However, Pulaski did not plan to engage General Prevost's whole army. His purpose was to strike the lead elements and cause a delay as the British assessed the unexpected threat. Furthermore, he wished to demonstrate for the benefit of General Prevost that, although the civilian government was on the verge of capitulation, the military leaders opposed surrender and would make him fight for Charleston. Many plantation owners lacked the spirit of resistance. They were more concerned with protecting their property rather than saving Charleston. Pulaski had run into the same problem in Poland, where some magnates valued their vast holdings of land rather than the sovereignty of the nation. He had fought for liberty of his country, free of Russian domination. He was willing to suffer casualties and lose battles for a broader goal. Liberty firmly took possession of his soul. In America, the noble goal of independence motivated his conduct. As historian Jared Sparks writes of Pulaski's clash with the British: "His coolness, courage and disregard of personal danger, were conspicuous throughout the encounter, and the example of this prompt and bold attack had great influence in raising the spirits of the people and inspiring the confidence of the inexperienced troops then assembled in the city."[8]

Pulaski's bold attack of the British cost his Legion dearly. Nevertheless, he achieved the larger purpose of saving Charleston. While Prevost was deciding whether to fight and capture Charleston, he received disturbing reports of the approach of General Lincoln's army. He concluded the risk was too great to remain before Charleston and be caught between the defenders of the city to his front and Lincoln's army to his rear. During the night of 11–12 May 1779, Prevost quietly withdrew his soldiers to the Islands of James and Johns.[9]

At dawn of 12 May, American soldiers on the defense lines were surprised to note an absence of the enemy. At once, Pulaski mounted his horse and galloped through the area of the former British encampment. Indeed, the British had withdrawn. And General Moultrie reported to General Lincoln: "The next morning at day-light, to the great joy of the citizens, it was cried out along the line, 'The enemy is gone.'"[10]

Historian Page Smith, hostile to Pulaski, insultingly describes the cavalry commander's reconnaissance: "Pulaski, always a showoff, mounted his horse and dashed out, making 'two or three circuits at full speed.'" At the time, Pulaski was not feeling well. John Frederick Lewis writes: "During all this time Pulaski was suffering under a severe attack of fever and ague, but with his inimitable courage kept on reconnoitering and harassing the enemy." Undoubtedly the fever-ridden Pulaski would not ride out just to show off, and Smith sees no military value in Pulaski confirming the withdrawal of the British.[11]

After informing Moultrie of the British departure, Pulaski decided to locate the enemy. He first returned to camp for his cavalry. Without giving the dragoons any respite from the hard fighting of the day before, he searched for the soldiers of General Prevost. The British retreat during the night gained them some distance. Pulaski followed their trail to the Ashley River, which they had already crossed. Prudently Pulaski did not advance any further with his small force. He rode to meet with Lincoln's advancing army. He paused at Dorchester on the Ashley River some twenty miles northeast of Charleston. From there he sent a message to Moultrie, telling the general that he would remain in the vicinity of Dorchester until he got news of Lincoln's advance. He reported that he had only forty dragoons available and that all the militia had left him. Nevertheless, he sent out a party to patrol the Ashley River.[12]

In New York, General Sir Henry Clinton became alarmed over General Prevost's invasion of South Carolina. Clinton believed that Prevost was too weak to engage in such a bold action. "The force Major General Prevost had with him in Georgia," he explained, "was fully sufficient to repel all attempts of the rebels to dispossess him of that province, but was not equal to more." He was concerned that Prevost could have exposed Savannah to recapture by the Americans, and if Prevost had been defeated in South Carolina, he might well have destroyed the British strategy for the conquest of the South. Clinton also explained that Prevost's risky effort probably had roused the South Carolinians to fortify their capital and make the capture of Charleston more difficult in the future. Indeed, Clinton was planning a major undertaking for the capture of Charleston in 1780. The British Commander-in-Chief was not displeased that Prevost failed to capture Charleston but rather relieved that he safely returned to Savannah.[13]

Smith, writing of the arrival of Pulaski's Legion at Charleston, pauses to deride the commander: "Pulaski, who was obstreperous and moody by turns, had presented Washington with one of his most worrisome foreign-officer problems." Evidently Smith did not bother to research and understand the difficulty that Pulaski experienced with his regimental commanders of the Continental cavalry: Colonels Baylor, Sheldon, and especially Moylan (Colonel Bland was an exception to the lot). The three colonels resented Pulaski as a foreign officer. They were representative of many other American officers who were highly critical of foreigners for taking officer positions that the Americans felt belonged to them. In addition, the regimental commanders were suspicious of each other and quarreled among themselves. For this reason, Washington never recommended any one of them for brigadier general after Pulaski's resignation. Washington disclosed his misgivings to the President of Congress, 3 August 1778: "To promote any gentlemen now in it, to general Command, would not be acquiesced in by the rest (nor do I know that any of them wish it) and it would increase their misunderstanding and of course disorder." Indeed, Pulaski was not obstreperous; he tried to get along. The Americans were the unruly ones. Furthermore, Smith writes that Washington solved the disharmony in the cavalry corps by authorizing Pulaski to recruit his own legion. Smith again reveals his shallow research when he then says that Pulaski's staff consisted of Polish officers he had brought with him and that the soldiers were, for the most part, Hessian deserters. This author found only two Poles in the officer corps of the Legion, Captains Zielinski and Paschke (omitting Kotkowski who served briefly). An all-Polish officer corps would have undoubtedly delighted Pulaski. Historian Franklin Kemp describes the composition of the Pulaski Legion:

> It is generally believed by many, especially in Europe, that the Pulaski Legion was a Polish military Unit. This is incorrect. While Count Pulaski and one or two of the officers of the Legion were of that nationality, an examination of the roster of the Legion reveals that most of the members were of Anglo-Saxon descent. There was also a fair representation of French and German names.[14] (See Figure 1, page 68).

The withdrawal of the British army from South Carolina removed the great threat that had hung over the fate of Charleston.

The patriots were overjoyed. Nevertheless, the outcome had swung precariously between capitulation and fighting. Had Pulaski not attacked the British at a very critical moment, General Prevost assuredly would have been master of the key Southern city in America. Pulaski strengthened the resolve of South Carolinians and stalled the British just long enough for General Lincoln's advancing army to loom as a threat to Prevost. Colonel Frederic Gilbert Bauer, writing in *The Cavalry Journal*, states, "Pulaski's Legion by its sixty-day march south helped relieve Charleston in May, 1779." Historian Roger Bruns writes more conclusively, "Charleston was saved at the last minute by a mounted unit led by Casimir Pulaski, a Polish cavalry officer who, like Lafayette, had come to America to fight for the revolutionaries." Indeed, General Pulaski saved Charleston.[15]

· 9 ·

THE SIEGE OF SAVANNAH

GENERAL PREVOST WITHDREW his army from near Charleston on 12 May 1779 and crossed the Ashley River to the southern bank. After camping three miles above Ashley's Ferry for a few days, he retreated to James and Johns Islands. General Pulaski and his cavalry continually followed his movements, keeping General Moultrie informed. Moultrie immediately passed this intelligence to General Lincoln. Moultrie wrote Lincoln: "All my intelligence hitherto has been from Count Pulaski." The Legion Commander was very satisfied with the manner his cavalry was being employed. As Lincoln neared the British, Prevost assembled his army on Johns Island and built redoubts at Stono River Ferry. The enemy action challenged Lincoln who ordered Brigadier General Isaac Huger with a thousand infantry, and supported by Pulaski's and Colonel Daniel Horry's South Carolina cavalry, to attack the British at Stono Ferry. As he instinctively behaved before engaging in battle, Pulaski first reconnoitered the British position. He found the enemy strongly entrenched. Their flanks were protected by artillery batteries, fully manned and ready to fire. In addition, Prevost reinforced his position at Stono Ferry. Pulaski concluded that the British were posted too strongly for the attempt. As senior officer, Pulaski ordered Huger to retire. Shortly thereafter a British deserter informed the Americans that General Prevost's brother, Colonel Mark Prevost, commanded the position at the ferry with 1500 troops and was confident of repelling the Americans. During his reconnaissance, Pulaski attacked an exposed party of British soldiers near the ferry where two of his officers were wounded in the fight. The British broke off the engagement and retreated to a thick woods. Pulaski planned to attack them a second time, but thought otherwise when his intended target received sizable reinforcements. A stalemate of several days occurred while Pulaski awaited Lincoln's next decision.[1]

Camped on the road to Jacksonborough, six miles from Stono Ferry, Pulaski wrote Congress, 4 June 1779. The Legion Commander felt great satisfaction from fighting the British daily. "I am charmed with being able to inform you in particular," he wrote, "that the Conduct of my Corps in this Country is as useful as it was displeasing in Pennsylvania." He reported losing forty soldiers "on the Fields of Battle" and the same number of deserters. He said he still had a fighting Legion of 180 soldiers. Pulaski was happy to be among the people of South Carolina who extended a warm welcome to his Legionnaires and to him personally. Governor Rutledge rode out immediately to meet Pulaski as soon as he encamped his cavalry outside the town. Rutledge cordially welcomed Pulaski while sizing up the capability of the Legion with a discerning eye. Pulaski's bold attack on a superior British force at Charleston, 11 May 1779, impressed the South Carolinians. He wanted Congress to know of the effective performance of his Legion in the Southern Department. Therefore, his letter of June 4th was one attempt. In addition, he was anxious to remove any unfavorable impression of himself with the delegates of Congress over Joseph Reed's sharp criticism of the behavior of his Legionnaires. Pulaski asked Rutledge whether he would be willing to inform the delegates from South Carolina about his performance in the South. Rutledge readily agreed. On 22 July 1779, the Governor wrote his delegates: "I am perfectly satisfied with his Demeanor. I have a high opinion of his military abilities & am persuaded that his Corps has rendered essential service against the enemy." Rutledge closed the letter with a request, "This you will be pleased to make known (where necessary or proper to Congress)."[2]

On 15 June 1779, General Lincoln came to Charleston to consult with Governor Rutledge and the State Council on a plan of attacking the British at Stono Ferry. After reaching agreement, Lincoln ordered Moultrie to prepare his troops in Charleston "to march on the shortest notice." For his part, Rutledge instructed Moultrie to ready 1200 soldiers for the attack. The Governor also asked Moultrie to inform Pulaski and the cavalry to join Lincoln. But Lincoln believed that Moultrie needed Pulaski's cavalry more than he. Lincoln told Moultrie, "I have written to Count Pulaski to aid you in your movements." In his letter of 17 June 1779, Lincoln gave Moultrie specific directions to carry out a flanking attack from the direction of James Island. He told Moultrie "to throw over on James Island all the troops which can be spared from town" and let the British on Johns Island see the Americans. Lincoln also instructed Moultrie to bring boats for the crossing to Johns Island "in case an opportunity should offer without risking too much." Lincoln's plan, therefore, called for Moultrie to make a diversionary attack for the purpose of pinning down British troops while Lincoln made the main attack at Stono Ferry. Moultrie's signal to attack would be the sounds of firing coming from the directions of Stono Ferry and any movement of the British away from him. If these conditions developed, Moultrie was to tread on the heels of the retreating enemy.[3]

Moultrie managed to get about 700 soldiers onto James Island on the morning of 20 June 1779. To his surprise, he discovered Lincoln had attacked that very morning without waiting for him. After the battle Lincoln explained that he had received information which later proved to be false. Deserters and a trusted individual reported to Lincoln that the British at the ferry numbered not more than 600 soldiers and they appeared to be on the verge of retreating. Lincoln felt compelled to strike a blow before

Prevost got away. In actuality, the enemy force at the ferry consisted of British and Hessian troops, some 900 strong, under the command of that fighting officer Lieutenant Colonel John Maitland. On the American side, Lincoln's army totaled between 6000 and 7000 soldiers. Notwithstanding his superior strength, Lincoln employed only 1200 and began the battle without Moultrie's diversion. Lincoln attacked with two columns against very stiff British resistance. Maitland repulsed the attack. Lincoln explained that Maitland was reinforced during the fighting. Along the line of redoubts on the British right, a creek formed a protective barrier. Lincoln had not known of it. He claimed the creek "was the real reason why our continental troops did not storm the works as was intended." After an hour of indecision, Lincoln halted further attacks and withdrew. On James Island, meanwhile, Moultrie's situation turned ominous when British troops began crossing to his side. He, too, withdrew his force. The American defeat at Stono Ferry resulted in heavy casualties: 146 killed and wounded, and 115 missing. The British lost three officers, twenty-three soldiers killed, ten officers and ninety-three men wounded. Historian Ward severely criticizes Lincoln's generalship. Ward points to the Southern Army commander's poor judgment when he employed only 1200 men, largely militia, from a much greater available army against 900 British and Hessian regulars entrenched in prepared fortifications. Nevertheless, Lincoln's attack hastened the retreat of General Prevost to Savannah. At Beaufort on Port Royal Island, Prevost stationed Colonel Maitland's regiment of 800 soldiers while he continued with the remainder to Savannah. Fighting subsided for the time being. Pulaski returned to Charleston in early July 1779 to recuperate from sickness. His health had suffered from exposure in the marshy country. Many of his Legionnaires were also sick. Southerners contended that the heat of the summer would put an end to fighting and compel the armies to retire into summer quarters.[4]

Prior to the American assault on the British at Stono Ferry, 20 June 1779, General Lincoln planned but countermanded an earlier attack. In his *Memoirs,* Moultrie does not personally write of the attack that did not take place, but it involved General Pulaski. Moultrie enclosed a letter of Colonel John F. Grimke to J. Kean, Esquire, 21 June 1779. Grimke wrote that Lincoln planned "a proper and well concerted attack upon the enemy at Wappoo" (Wappoo-cut, a waterway between the Ashley and Stono Rivers and which separates James Island from the mainland). Nevertheless, Lincoln revoked his order "almost at the very moment of the assault on their works." Grimke does not explain why in his letter. However, he adds that "in consequence of which, General Pulaski had withdrawn his legionary corps from the service, in disgust." What upset Pulaski is not known. Perhaps he played a role in formulating the attack. In any event, Pulaski did not quit. Grimke also paints a picture of a disintegrating Southern Army camped at Sommers "mouldering away." The South Carolina militia were leaving for home individually. The enlistments of the Virginia and North Carolina militia were about to expire. Faced with this situation, Lincoln called a Council of War on the evening of 19 June and announced his plan to attack the British at Stono Ferry the very next morning. As noted, Lincoln explained the attack as a compelling desire to strike a retreating enemy. Grimke offers another explanation: Lincoln's Southern Army was disintegrating. It appears, therefore, that Lincoln felt compelled to hasten his attack whether he was ready or not.[5]

In mid-July 1779, General Moultrie predicted the beginning of a new campaign. His fears of more fighting troubled Lincoln, for the Southern Army was in no condition to renew the fighting. He told Moultrie that he hoped his conjectures "are without foundation, for we are by no means prepared for such an event." He explained that at present he had neither men, stores, nor money. And "the continental currency is so depreciated and worthless," he added, "that it will not answer the purpose of prosecuting the war." As if to reinforce Lincoln's concern for the weak condition of his army, Moultrie informed him on 17 July 1779 that the 3rd South Carolina Regiment mutinied for lack of pay and clothing, after waiting for four to five months.[6]

The lull in fighting gave Pulaski time to think about the difficulties he had experienced in America. On 19 August 1779, he unburdened himself in a long letter (and his last one) to Congress. The letter can be considered the Pole's dying testament. He pointed up the constant harassment from the auditors of Congress over the accounts of his Legion, the ill-treatment from some members of Congress and officers of the Continental Army, and the abuses and slurs against himself and his Legion. When the letter reached Philadelphia on 1 October 1779, a secretary of Congress recorded the letter in a register of correspondence and callously labeled the contents "Complaints." Pulaski wrote that he was baffled by the inability of the members to understand his motives in volunteering to fight for American independence. He said that everything he did was suspect and that he had to justify every move he makes. It seemed to Pulaski "that there is Some Malignant Spirit Constantly Casting Such an impenetrable might before your Eyes, as to render it impossible for you to See and judge my Conduct with propriety, and as becomes the Character of Gentlemen in Your Exalted Stations." He explained that his zeal for the American cause and a contempt for death motivated him to come to America. He believed that here he could gain honor and contribute to victory on the battlefield. However, he lamented that "Such has been my Lot, that nothing Less than my honour, which I will never forfeit, retains me in a Service, which ill treatment makes me begin to abhor."

Pulaski stressed the many times he demonstrated his devotion to the American cause. He asked, "Is there any one act of mine, Ever since the battle of brandywine down to the present period, the campaign of Charlestown, that has not demonstrated the most disinterested Zeal for the public cause?" Therefore, he asks, "Whence comes it then that I have so Little Credit among you Gentlemen?" Pulaski believed he had been hounded since the origin of his Independent Legion. He reminded Congress of his remarkable achievement of recruiting, clothing, and organizing a unique legion in the space of three short months. But then his achievement provoked questions that he had to address and defend. He brought up the event the year before in Philadelphia

The Siege of Savannah

when a few Legionnaires refused to pay exorbitant prices for items for the Legion. "I cannot Express my indignation," he wrote, "when I recollect the infamous chicane by which I was compelled to appear before a Court like a criminal." Pulaski's anger welled up again over the Reed affair in October 1778. Congress frustrated him over the delay in ordering the Legion out against the enemy due to the alleged misbehavior of his Corps among the inhabitants of Pennsylvania. The misbehavior was alleged because Pulaski revealed previously unknown data—that the Legion had obtained certificates from the magistrates, wherever his troops were quartered, that commended their behavior. He now disclosed that some Americans seized upon the British surprise attack on the Legion at Little Egg Harbor to insinuate negligence on his part. "Although my Corps behaved with firmness at Little Egg Harbor and several officers and soldiers fell or were wounded, their only reward was slander," Pulaski charged.

Although the author closely researched the activities of the Legion from primary source documents, he learned from Pulaski's letter to Congress of 19 August 1779 that Captain Bedkin's company of dragoons was not present with the Legion in South Carolina. Pulaski had left Bedkin behind to gather sick Legionnaires and those on furlough who kept the expensive horses of the Legion. He also entrusted Bedkin with $5000 to carry on additional recruiting. Pulaski's effort was thwarted, however, when the Board of War detached Bedkin's company and made him independent. For what purpose is not clear. The action of the Board seemed like a deliberate move to cripple the Legion. Pulaski felt as if the Board had cut off an arm from his body. He reacted indignantly: "Has it not the appearance of an insidious design of disaffected persons to urge me to quit the Service in disgust, without minding the justice of their proceedings?"

Pulaski devoted a good part of his letter to the unresolved accounts of his Legion during the organizational period. (The author discusses this matter in Appendix A). However, a few important facts should be disclosed here. From his first arrival in America, 23 July 1777, Pulaski spent his own money to maintain himself and much of the Legion's expenses. He never drew the pay of a brigadier general, $115 per month. "You cannot be ignorant," Pulaski explained, "that I have spent considerably more than the sum in question of my own for the pleasure of advancing your cause; you must be sensible also, that I did not come to America destitute of resources, to be a burthen on you." He disclosed that, in several letters from his family in Poland, the family dispatched the sum of 100,000 French *livres* in hard money to him. "Should it fortunately come safe," he said, "the pleasure to me will be truly great, to repay you to the utmost farthing the whole charge of my legion."

Pulaski's final letter to Congress contains his noble statement of purpose, and it bears repeating:

> Know that as I could not submit to stoop before the sovereigns of Europe, so I came to hazard all for the freedom of America, and, desirous of passing the rest of my life in a country truly free, and, before settling as a citizen, to fight for liberty.

Despite his frustrations and difficulties with Congress, he never faltered in his great devotion to freedom. His passion for liberty elevated him above all pettiness and sustained him to the end of his life. He closed his letter, still optimistic: "The campaign is at hand [Savannah]; perhaps I may still [have] an occasion of showing that I am a friend to the cause without being happy enough to please some individuals."[7]

Pulaski was eager to begin the next campaign. Again he would be fighting the British, the real enemy. He was also pleased with the active role his Legion had performed in the South. In contrast, he had little to show for the several months of service in the North. Washington was to blame. Not understanding the proper manner of employing the cavalry, he squandered its capability. He considered it a secondary arm. For Washington, the infantry was the king of battle, with artillery in a supporting role. In addition, the Commander-in-Chief believed that cavalry was too expensive. He maintained that he could recruit and equip three infantry for the cost of one cavalryman.

Meanwhile, the opposing armies in the South ceased active operations to escape the steamy heat of the summer. When the militia went home, the Southern Army melted down to an emaciated force. Only Pulaski's Legion and two battalions of South Carolina Continentals remained. Under the command of General Moultrie, the small army occupied Shelton, South Carolina, in a position to watch Colonel Maitland's 800 British troops at Beaufort on Port Royal Island. Shelton lay only about ten miles from Beaufort, but a waterway offered the island a protective barrier. General Prevost and the remainder of the British Army rested in Savannah.[8]

In the West Indies, the French Fleet of Admiral Count D'Estaing scored a few victories against the British. Americans seized upon the idea of inviting the French admiral to employ his powerful force in the capture of Savannah. Governor Rutledge invited the admiral; Colonel De Bretigny, a French officer of the Continental Army, also urged the Admiral. The French consul in Charleston, Monsieur Plombard, added his plea. They told D'Estaing that the British force at Savannah was weak, since Prevost had divided his army between Georgia and South Carolina. D'Estaing agreed, perhaps moved to erase the bad impression he had created the year before when he abandoned the attack on Newport, Rhode Island. He stressed, however, that the capture of Savannah must be done quickly, perhaps in ten days; his fleet could not remain in the South Atlantic for long because of the approaching hurricane season. D'Estaing sent General Viscount de Fontages to Charleston to coordinate a plan of attack on Savannah. Lincoln immediately gathered his scattered army for the march to Savannah. Historian David Ramsay writes: "The fall of Savannah was considered as infallibly certain. It was generally believed that in a few days the British would be stripped of all their southern possessions."[9]

Meanwhile, the French Fleet, consisting of twenty-two ships of the line and eleven frigates, reached the mouth of the Savannah River on 8 September 1779. D'Estaing carried some 4000 French and colonial soldiers. Including the Americans, the allies would have a considerably greater force than the British. Historians Commager and Morris write: "The combined Franco-American attacking forces numbered 5000, along with Pulaski's Legion, as against 3200 defenders."[10]

With Pulaski's cavalry leading the way, General Lincoln marched his small army to the Savannah River. He commanded a force of 1,000 soldiers, consisting of South Carolina Continentals and militia. Upon reaching Zubly's Ferry, a few miles above Purrysburg, 11 September 1779, Lincoln met an unexpected problem—there were no boats to ferry the troops. He had issued a call to all units to obtain boats for the crossing, but none was to be had. He found only one canoe capable of carrying three infantrymen. Lincoln was anxious to get Pulaski's cavalry across the river in order that he reconnoiter and find the enemy. As Captain Bentalou relates the day at the ferry site, Pulaski accomplished the laborious task. With his accoutrements, only one dragoon could be carried in the canoe, while his horse swam alongside. In this manner, almost thirty cavalry and horses crossed to the opposite bank. Placed in command of this unit, Bentalou followed a causeway for about three miles through a swamp before reaching firm ground. Along the causeway, Bentalou had to repair several small bridges before the horses could continue. At the end of the causeway, Bentalou observed two redoubts (temporary field fortifications of earth and logs). He grew wary. There was no way of going to the right or left of the redoubts. A cautious approach to the redoubts disclosed that the British had abandoned them. Bentalou became more concerned about his environment. He commanded only a tiny force in enemy territory, without the possibility of assistance from an army stranded on the opposite shore of the Savannah River. His safety lay in being wakeful and alert. As he rode on, Bentalou found additional redoubts. Fortunately again, the British had evacuated them all. In the evening of the next day, Bentalou came within sight of Savannah. His men and horses were exhausted. Nevertheless, he had gathered important intelligence—General Prevost had withdrawn all his soldiers within the defense lines of

Savannah. Bentalou started back to the ferry. About midnight of the same day, he was challenged. To his great relief, it proved to be Pulaski, who, taking the remainder of the Legion's cavalry and some volunteers, followed rapidly after Bentalou. Pulaski and the cavalry spent the night at a nearby plantation.[11]

As to the movements of the French, Admiral D'Estaing's fleet cast anchor off Tybee Island, and the Admiral prepared to land soldiers on the mainland. Four days later he brought ashore 1200 troops at Beaulieu, located twelve miles from the mouth of the Ossabaw River and about thirteen to the south of Savannah. The landing was unopposed. D'Estaing immediately dispatched a messenger with information of his landing to Lincoln. Knowing of Pulaski and believing that he would be in the vicinity of Savannah, D'Estaing added a special letter to the cavalry commander. At Pulaski's camp the next morning, the dragoons spotted a man in a red coat, riding through the woods. The dragoons pursued the unknown rider and brought him to Pulaski. The stranger proved to be D'Estaing's messenger. According to Bentalou, D'Estaing wrote laudatory remarks about Pulaski and said that he expected Pulaski to be the first to greet him. Pulaski immediately dispatched a message to Lincoln, 14 September 1779, informing him of his contact with D'Estaing and of his plan to join the Admiral as soon as possible. Notwithstanding the heavy rain that day, Pulaski rode to Beaulieu where D'Estaing and Pulaski "cordially embraced and expressed mutual happiness at the meeting." Pulaski informed the Admiral that General Lincoln with about 600 infantry and artillery was in the act of crossing the Savannah River and that Lincoln's subordinate, Brigadier General Lachlan McIntosh with three companies of Georgia troops, was marching from Augusta to join Lincoln. In all, Pulaski told Comte D'Estaing the American Army consisted of about 1000 infantry, 260 cavalry, and eight pieces of cannon.[12]

Meanwhile, French soldiers continued to come ashore, some 4000 in all. The initial 1200 marched from Beaulieu to a camp three miles from Savannah. D'Estaing did not wait for Lincoln. He would capture Savannah on his own and even the score with

Casimir Pulaski

> Dear General
>
> I have take[n] my quarter about seven miles from Savannah, at the widow Gibbon's house, on the way to Ogeechee's ferry, it is very essential post, the Ennemies got an advanced one about two miles from the town, that they have posted there since last night, being alarmed by the Detachment wich was on their Lines yesterday, it will be necessary that my detachment should be reinforced not only by the cavalry, but with some infantry to give me the paisibility of attacking their picques. I shall pursue two miles further on the Sunburry's road to keep a free communication with Count D'estaing. The enemies land on the road very often some parties.
>
> > I have the honor to be
> > with respect, Dear General,
> > Your most humble servant.
> > C Pulaski, Gen.
>
> September 14th 1779
> at three o'clock in the morning

Printed version of General Pulaski's report to General Benjamin Lincoln on the results of his reconnaissance of the British near Savannah. (The original letter is in the possession of the Polish Museum of America, Chicago)

General John Sullivan who had upstaged him in the aborted attempt to seize Newport, Rhode Island, the previous year. Earlier, at the meeting with Pulaski at Beaulieu, D'Estaing told the cavalry commander that he would march on Savannah at once, and he counted on the Legion to lead the way. "In pursuance of this wish," Bentalou said, "we set out immediately and reached Savannah sometime before D'Estaing, where we engaged and cut off an advanced picket of the enemy's infantry." True to his decision, D'Estaing on the morning of 16 September summoned General Prevost to surrender. The British general stalled for time. He answered the Admiral that he first had to consult with the Royal Governor. Then he wanted to know the terms of surrender. When D'Estaing refused, Prevost asked for a truce of twenty-four hours in order to consider the question of surrender. D'Estaing naively consented, and the British engineers feverishly continued to ring the city with redoubts and other fortifications. "Captain [James] Moncrief, distinguished engineer," historian Carrington writes, "had charge of the preparations; and every hour of protracted delay in making the investment was earnestly improved by the garrison in preparation to resist the attack." To bolster his defense of Savannah, Prevost ordered Maitland's 800 soldiers at Beaufort to Savannah. Marching and sailing along the inland waterway, the resourceful Maitland strained to reach Savannah. Had D'Estaing attacked at once before Maitland reinforced Prevost, the French and Americans more than likely would have captured the city. However, when Maitland eluded the Americans and reached Savannah, Prevost felt strong enough to refuse surrender. He was surprised that D'Estaing had allowed him to procrastinate. The thought of an easy capture of the beleaguered city was dashed to pieces by British finesse and courage.[13]

D'Estaing decided to lay siege; Lincoln concurred. They surrounded the town with entrenchments and placed cannon in position. The Admiral did not employ Vauban's siege tactics, that is, to approach the enemy fortifications with a series of parallel trenches for a final assault. Instead, his plan rested on a massive

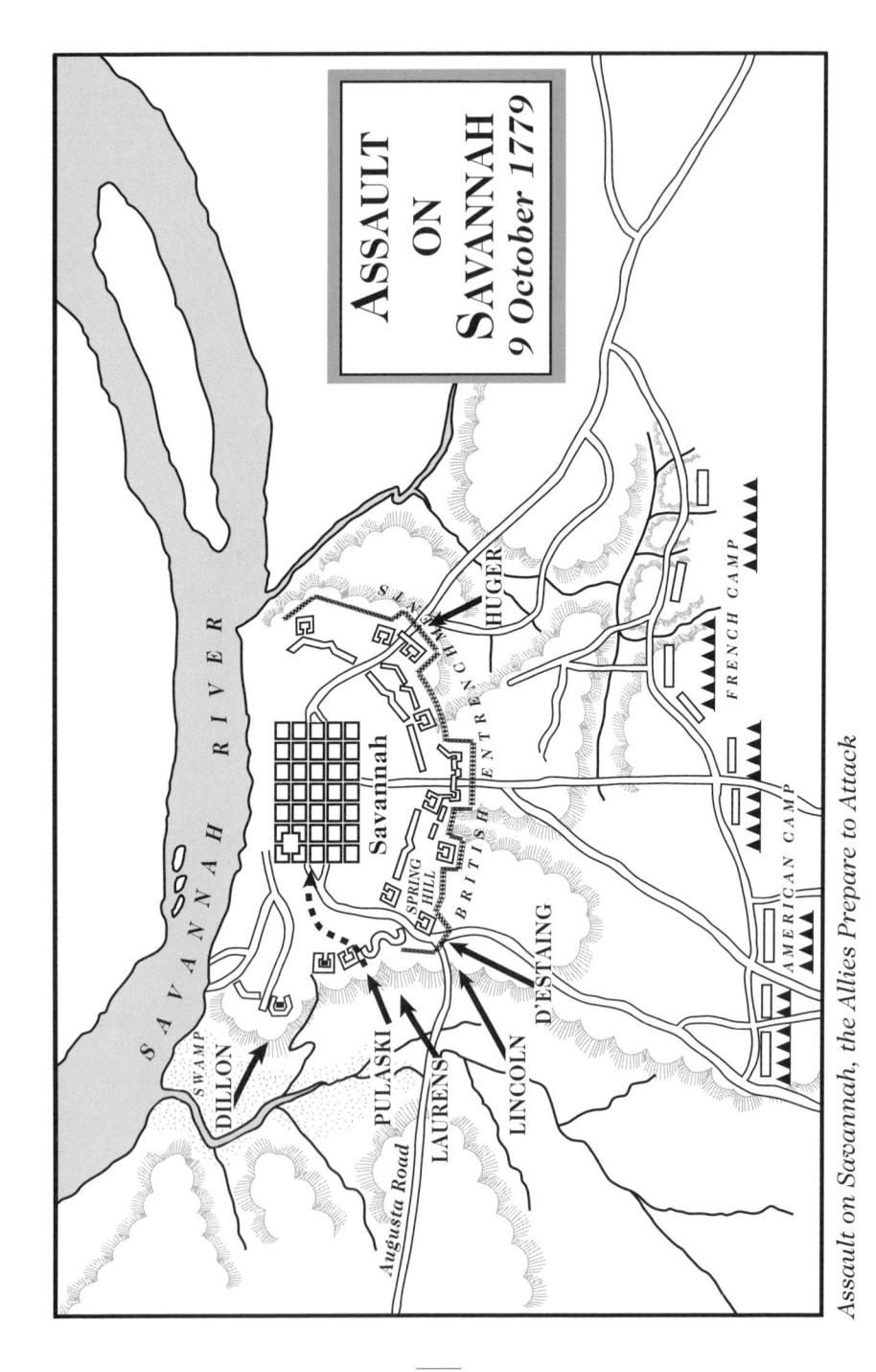

Assault on Savannah, the Allies Prepare to Attack

bombardment of Savannah. At the time, Savannah contained about 430 houses and encompassed about one-half the Historic District of today. The town was bounded on the north by Bay Street (near the river), Lincoln Street on the east, Oglethorpe Street on the south, and Jefferson Street on the west. The French occupied siege lines about 300 yards from the British fortifications. On 3 October 1779, the cannonading began, with thirty-five cannon and nine mortars. The roar of the cannon and explosions within the city threw the residents into panic. Prevost asked for a truce to evacuate women and children, but D'Estaing refused. His attitude had hardened. Perhaps he now realized that he should have attacked earlier. For five days the bombardment continued. During the siege, Lincoln received a report of a party of British troops that ascended the Ogeechee River and landed a short distance below the ferry. Lincoln ordered Pulaski's cavalry to attack the enemy. Pulaski burst upon the British camp, took several prisoners, and dispersed the remainder who escaped to their vessels. Despite the intense bombardment, British resolve did not break, and D'Estaing decided to assault the town. He had long exceeded the two weeks that he could spare for the capture of Savannah. He worried about the safety of his ships. Hurricanes could suddenly appear without warning.[14]

In association with Lincoln, Pulaski, and his own senior officers, D'Estaing developed a plan for a frontal attack. In addition, Pulaski offered a plan of his own. In a written proposal on 6 October 1779, the Legion Commander recommended three points of attack. First, on the British right flank along the Augusta Road. The second on the left by Americans under General McIntosh. The third and main attack at the right center of the British line. Pulaski admitted he developed his plan with the little knowledge of the terrain he was able to obtain from the Americans. Pulaski's plan was straightforward—a feint on either flank and the main thrust in the center (and D'Estaing's assault was attempted in this manner). On the day before the attack, 9 October, the two allied commanders agreed on the details of the plan. However, D'Estaing's senior officers opposed the plan, and Lincoln had concurred grudgingly. He had little choice: make the assault or lift the siege. The line of attack pointed directly at the British right center, where Pulaski had recommended. Historian David B. Mattern, Lincoln's biographer, writes that four columns, two French and two American, would attack against the strong Spring Hill Redoubt and adjacent redoubts; Pulaski's cavalry would sweep to the left of the attacking columns, in an attempt to flank the entrenchments. Historian Henry B. Carrington writes of a main attack of two columns, one French and the other American. The French employed 3500 troops; the Americans fielded a smaller number—600 Continentals including Pulaski's cavalry and 250 Charleston militia commanded by Colonel John Laurens. D'Estaing positioned Colonel Dillon's Irish unit on the extreme left. General Isaac Huger with 500 soldiers of the First and Second Brigades of militia, General James Williams' brigade, and the Second Battalion of militia were to execute feints on the north and east sides of the town. The main attack fell to D'Estaing and Lincoln against Spring Hill and its flanking redoubts. Pulaski would pierce the redoubts on D'Estaing's left. With respect to Pulaski's role, historian Alexander A. Lawrence writes: "The cavalry under Pulaski [his own and South Carolinian] was to endeavor to reach Yamacraw by penetrating between the battery and the redoubt nearest the river."[15]

Despite the excellent plan, the combined French-American attack was doomed from the start. Too many problems and difficulties threatened success. Many of D'Estaing's officers disliked him and withheld or gave only grudging support. The Admiral would not listen to his officers when they offered advice that he did not agree with. He was prone to end discussions abruptly by asserting his superior rank (and wisdom). The French army was a motley group of Frenchmen, as well as free blacks and mulattoes from the West Indies. The French despised the blacks who resented the white soldiers' superior airs. Then, too, class divisions existed between the blacks and mulattoes. Many of the French officers came from the nobility, and they expected everyone else to accord them preferential treatment. Disregarding their assigned positions for the attack, they arbitrarily moved their units to the front, the position of honor. Their hateur insured confusion. A serious problem was the language barrier. There were too few American officers, like Colonels Laurens and Thomas Pinckney, to bridge the barrier. Between the two commanders, General Lincoln disliked D'Estaing because of his haughty behavior. In turn, the Frenchman treated the American as a junior partner. Perhaps D'Estaing felt justified. The French employed four times the number of troops as the Americans in addition to a powerful naval force. Recriminations also continued between them over the failure to bottle up Maitland at Beaufort. D'Estaing pointed his finger at Lincoln. "D'Estaing blamed it all on the Americans," Lawrence writes, "accusing General Lincoln of having brought his army to Georgia, instead of containing the British at Beaufort, because of his selfish desire to be in on the capture of Savannah." Nevertheless, the allies made the attack. D'Estaing felt honor-bound; Lincoln agreed reluctantly for the sake of the alliance.[16]

· 10 ·

The French-American Assault on Savannah

Pulaski Suffers Mortal Wound

❧

The final blow that insured the defeat of the allies occurred on the night before the attack, set for dawn of 9 October 1779. On the previous evening, Sergeant Major James Curry of the Charleston Grenadiers deserted to the British. He disclosed to General Prevost the plan of operations of the allies, including the main point of attack, Spring Hill Redoubt. As a consequence, Prevost shifted soldiers from his left flank and reinforced the defenders at and around Spring Hill. Here he placed his most capable officer, Colonel Maitland, in command. The British general kept only a small force to guard the left of his line. During the early hours of 9 October, French and American soldiers marched through swamps and rice fields to their assigned starting areas. They were slowed by unfamiliar ground. Despite the confusion of darkness, most units reached their positions, but late. Colonel Dillon's French division faced the British right near the Savannah River. General Isaac Huger moved his American force of some 500 soldiers to the British left. The main attack of French and American columns approached Spring Hill. To inspire the French troops, Admiral (General) D'Estaing led them in person. Pulaski's cavalry occupied a position between the American center and Dillon's division. Once the British fortifications were breached, Pulaski would charge with his cavalry through the opening into the city, causing alarm and confusion behind the British defensive line, while the allies pressed forward over the fortifications in the expectation of a British collapse. Colonel Laurens' light infantry force would follow closely in support of Pulaski, who would deliver the coup de grâce. D'Estaing and Lincoln developed an excellent plan, and they expected to surprise the enemy at their main point of attack. However, they did not know, as yet, of the American soldier's betrayal. They would soon learn the bitter and bloody truth.[1]

A French vanguard of 250 soldiers under Colonel de Bethísy struck at Spring Hill, but the British repulsed the Frenchmen before they could be reinforced. Meanwhile, the two main columns had inadvertently shifted too much to the left, and Bethísy's troops retreated. On the British far right flank, Dillon moved forward with about eighty soldiers; the rest of his division was bogged down in a swamp. With no follow-up support, Dillon fell back. Directing the attack in the center, D'Estaing was wounded in the arm and leg as the British poured a tremendous volume of musketry and cannon fire into the attackers. Even British warships anchored in the Savannah River added to the cannonade. The few times that French and American soldiers lodged themselves on the redoubt, the British counterattacked savagely and pushed them back. Blood on the allies' side flowed profusely. Following behind the French, the American column plunged into a sea of confusion. When confronted with reality, the American militia ran away. A French naval officer recorded in his *Journal:* "The militia fled in a cowardly manner in the woods even before the action commenced." However, the Charleston militia stood out in contrast; D'Estaing praised them for their bravery. The American Continentals also fought well. Notwithstanding, the odds for success greatly favored the British. Soon the attack sputtered out, as the killed and wounded piled up before the Spring Hill redoubt.[2]

The French-American Assault on Savannah

Meanwhile, Pulaski anxiously awaited word of an opening in the British line of fortifications. Receiving a report that D'Estaing had been grievously wounded, he decided to check personally. As Captain Bentalou noted, "Aware of the fatal effects which such a disaster was likely to produce on the spirits of the French soldiers—and hoping that his presence would reanimate them, Pulaski rushed on to the scene of disorder and bloodshed." He galloped away in search of the Admiral, taking Bentalou with him. As Pulaski approached Spring Hill, he entered the area of intense shelling. Many times the fearless commander had faced enemy bullets in Poland and America. Each time he escaped death almost miraculously. On 9 October 1779, however, his luck ran out. Shortly Pulaski gasped with pain and fell off his horse. He had been struck by a grapeshot in the groin that may have been fired from a British warship in the Savannah River. Bentalou, who also was wounded by a musket ball, says that Pulaski "received a swivel shot in the upper part of his right thigh." As Pulaski was carried away from the hail of bullets, Colonel Daniel Horry, his second in command and in charge of the South Carolina cavalry, asked him for further orders. Pulaski answered, "Follow my lancers to whom I have given my order for attack." The cavalrymen, however, were devastated by the loss of their general and became hopelessly entangled in the confusion of the battlefield. On the field Dr. James Lynah of Charleston quickly reached the wounded Pulaski. Lynah served as the chief surgeon of Colonel Horry's Regiment of Light Dragoons. With the help of his eighteen-year-old son, surgeon's mate Edward Lynah, and a black servant named Guy, the doctor lifted and carried Pulaski out of range of fire. Dr. Lynah operated immediately and removed the shell from the general (the grapeshot is on display at the Georgia Historical Society in Savannah). Although the operation caused Pulaski great pain, he bore it "with inconceivable fortitude." Dr. Lynah always maintained that he could have saved Pulaski's life had the general remained under his care. Still in great pain but conscious, Pulaski asked Bentalou to be taken beyond the reach of the enemy. He strongly believed that if the British captured

CASIMIR PULASKI

him, they would eventually turn him over to the hated Russians, who would exploit his capture for propaganda purposes and then execute him. Acceding to the pleas of his commander, Bentalou had Pulaski carried to the safety of an American ship, the *Wasp,* where French surgeons tried but could not establish suppuration, and gangrene set in. After being wounded, Pulaski died five days later, 15 October 1779. In his *Memoirs,* Henry "Light Horse Harry" Lee singles out the action of General Pulaski: "The daring effort of the intrepid Pulaski to retrieve the fortunes of the day, failing with his much regretted fall, presents additional proof of the high spirit which actuated the besiegers, demonstrating that every difficulty was encountered, every danger braved, to crown the enterprise with success." During the impetuous allied attack, the soldiers planted two standards on the Ebenezer redoubt. Unfortunately, the attack sputtered to a halt. The British captured one standard, but the second one was brought off by the brave Sergeant William Jasper of the 2nd Regiment of South Carolina Continentals, who at the time was suffering from a mortal wound.[3]

According to Bentalou, Pulaski's remains were buried at sea. The *Wasp* sailed to Charleston and entered the harbor with its flag at half staff. Other ships in the port repeated the mournful signal, and batteries of the forts fired salvos in honor of the fallen general. Governor Rutledge and the Council of South Carolina, along with the officials of Charleston, jointly adopted resolutions to honor the memory of General Pulaski with the most respectful and splendid funeral honors. They set aside 21 October 1779 for the observance while the Quartermaster General of the United States at Charleston carried out the preparations. On the designated day, the people formed a magnificent procession, so very long that it circled the city before reaching St. Michael's Church. A black cloth, normally draped over a coffin, was carried by three American and three French officers of high rank, and they were followed by the splendid horse that Pulaski rode into battle. The procession moved solemnly to the slow pace of a dirge played by a military band. During the church service, the chaplain of the army delivered a fitting eulogy. Ann Manigault of Charleston noted in her *Journal* for the day of remembrance: "A procession in honor of Count Pulaski." The editor of the *South Carolina Historical and Genealogical Magazine* that published the *Journal* in 1907 added a note from a newspaper account: "The gallant Count Pulaski died at Sea, on his return from Georgia, of his wound; and on Thursday last week his funeral rites were performed here in a manner suitable to the rank and merit of that intrepid and much lamented Officer." Many more honors followed the outpouring of respect in Charleston. A verse from the poem "Ode to Youth" by Poland's national poet Adam Mickiewicz (1795-1855) extols a hero's ultimate sacrifice as an inspiration for others in the pursuit of noble goals:

He, too, is happy who unsuccessful fell
If the life laid down
Has been to others a rung in the ladder of fame.[4]

Although Bentalou maintained that Pulaski was buried at sea, others asserted that his gravesite was on land. In 1851, Dr. Joseph Johnson wrote that, based on an account of his friend, I. K. Tefft of Savannah, the remains of Pulaski were buried on land. Tefft claimed that Pulaski's countryman and aide-de-camp, Lieutenant Charles Litomisky [Litomski], assisted at the burial of his commander under a large tree upon the bank of a creek leading from Savannah to Charleston. Actually, Pulaski was buried on the Greenwich Plantation of Jane Bowen, three miles from Savannah. Historian Edward Pinkowski uncovered convincing evidence in the 1960 decade when the long-dormant *Benjamin Lincoln Papers* were microfilmed and made available by the Massachusetts Historical Society. Pinkowski found the letter of Samuel Bulfinch, captain of the privateer *Wasp,* to General Lincoln of 15 October 1779. Bulfinch told the general of the military cargo he had loaded on board. In particular, one statement is especially important. Bulfinch wrote: "I likewise took on board the Americans that were sent down, one of which died this day, and I have brought him ashore and buried him." Pulaski's body was placed in a wooden coffin crafted by Eleazar Phillips, purser/

steward of the *Wasp* and a former cabinet maker in Charleston. The general was laid in the coffin in his military uniform and transferred quietly at night from the *Wasp* to the plantation where he was buried in a torchlight service. The secret burial has been overshadowed by the claim of Bentalou's sea burial. Nevertheless, the story of Pulaski's burial on land persisted for more than two hundred years, and it received much credence, when a metal box was discovered inside the Pulaski Monument in Savannah as the monument was disassembled for restoration in 1996. Officials of Savannah found two cornerstones and a metal box bearing a plate with the inscription "Brigadier General Casimer Pulaski." The box contained the bones of a man matching Pulaski in height and physical characteristics. Pinkowski took a leading role in supporting a determined search for the identity of the bones by DNA testing. The author discusses the effort in Appendix C.[5]

Several American historians differ with Bentalou over the circumstances of Pulaski's mortal wound. The Battle of Savannah, indeed, was a violent and confusing affair. That other interpretations have emerged is understandable. William W. Gordon makes the same observation, and he presents some details of Pulaski's initial movements:

> General Pulaski left his camp to the Southwest of the city on the morning of October 9th and at the head of Lieutenant Colonel Laurens' column [Charleston militia] advanced to a point on Bull Street extended South of the city. At the edge of the woods, he halted and took a position for observation.
>
> From this time onward, the accounts of his movements and especially of the kind of shot which killed him, materially differ according as the different narrators viewed them. It must always be borne in mind that in making the charge of cavalry across open ground in the face of armed entrenchments, General Pulaski was acting under the express orders of General Lincoln.[6]

Historians Dupuy and Dupuy write: "While the battle was raging there [Spring Hill redoubt], Pulaski and his cavalrymen attempted to break through *abatis* protecting a weakly-held portion of the British line, but they, too, were stopped and Pulaski was mortally wounded." Commager and Morris state: "Count Pulaski, who with the cavalry preceded the right column of the Americans, proceeded gallantly until stopped by the abbatis, and before he could force through it, received his mortal wound." Colonel William P. Bowen, grandson of Jane Bowen, relates a magnanimous gesture of the British when Pulaski was struck and toppled from his horse. Bentalou and other Americans surrounded the fallen general. All were within firing range of the British who knew that the casualty was Pulaski. They withheld their fire until the wounded commander could be carried away. The British firing pause was a tribute to Pulaski's gallantry in battle. Recall that Major F. Skelly in his *Journal* praised Pulaski as "a great partisan" and his Legion as "the best Cavalry the rebels ever had."[7]

Historian Joseph Johnson reinforces Bentalou's version of Pulaski's mortal wound. He writes that, when Pulaski learned of D'Estaing becoming a casualty, he galloped up to the French column with one or two of his officers. He planned to lead the French soldiers back against the British line. "Being thus exposed on horseback," Johnson says, "he became the target for every marksman and sacrificed his life, by fruitless and unnecessary exposure." As a seasoned combat commander, Pulaski possessed courage and determination. Undoubtedly he would have led the French soldiers in one more attempt to break through the British line. Often the second effort succeeds. Unfortunately, a gaping wound in the groin immobilized him; confusion and indecision continued on the battlefield. Historian Carrington upholds the view that Pulaski attacked the British line. He writes: "Count Pulaski promptly took his position, and by the impetus of his attack was carried into the face of superiors numbers where he fought without yielding, until he was mortally wounded."[8]

Another account of the manner in which Pulaski was mortally wounded comes from Major Rogowski, whom historian Charles C. Jones, Jr. quotes:

> For half an hour the guns roared and blood flowed abundantly. Seeing an opening between the enemy's works, Pulaski resolved with his Legion and a small detachment of Georgia cavalry, to

charge through, enter the city, confuse the enemy, and cheer the inhabitants with good tidings. General Lincoln approved the daring plan. Imploring the help of the Almighty, Pulaski shouted to his men "Forward," and we two hundred strong rode at full speed after him, the earth resounding under the hoofs of our chargers. For the first two minutes all went well. We sped like Knights into the peril. Just, however, as we passed a gap between the two batteries, a cross fire, like a pouring shower, confused our ranks. I looked around. Oh! sad moment, ever to be remembered! Pulaski lies prostrate on the ground. I leaped towards him, thinking possibly his wound was not dangerous, but a *canister shot* had pierced his thigh, and the blood was flowing from his breast, probably from a second wound. Falling on my knees I tried to raise him. He said in a faint voice, *Jezus, Maria, Jozef!* Further I know not, for at that moment a musket ball grazing my scalp blinded me with blood, and I fell to the ground in a state of insensibility.[9]

Although Rogowski was an eyewitness to Pulaski's fateful moment, he was not an officer of the Continental Army. Perhaps he served as a volunteer on Pulaski's staff. The Legion Commander welcomed officers that he had known in Europe, and especially those that had served under him in the Army of the Confederation of Bar, 1768-1772. According to his *Memoirs* published in 1847, Rogowski served as a cavalry officer in the insurrection against Russian-occupying forces in the Kingdom of Poland. Rogowski looked every inch a soldier. He was tall and lean, and sported an imposing white mustache. He claimed that he sailed for America with Pulaski, and they reported to General Washington at his headquarters at Neshaminy Creek just north of Philadelphia in August 1777. He also claimed that, when Congress appointed Pulaski brigadier general and Commander of the Horse, he received a Congressional appointment as major. However, there is no evidence to prove Rogowski's appointment. He discloses some confusion with names of American and French officers in his *Memoirs*. For example, he criticizes Fleury for mishandling Pulaski's ambush at Charleston. However, the commander of the Legion infantry was Bedaulx, or Verney in his absence. By this time, Fleury was long gone to become Lafayette's division engineer. Nevertheless, Rogowski's details of Pulaski's service are quite accurate. He makes a revealing statement when he speaks of American difficulty with Polish surnames. "Americans pronounced Pulaski's name rather well," he wrote, "but they always mispronounced my name, once Kokoski and a second time Kolkoski." It is possible that Rogowski had been Count Kotkowski who joined Pulaski's Legion as captain on 10 December 1778. He served briefly, getting into trouble at Minisink. When General Hand preferred court martial charges against him, Kotkowski disappeared before the trial and next showed up in Philadelphia, where he told Washington's staff that he was resigning and returning to Europe. Perhaps he did not depart America but, subsequently and quietly, attached himself to Pulaski's staff and marched with the Legion to Savannah. That he took part in the Battle of Savannah is verified by his being listed as wounded in a French naval officer's contemporary *Journal*.[10]

It seems that historians will continue to differ over the manner in which Pulaski suffered his mortal wound. As late as 1997, historian Benson Bobrick writes: "Among those most conspicuous for valor in the action that followed was Kazimierz Pulaski, who returned repeatedly to the assault in a vain attempt to charge through an opening in the enemy's lines." In contrast to Bobrick's praise of a brave officer, William Johnson charges in his 1825 *Remarks Relating to Count Pulaski* that Pulaski foolishly stormed the redoubts at Savannah with his cavalry, when, in fact, Pulaski had no opportunity to make any charge. Johnson undoubtedly misinterpreted General Lincoln's "Evening Orders" for the battle, and Bentalou rebuts Johnson's incorrect account. Bentalou explains, "The cavalry under the command of Pulaski were to *follow* the left column of French troops, and the light troops [American], who are to follow the cavalry, will attempt to enter the redoubt on the left of Spring Hill, by escalade" [that is, by scaling up the embankment of the redoubt]. Bentalou asserts that "Certainly there is not a word here of the cavalry's attempting the escalade." He further explains that had the French troops succeeded in their escalade, the way would have been opened, and the cavalry would have galloped through. He adds that if the column of light troops succeeded in seizing the neighboring redoubt by escalade, the American supporting column would have followed the cavalry into the town. Bentalou points to the intensive and bloody fighting at Spring Hill and the adjacent redoubt. The British were prepared for the allies, and they repelled all attacks with fearful allied losses. Had Pulaski's cavalry stormed the redoubts with the French and American infantry, Bentalou asserts, the cavalry corps should likewise have suffered heavy casualties. Bentalou refers "to the returns of the killed and wounded of that day, among whom will be found, I believe, none of the cavalry save Pulaski and myself." Bentalou's argument is very convincing, and his claim is reinforced by the published account of the killed and wounded at Savannah in *The South Carolina and American General Gazette,* Charlestown, of 29 October 1779. In the long list of casualties, the *Gazette* reported: "Wounded, Cavalry. Brig. Gen. Count Pulaski, Capt. Bendelo, and Capt. Giles." It is clear that Johnson wrote nonsense, for he possessed little, if any, knowledge of military operations. His false accusation of Pulaski's storming a fortified position with horses, and the story growing into a myth, may have lingered into the twentieth century. Some American historians readily picked up and spread the German propaganda of World War II that Polish horse cavalry attacked German tanks, like the editors of Time-Life Books in *Blitzkrieg* (1977).[11]

II

DEMISE OF THE PULASKI LEGION

⁂

FOLLOWING THE DISASTROUS DEFEAT of the allies at Savannah, Admiral D'Estaing called off any further attempts to take the town. The stormy season was fast approaching, and he believed that he had satisfied the matter of honor. Assembling his army at Thunderbolt on the Wilmington River, he began embarking the troops. The first ships sailed away on 21 October 1779, and departures continued for several days. General Lincoln's army began evacuating Savannah, too. By 15 October the Virginia and Georgia militias left for home. Lincoln's Southern Army shrunk to Pulaski's Legion and two Continental regiments. The defeat was costly for the allies. According to the returns of participating units, D'Estaing determined that the French suffered 821 men killed and wounded, among them sixty-one officers. The same French report lists 312 Americans killed and wounded. Defending behind their fortifications, British losses were minimal: eighteen killed and thirty-nine wounded. Frank Moore's *Diary of the American Revolution* quotes a British report: "It is almost incredible the trifling loss we sustained; the only officer killed was poor [Captain] Tawes, and there were not twenty privates killed and wounded." The same report calls the enemy's loss "astonishing." The report continues: "I never saw such a dreadful scene, as several hundreds lay dead in a space of a few yards, and the cries of many hundreds wounded was still more distressing to a feeling mind." The British noted that Pulaski was dangerously wounded by a grape-shot in the groin. Historian Ward characterizes the assault on Savannah as "the most severe fight of the war since Bunker Hill—a magnificent attack and a superb defense." Lieutenant Colonel Cruger, who defended Savannah, saw the French-American defeat as a catastrophe for the allies. After the debacle, he wrote on 8 November 1779: "I may add that never did a sett [sic] of people meet with a greater Disappointment than did on this occasion the Rebel Gentry and their great & good Allies. They came in so full of Confidence of succeeding, that they were at some loss where to lay the blame, each abusing the other for deceiving them."[1]

The failure of the allies can be attributed mainly to D'Estaing's inept leadership. He allowed Prevost to procrastinate instead of launching an immediate attack on Savannah, before Prevost was reinforced by Maitland's 800 battle-tested soldiers and Cruger's unit from Sunbury, Georgia. Then, too, D'Estaing was too impatient to continue the siege that Lincoln advocated. The siege would have been much less costly. Time-consuming, of course. In the end, however, it would have undoubtedly achieved the desired result. However, the nail in D'Estaing's coffin was driven in by the American deserter who betrayed the allies' plan of attack.[2]

The capture of Savannah could have thwarted the British southern strategy. Instead, the failure of the French and Americans led to dire consequences. Historians Scheer and Rankin succinctly sum up the importance of Savannah: "The failure of the allies to oust the British from Georgia was nothing short of calamitous for the rebellion. A victory at Savannah would have deprived Clinton of a base from which to invade the rest of the South, and the whole plan of the King for reducing the colonies one by one, working northward, would have gone awry." General Henry Clinton was in the process of planning a massive expedition to South Carolina. "I had long determined...on an expedition against

Charleston, the capital of South Carolina," he wrote, "which every account I had received from Georgia convinced me was necessary to save the province from falling again into the hands of the rebels." Leading the expedition in person, Clinton landed some 8500 troops, first at Savannah and then on Johns Island. He bottled up Lincoln's army in Charleston, laid siege, and captured the entire command of 5500 Continentals and militia, 12 May 1780.[3]

Following the debacle of the French and Americans at Savannah, the Pulaski Legion seemed dazed by the loss of its fearless commander and several key officers, Colonel Kovatch, Captain Zielinski, and several lieutenants. The command devolved on the senior officer, Lieutenant Colonel Charles Bedaulx, who had the unenviable duty to inform the President of Congress of the death of Pulaski. Writing from Charleston on 25 October 1779, Bedaulx said, "I am now Commander of the sad remainder of the Legion which he had under his command." Bedaulx took over only the remnant of the Legion and not the Georgia and South Carolina cavalry that were part of Pulaski's command in the Southern Army. He told the President that he would report to the Board of War the condition of the Legion "where the officers are more numerous than the Privates."[4]

The news of the devastating defeat of the allies at Savannah reached Philadelphia on 10 November 1779. General Lincoln had reported the Savannah campaign to President Samuel Huntington from Charleston on 22 October 1779. The general lamented the heavy casualties suffered by the Southern Army. "Our disappointment is great," he said, "and what adds much poignancy of our grief is the loss of a number of brave officers and men—among them the late intrepid Count Pulaski." Congress rose up in praise of Pulaski. The delegates resolved to erect a monument in his honor, 22 November 1779, but promptly forgot about it. Not until 1910 did the Federal government carry out the resolution of the early Congress, when the government erected an equestrian and imposing statue in the heart of Washington, D. C. At his headquarters at West Point, 17 November 1779, Washington called

CASIMIR PULASKI

PULASKI MONUMENT. On Monterey Square in Savannah, Georgia. The people of Savannah erected the monument by private subscription in 1854 to honor the intrepid cavalry commander General Casimir Pulaski who gave his life for American independence at the Battle of Savannah, 9 October 1779. (Photo, Circa 1900. Courtesy of The Georgia Historical Society, Savannah)

attention of the army to Pulaski's sacrifice. He issued general orders in which he designated the watch-word "Pulaski" for the day's guard and the countersign "Poland."[5]

The citizens of the South have always been grateful to Casimir Pulaski for his unselfish devotion to their freedom. In 1825, Savannahians prepared to welcome General Lafayette to their city. The editor of *The Savannah Georgian* seized the occasion to urge the residents to honor the sacrifice of General Pulaski for their freedom. "Let a plain cenotaph with suitable inscriptions," he wrote, "characterized rather by durability than show and during the sojourn of the General [Lafayette] here, let the same with due ceremony and in his presence, be placed on the spot where the brave Polander fell." On 21 March 1825, Lafayette laid the cornerstone in Chippewa Square. The site was moved to Monterey Square where the cornerstone was laid again on 11 October 1853. During the ceremony, a distinguished son of Savannah, Henry Williams, delivered an inspiring oration. He succinctly gave the reason for the occasion:

> The solemn ceremonies which are about to be performed in our presence, will indicate to us, that upon this massive foundation at our feet, is destined to rise in marble beauty a lofty column, which shall fitly commemorate the gallant achievements and melancholy fate of that heroic son of Poland, that worshipper of Liberty and martyr in her cause, the friend and fellow-soldier of Washington, the noble and chivalrous Pulaski.

The completed 55-foot-high monument was dedicated on 8 January 1855. Robert Eberhardt Launitz, an eminent sculptor of New York, won the $17,000 commission for designing and sculpturing the graceful and beautiful monument. He placed a statue of Liberty at the top, adding the arms of Poland and Georgia on the cornice, inverted cannons on the corners, and bas reliefs of the wounded Pulaski falling from his horse. The committee consisted of Dr. Richard D. Arnold, Chairman; William Robertson, Treasurer; and William P. Bowen, Secretary and Commissioner. The monument stood the ravages of weather and time until 1996, when the City of Savannah determined that the monument must be renovated, if it was not to collapse. The author relates the story of the restoration and the discovery of suspected remains of Pulaski in Appendix C.[6]

Without its dynamic commander, the Pulaski Legion rapidly disintegrated. While fighting in South Carolina and at Savannah, Pulaski commanded a respectable cavalry corps, since he also assumed command of South Carolina and Georgia cavalry. Only an emaciated Legion now remained. To add to the Legion's problems, Lieutenant Colonel Charles Bedaulx was seriously ill. He told Congress in a letter from Charleston, 25 October 1779: "I am entirely disabled…and incapable of continuing any longer in the military service." He explained that he consulted several physicians who "all agree that I must go and breathe the Air of my Native Country." He had been forced to spend his own money to support himself in America. As a consequence, the financial demands "have reduced my little Fortune almost to nothing." Knowing of the recent resolve of Congress to grant pensions of half pay to officers, he petitioned Congress "to grant me the favor of being put at the half pay in Europe, from any of the Ministers or Agents of the States there." General Lincoln penned his own letter to Congress, 31 October 1779, enclosing Bedaulx's letter and adding a favorable recommendation to Bedaulx's petition. Lincoln wrote, "I think this Gentleman very deserving of the indulgence." Lincoln also took occasion to offer his own recommendation on the future of the Pulaski Legion: "As the Legion commanded by the late Count Pulaski is much reduced—the time for which many of his men engaged expired last month, and they have left the Service, and as it cannot be recruited, I think it would be for the good of the Service to incorporate it with some other Corps." Had Pulaski lived, he could have recruited replacements for his Legion; he demonstrated this dynamic quality repeatedly.[7]

Before Congress acted on Bedaulx's request, however, he died in Charleston barely two months after the Battle of Savannah. Major Isaac Hayne recorded in his Journal the death of Bedaulx in December 1779. Bedaulx was buried in the parish cemetery

Historic Pulaski Monument Marker in Monterey Square, Savannah, Georgia

The inscription on the marker reads as follows:

The monument erected in this Square to the memory of General Casimir Pulaski, who fell at Savannah in the cause of American independence, was erected in 1854. The corner-stone was laid, with impressive ceremonies, October 11, 1853—the 74th anniversary of the traditional date of the death of the famous Polish patriot.

Dr. Richard D. Arnold was chairman of the Commission in charge of the erection of the memorial for which $20,000 was collected by public subscription.

The designer of the monument, which is of Italian marble, was the eminent Russian-born sculptor, Robert Eberhard Launitz of New York. At the conclusion of his explanation of the elaborate design and its symbolism, Mr. Launitz stated:

"The monument is surmounted by a statue of liberty, embracing with her left arm the banner of the Stars and Stripes, while in her right hand is extended the Laurel Wreath. The love of liberty brought Pulaski to America; for love of liberty he fought; and for liberty he lost his life. Thus, I thought that Liberty should crown his monument, and share with him the homage of the free."

Erected by the Georgia Historical Commission, 1954.
(Photo by the author, 31 May 2000)

CASIMIR PULASKI

HISTORIC CASIMIR PULASKI MARKER IN SAVANNAH, GEORGIA

Located at the Pulaski Monument, the second marker reads:

The great Polish patriot to whose memory this monument is erected was mortally wounded approximately one-half mile northwest of this spot during the assault by the French and American forces on the British lines around Savannah, October 9, 1779. General Pulaski was struck by a grapeshot as he rode forward with customary ardor, from where the cavalry was stationed to rally the disorganized Allied columns. The fatal ball was removed from his thigh by Dr. James Lynah of South Carolina. Doubt and uncertainty exists as to where Pulaski died and as to his burial place. A contemporary Charleston, S.C. newspaper item and other sources indicate that he died aboard a ship bound for that port. It was generally believed that he was buried at sea. A tradition persisted, however, that General Pulaski died at Greenwich plantation near Savannah and that he was buried there. When the monument here was under erection the grave at Greenwich was opened. The remains found there conformed, in the opinion of physicians, to a man of Pulaski's age and stature, and were re-interred beneath this memorial in a mettalic case in 1854.

Erected by the Georgia Historical Commission, 1954.
(Photo by the author, 31 May 2000)

Demise of the Pulaski Legion

HISTORIC MARKER "GENERAL CASIMIR PULASKI"
AND "SERGEANT WILLIAM JASPER"

Located outside the Savannah Visitors Center and at the approximate location of Spring Hill Redoubt where Pulaski and Jasper were mortally wounded in the Battle of Savannah, 9 October 1779. The inscription on the marker reads:

Near this spot two notable heroes of the American Revolution were mortally wounded in the ill-fated assault by the American and French forces upon the British lines here, October 9, 1779.

Brig. Gen. Casimir Pulaski, the famous Polish patriot, was fatally wounded by a grapeshot as he rode forward into the heavy fire from the British defenses located in this area.

Sergeant William Jasper fell a short distance west of this marker while attempting to plant the colors of the 2nd Regiment of South Carolina Continentals upon the British entrenchments.

To their memory and to the memory of hundreds of gallant soldiers of America and France—including the French commander-in-chief, Count D'Estaing—who shed their blood here in the cause of Liberty, this marker is erected.

Georgia Historical Commission, 1952.
(Photo by the author, 31 May 2000)

Casimir Pulaski

of St. Phillips Church on 8 December 1779. The command of the Legion passed to Major Peter Verney. His small force, along with the remnants of Bland's, Baylor's, and Moylan's regiments of Continental cavalry, were united under the command of Lieutenant Colonel William Washington, who operated along the Ashley River in the spring of 1780. On April 14, Washington's cavalry, as part of General Isaac Huger's command, was struck at Monck's Corner by the aggressive British cavalryman, Lieutenant Colonel Banastre Tarleton. The Briton was reinforced by Major Patrick Ferguson's seasoned loyalist volunteers and a corps of riflemen. Tarleton surprised the Americans at three o'clock in the morning. Driving in Huger's outposts, Tarleton charged into the American camp with such suddenness and force that he routed the American cavalry completely. Tarleton's infantry immediately attacked a meeting house where American militia were quartered for the night. The bayonet-wielding British killed or dispersed the unsuspecting militia. The attack seemed like a repetition of Little Egg Harbor. The American losses were very severe. Major Verney was killed. Four other officers and fifteen soldiers were killed or wounded; seven officers and sixty men were captured. General Huger, Colonel Washington, and several others escaped capture by fleeing into the swamps. With the death of Verney, Captain De Segond became the senior officer in the Legion. Unfortunately, the remaining Legionnaires were captured by the British when General Lincoln's 5500-man army was besieged in Charleston. Lincoln surrendered to General Clinton, 12 May 1780. Some Legionnaires happened to be away from Charleston, like Captain Bedkin's company. They were incorporated into Colonel Charles Armand's corps by the action of Congress, 14 November 1780. Thus, the tempestuous life of the Pulaski Legion in the American Revolution came to an unheralded end.[8]

Several of Pulaski's officers continued to serve with distinction in the Continental Army. Others left before the end of the war, 3 September 1783. Major De Segond, who had been promoted to major in 1783, was honorably discharged from the service on 22 January 1784. Becoming a soldier of fortune, he served in a military capacity first in Holland followed by Russia and Austria where the government granted him a pension and the rank of major general without assignment. He returned to France in 1810 and became a founding member of the Society of the Cincinnati in France. In July 1782, Dr. Felix Texier, surgeon, and Captain Celeron were discharged from the Continental Army. Celeron emigrated to the French island of Guadaloupe where he served as a commissioner until 1807. He met De Segond in France and joined him in becoming a founding member of the Society of the Cincinnati. Lieutenant De la Close left America early, July 1780. Congress promoted him to brevet captain and granted him a year's pay. De la Close was followed in 1781 with the retirements of Captains Alexander O'Neil and Jerome de Bellecour, General Pulaski's aide-de-camp.[9]

Captain Paul Bentalou, not having recovered from his wound at Savannah, applied to Congress to retire from the army. On 21 February 1781, Congress voted him three months pay and discharged him from the service. He carried the Pulaski Banner to Baltimore and safeguarded it until his death in 1830. He is remembered for his close association with the two visits of the Marquis de Lafayette to Baltimore in 1824 and 1825. Bentalou made a significant contribution to history with two publications in defense of the service of General Casimir Pulaski in the American Revolution.[10]

Lieutenant Louis de Beaulieu endured a long period of recovery from two deep saber cuts to the face in Tarleton's surprise attack on General Huger's command at Monck's Corner. He was captured either during Tarleton's raid or a short time later with Lincoln's army at Charleston. The British paroled him and many others. He was now anxious to return to France, but the conditions of his parole prevented him. As he was in dire financial straits, he traveled from South Carolina to Philadelphia and there petitioned Congress to reimburse him for expenses and other obligations. Congress responded sympathetically, voting on 6 September 1780 the sum of $5000 "to reimburse his expences while under the cure of wounds he received in the service of these states, and to defray the charges of traveling from South Carolina to Philadelphia."[11]

Captain Frederick Paschke at first found himself without an assignment in 1780. When Congress merged the remainder of the Pulaski Legion with Armand's, the men were easily absorbed; vacancies were abundant, but not in the officers' ranks. Congress approved the mode recommended by the Commander-in-Chief of "incorporating the remainder of the men of the late Brigadier General Pulaski's legion, and as many of the officers as there are vacancies for, into Colonel Armand's corps." With no assignment and devastated by the loss of Pulaski and the demise of the Legion, his commander's pride, Paschke felt unwanted and depressed. The Board of War acknowledged that Paschke despaired of being employed in the American Army. Paschke decided to return to Europe. He applied to Congress for a sum of money to enable him to pay for his travel. Congress, therefore, resolved on 16 May 1780: "That the sum of three thousand dollars currency of these United States [depreciated money], and a bill of exchange for two hundred and fifty dollars in Specie be paid to Capt. Paschi, late of Count Pulaski's legion (which being dissolved Congress have no means of employing Capt. Paschi, tho' a deserving Officer) to enable him to return to Europe." However, Paschke remained in America. He was reluctant to abandon his original purpose: to fight for American independence, and the fighting was not over. When General Baron De Kalb invited Paschke to join his division as quartermaster officer, Paschke seized the chance. De Kalb's division joined the Southern Army of General Gates, and Paschke continued to serve in the Quartermaster Department of Gates' and General Nathanael Greene's commands. On 22 January 1781, he wrote Congress again about his service in the Continental Army. He said he did not consider the initial lack of an assignment to be the equivalent of a discharge. (Paschke held a valid conclusion since discharging an officer normally is a deliberate act). Therefore, Paschke told Congress that he would like to be considered eligible for the half pay pension plan that

Congress had passed for officers. Congress, however, rejected his request but noted "that something is due him for his service with the Southern Army." Congress then ordered "the Board of Treasury report a warrant in favor of Captain Paschke, late of the army of these states, for three hundred dollars of the new emissions for his service with the southern army since the resolution of the 16 day of May last" (the sum equaled six months pay without subsistence). Notwithstanding, Paschke continued his duty in the Southern Army under the quartermaster, Lieutenant Colonel Edward Carrington, until the end of the Revolution and the dissolution of Greene's army on 13 July 1783. Upon Paschke's departing the South, Carrington wrote a testimonial, lauding his loyal and effective service and calling on Congress for a consideration that "his great merits entitle him to." General Greene endorsed Carrington's testimonial favorably. In Philadelphia, on 18 December 1783, Colonel Timothy Pickering, Quartermaster General, added his strong endorsement, saying that "My knowledge of Capt. Paschke's worth & integrity induced me to give him the appointment mentioned by Lt. Col. Carrington." Armed with Carrington's letter as bolstered by Greene's and Pickering's endorsements, Paschke asked Congress, 11 January 1784, for a promotion to major by brevet in recognition of his long and faithful service of six years. Unfortunately, Paschke's request was met with indifference. The war was over, and Congress now showed little concern for the military. It rejected Paschke's petition for a brevet promotion, 22 January 1784. A Committee of Congress consisting of James Tilton, Arthur Lee, and David Howell recognized that Paschke "has produced ample testimonials of his bravery, integrity, capacity, and industry in the service of the United States." Notwithstanding, the Committee concluded, and Congress agreed: "But as the definitive treaty of peace is ratified, nearly the whole of the army discharged, and the Commander in Chief has resigned his commission, it is inexpedient to make the promotion requested by Captain Paschke." The reasons of Congress are trite and irrelevant. The ratification of the treaty of peace in no way abrogated the authority of

CASIMIR PULASKI

Congress to appoint and promote officers. The fact that most of the army was discharged was irrelevant. The army made no promotions, only Congress could. That Washington had resigned and returned to Mount Vernon was irrelevant. The best that Washington could ever do was to recommend, and only Congress could promote. Congress callously cast aside an old soldier, justifying its decision on an innocuous word "inexpedient" that hides many sins. A promotion to an army officer is an important event. It recognizes his capability and rewards his faithful and commendable service. Perhaps Congress found it easier to reject this promotion because Paschke was a foreigner. Undoubtedly Paschke was deeply disappointed. In poor health, he returned to Charleston where he died three years later. The *South Carolina Gazette,* 16 June 1788, printed a short obituary:

> Died, on Wednesday last [11 June 1788], in the afternoon, after a long and afflictive illness, Frederick Paschke, Esq.; captain in the Legion under the command of the valiant Count Pulaski, in the late American army, aged 44. He was a native of Poland, and always supported the character of an irreproachable, honest man, and a brave soldier. His remains were, on the following day, respectfully deposited in St. Philip's Church Yard, attended by the society of the Cincinnati, of which he was a member.[12]

Many foreigners fought valiantly and gave their lives for American independence. In the Pulaski Legion, the officers faced the enemy bravely and without regard to personal safety (unlike the cowardly American militia that ran from the battlefield at Savannah and other battles). Killed in action were Lieutenant Colonel Carl von Bose and Lieutenant De la Borderie at Little Egg Harbor, Colonel Michael Kovatch and Captain Jan Zielinski at Charleston, General Casimir Pulaski at Savannah, and Major Peter Verney at Monck's Corner. Many other officers and enlisted men of the Legion were wounded. It seems that these foreigners understood and appreciated freedom more than many Americans, and they have not been forgotten. At the laying of the cornerstone of the Pulaski monument in Savannah, Henry Williams praised the assistance of foreigners to American independence.

He called attention to the dangers and the suffering in combat that they endured, and even the shedding of their blood. "So long as traditions, or record, or marble trophy, shall preserve the memory of the heroic acts of the Revolution," Williams said, "so long shall the names of De Kalb, Steuben, Lafayette, Kosciusko and Pulaski be cherished with those of Washington and Greene." Williams had special praise for Pulaski:

> His patriotic career in his own country, his eminent services in ours, his enthusiasm in the cause of Liberty, his chivalrous character, his impetuous courage, and his glorious but untimely fate, have so illumined his name, that it lends alike a lustre to romance and a dignity to history.[13]

Despite what some American historians maintain, the militia did not win the Revolutionary War. It was the soldier of the Continental Army. Inadequately clothed and starved by Congress, the Continental soldiers stood firm in their devotion to liberty, while taking casualties from the better equipped British soldiers. The Continentals endured extreme hardship, as General Nathanael Greene told Washington: "The miserable situation of the troops for want of clothing had rendered this march [to the Dan River] the most painful imaginable, several hundreds of Soldiers tracking the ground with their bloody feet."

· 12 ·

Evaluating General Pulaski's Service

❦

Early American historians praised Casimir Pulaski's service in the cause of American independence. For one, they were closer in time to the unprecedented experiment in North America that led to the formation of a free and independent country, governed by its people and guided by the remarkable Constitution of 1789, the first written constitution in the world. Consequently, these historians admired and appreciated those individuals who fought valiantly for independence and especially the ones who sacrificed their lives. Pulaski was one such outstanding American patriot. He told the members of Congress and his Commander-in-Chief, General George Washington, that he willingly faced enemy fire to gain freedom for the Americans.

The Reverend William Gordon, contemporary historian of the American Revolution, portrays Pulaski as a great freedom fighter whose bravery helped save Charleston, South Carolina, from imminent capture by the British in 1779. Gordon describes the dramatic event: The advance of 900 redcoats marching up to the outskirts of Charleston on 11 May 1779, and on the same day Pulaski's legionary corps of infantry crossing the Cooper River into Charleston. Although his Legion had been on the march for weeks from York, Pennsylvania, and had reached Charleston scarcely two hours earlier, Pulaski, without hesitation, led eighty of the infantry beyond the American defensive line and positioned them in a valley behind a small breast work for the purpose of drawing the British into ambush. Taking his cavalry and assisted by South Carolina mounted militia called "Raccoons," he advanced about a mile beyond the infantry and attacked a superior force of British cavalry. He then broke off the fight and drew the pursuing British horsemen to the position of his screened infantry, "who from an eagerness to engage," Gordon writes, "had quitted their breast work, and so rendered abortive the advantage of the intended ambuscade, and were by superior numbers compelled to retreat." His excellently-planned trap having failed, Pulaski's horsemen and infantry found themselves overwhelmed by the vastly superior enemy. Nevertheless, Pulaski rose to the challenge and demonstrated his mastery of cavalry fighting that gained the grudging admiration of the British. Pulaski lost the fight and many brave soldiers, but he achieved a significant objective, as Gordon relates:

> Pulaski however by discovering the greatest intrepidity, and by successful personal recounters with individuals of the British cavalry, had a considerable influence in dispelling the general panic, and in introducing military sentiments into the minds of the citizens.[1]

The eminent nineteenth century historian Jared Sparks wrote approvingly of Pulaski. In his monumental work, *The Library of American Biography* (1845), Sparks devotes an entire volume, XIV, to Pulaski's tumultuous life in Poland and accomplishments in the American Revolution. At the end of his long essay, Sparks evaluates Pulaski's character. "In his private qualities," Sparks writes, "he seems to have been amiable, gentle, conciliating, candid, sincere, generous to his enemies and devoted to his friends." Sparks' words are in sharp contrast to the remarks of some American historians of the twentieth century. Sparks says that Pulaski

Evaluating General Pulaski's Service

never embroiled himself with political factions of the Revolution. He guided himself by his role of military officer. His leadership qualities were evident. "His soldiers adhered to him as to a brother," Sparks continues, "and willingly endured fatigues and encountered perils the most appalling, when encouraged by his approbation or led on by his example." Sparks asserts that Pulaski possessed, in a remarkable degree, the power of winning and controlling men. He was energetic, vigilant, untiring in the pursuit of an object, fearless, fertile in resources, calm in danger, resolute and persevering under discouragements. How the loss of his key officers, Baron Von Bose, Michael Kovatch, and Jan Zielinski must have wrenched his heart! Likewise, the many Legionnaires killed at Little Egg Harbor and Charleston profoundly saddened him. Still, the severe losses did not cause him to back away from fighting the enemy for the ultimate goal of freedom. "He was true to his principles and firm in maintaining them," Sparks states. Pulaski gained the respect of General Washington who commended the cavalry leader for his zeal and bravery more than once. Pulaski demonstrated courage on every occasion in which he had an opportunity to meet the enemy. Sparks notes that Pulaski embraced the American cause as his own. The Pole harmonized the American Revolution with his principles and the noble impulses of his nature, the cause of liberty, and of human rights. Sparks points to Pulaski's final sacrifice. He lost his life in defending freedom, and thus gained the highest of all claims to a nation's remembrance and gratitude.[2]

During his two years of service in the Continental Army, Pulaski supported himself. He never drew the authorized pay of a brigadier general of $115 per month. He bought his own cavalry horses, selected from the best animals he could find, and the accoutrements of cavalry. He paid for his smartly-tailored uniforms. He expended greater sums on his Legion. Early in the recruiting, equipping, and organizing of the Pulaski Legion, he told Congress he had spent $16,000 of his own money. This sum grew to around $50,000. When his Paymaster, Captain Joseph Baldesqui, could not produce an invoice for every expenditure for the Legion, as demanded by the auditors of Congress, Pulaski wrote his family in Poland to send him a sufficient sum of money to pay for every outstanding debt. Pulaski was no adventurer. Indeed, he was truly altruistic.[3]

Historian William W. Gordon penned a well-researched and thoughtful article "Count Casimir Pulaski" published in *The Georgia Historical Quarterly* in September 1929 on the sesquicentennial of Pulaski's death at Savannah. William Washington Gordon III (1866-1932) was an outstanding citizen of the South. A graduate of Yale University, he became a respected lawyer in Savannah. Like his grandfather and father before him, he carved out a distinguished career of public and military service. Grandfather William Washington Gordon I became the first graduate of West Point in Georgia (Class of 1815). He built the Georgia Central Railroad and served as the first president. The father (Gordon II) served as Mayor of Savannah. In the Civil War, Captain Gordon II joined Jeb Stuart's famous cavalry corps. In the Spanish-American War, Brigadier General Gordon commanded a brigade of United States Volunteers, and the son, Lieutenant Gordon III, assisted his father as aide-de-camp. Gordon III gained additional military experience when he served in the Georgia State cavalry for twenty years and retired as a major. Along with several other magazine articles, he wrote "Cavalry in the South" for the *U. S. Military Journal* in 1905. At the time he researched and wrote his essay "Count Casimir Pulaski," he was President of the Georgia Historical Society. Thus, the military qualifications, experience, and family tradition of William Washington Gordon III prepared him well for evaluating General Pulaski's service in the American Revolution.[4]

Speaking of Pulaski's character and achievements, Gordon states that "General Pulaski bore an unblemished reputation in private as well as public life." He points to Pulaski's notable qualities as a leader: "In all the military engagements of which we have record, he has been distinguished for his extraordinary personal bravery and for his handling of cavalry, employing surprise and shock tactics by virtue of which he almost invariably

Evaluating General Pulaski's Service

met with success despite the use of small numbers against greater forces." Pulaski was the first officer to be given command of all the United States cavalry. Therefore, Gordon remarks that Pulaski may be considered the father of that branch of service. When Pulaski took command of the four Continental Army cavalry regiments, he was dumbfounded to find the American cavalry lacking in the most basic of fundamentals. Pulaski immediately began training the cavalry along sound military lines, despite the reluctance of his American officers to listen to a foreigner, albeit one possessing vast cavalry experience. Notwithstanding, Pulaski pressed on while provoking complaints from the Americans that they were being overworked (in contrast to their former lackadaisical behavior). He based his training methods on his own combat experience against the Russians and the drill regulations of Prussian cavalry, considered then a model in Europe. He had the Prussian regulations translated into English. Gordon observes that the knowledge Pulaski brought to the task was passed on to the other cavalry leaders. "So that it may be asserted," Gordon writes, "that his training of the cavalry was probably just as important to that arm of the service as that of Baron Von Steuben's training to the infantry."[5]

Some American historians such as Page Smith state that Pulaski as Commander of the Horse could not get along with the officers of his cavalry regiments. However, the fault lay more with the Americans than with Pulaski. The regimental commanders and most of their officers made no effort to get along with Pulaski. First and foremost, they were resentful that a foreigner was placed over them. Of the four regimental commanders, only Colonel Bland was respectful and obedient. Bland, a true officer and gentleman, understood and complied with the authority of Congress. In 1781, Virginia elected Bland to Congress where he served for two years. Other officers known to be courteous and respectful of the Commander of the Horse were Captains Henry "Light Horse Harry" Lee, Henry Bedkin, John Craig, as well as other officers of Colonel Bland's regiment (he set the standard for his regiment). One understands why Pulaski selected Bland's

CASIMIR PULASKI

regiment of horsemen to be stationed in Trenton during the winter of 1777-78. Trenton could not accommodate the four regiments. There were no more quarters available among the civilian households because of the earlier lodging of sailors. Therefore, three regiments were stationed at communities outside of Trenton. However, Pulaski kept Bland's small regiment in Trenton for the purpose of maintaining a rapid reaction force for emergencies, such as occurred at Haddonfield in support of General Wayne. In contrast to Bland, Colonels Stephen Moylan, John Baylor, and Elisha Sheldon obstructed Pulaski. They were the unruly ones. They not only opposed Pulaski but also mistrusted and snarled at one another. Their mutual distrust caused Washington to be wary of them. When Pulaski signaled his intention to resign from the Continental Army, Washington ordered General Edward Hand to replace him at Minisink, and Congress followed up with a resolution for another Commander of the Horse. On 24 November 1778, Congress *"Resolved,* That a brigadier general, out of the brigadiers of the infantry, be appointed by Washington to command the cavalry." Washington never did. To have placed another general over the four might have caused further dissension. Prior to Pulaski's appointment, the regimental cavalry commanders had operated independently of one another for a year and resisted any change in their status. When Congress and Pulaski changed that status, three of the four colonels turned their resentment on Pulaski. Upon Pulaski's resignation, Washington charged Moylan with overall supervision of the four regiments. Moylan, however, immediately proved himself incompetent and irresponsible. Washington feared giving the command of the four regiments to one of the cavalry commanders, believing that chaos would result. As he told the President of Congress: "To promote any gentleman now in it [cavalry corps] to general Command, would not be acquiesced in by the rest (nor do I know that any of them wish it and it would increase their misunderstanding and of course disorder)." The charge that Pulaski was unable to get along with his officers appears unjustified.[6]

Pulaski's contribution to military victory could have been much

Evaluating General Pulaski's Service

more effective had American military thinking matched that of European. Unfortunately, the young nation's was vastly inferior. Time and again Pulaski proposed to Congress and to General Washington a relatively large force of cavalry placed under the immediate orders of the Commander-in-Chief and employed by him at critical phases of battles. Such a mobile strike force was perfected by Napoleon Bonaparte about two decades after the American Revolution. He employed corps of cavalry divisions in the heat of battle that insured victory. For generations the employment of light and heavy cavalry (Winged Hussars) was standard practice in Poland. Not until the American Civil War did cavalry become of age when the South produced the brilliant Jeb Stuart and Nathan Bedford Forrest. At first, the North wasted its cavalry in the same naive manner as Washington had done. However, President Abraham Lincoln learned from the Confederates of the South. By 1863, the North also fielded powerful cavalry corps composed of cavalry divisions and commanded by intrepid cavalry commanders in the mold of Pulaski—Alfred Pleasonton, George Custer, James Wilson, and Philip Sheridan.

At the beginning of the American Revolution few generals had any military schooling or battle experience. Generals Charles Lee, Horatio Gates, and Arthur St. Clair had previously served in the British Army. Washington's military experience was limited to his service as a militia colonel with General Edward Braddock in the French and Indian War. Historian Noel B. Poirier in his excellent essay "Young General Lafayette" writes that Lafayette, the boy-general, at age twenty possessed more formal military training than most of Washington's generals combined. Some of them, however, developed skill as the Revolution continued. Most notable was Nathanael Greene, "the Fighting Quaker," who became one of the foremost tacticians and strategists. In the main, the Americans' lack of military schooling, battle experience, and tradition tended to close their minds to innovative measures that Pulaski advocated.[7]

As Commander-in-Chief, Washington placed his trust in the infantry and artillery. Consequently, Pulaski could not convince

CASIMIR PULASKI

FORT PULASKI NATIONAL MONUMENT
Named in honor of General Casimir Pulaski and built by U. S. Army engineers on Cockspur Island, Georgia, at the mouth of the Savannah River. Lieutenant Robert E. Lee served his first engineering assignment on the construction project, 1829-1831. The excellently-designed and strongly-built fort was considered impregnable until the American Civil War when the Union Army for the first time introduced rifled artillery and reduced the walls. The Confederate garrison surrendered the fort, 11 April 1862. (Photo courtesy of The Georgia Historical Society, Savannah)

Washington to employ cavalry as a special combat arm. The best Pulaski could do was to exact from Congress an Independent Legion of sixty-eight horse and 200 light infantry. Several times he tried to augment his small Legion, but Congress refused to go along. Pulaski's contribution to the Revolution, despite his knowledge of cavalry operations, became limited by the lack of understanding and encouragement from both Washington and the members of Congress. Historian Charles Francis Adams charges that "Washington did not evince mental alertness." As the author repeats here for emphasis, Adams expressed surprise that Washington did not learn from his mistakes made at the Battle of Long Island in 1776. With no cavalry to detect British troop movements, General Cornwallis' soldiers marched around Washington to his rear without detection and inflicted a disastrous defeat on the Americans. Adams wonders why Washington failed to understand from his mistakes that he must have "an adequate mounted force of some kind, attached to his command, at once the army's eyes and ears, its safeguard against surprise and his most ready weapon of offense." Adams' description of an effective cavalry corps and its purpose in battle is the kind of unit that Pulaski passionately advocated, but without success. The Pulaski Legion was the best that Congress agreed to, and Pulaski had to be satisfied with a partial realization of his thinking. The Pulaski Legion had little opportunity to demonstrate its capability in the Northern Theater, but it did so effectively in the South.[8]

Throughout the Revolutionary War, Washington never changed his opinion on the employment of cavalry troopers—they were just like the infantry and should be employed wherever soldiers were needed. Consequently, he ordered Pulaski to Minisink to fight Indians. The assignment was a misuse of the cavalry's capability. Naturally, in desperate situations a commander reaches out for all able-bodied soldiers regardless of their specialty. (At the Anzio beachhead in 1944, General Mark Clark thrust rifles into the hands of cooks and placed them in the front trenches to stem the threatened breakthrough of the Germans.) But Washington employed the cavalry as infantry in normal situations. Adams provides a striking example. Governor Jonathan Trumbull of Connecticut dispatched a body of four to five hundred "light horse" to New York. They were men of reputation and property. Nevertheless, Washington refused to allow them to keep their horses due to the expense of maintaining them. When they refused to do infantry duty, he abruptly sent them home. He told their commander: "They can no longer be of use here, where horses cannot be brought into action, and I do not care how soon they are dismissed." Washington, however, was not that curt with Pulaski. The Commander-in-Chief recognized the Pole's capability and personal bravery and approved the creation of the Pulaski Legion.[9]

Captain "Light Horse Harry" Lee, who first served in Colonel Theodorick Bland's First Continental Cavalry Regiment, knew Pulaski well. In his *Memoirs*, Lee writes: "This gallant soldier was a native of Poland...[he] hastened to the wilds of America, and associated himself with our perils and our fortune." Lee called Pulaski "indefatigable and persevering" in the cause of American independence. Lee describes Pulaski's character:

> He was sober, diligent, and intrepid, gentlemanly in his manners and amiable in heart. He was very reserved, and, when alone, betrayed strong evidence of deep melancholy. Those who knew him intimately spoke highly of the sublimity of his virtue, and the constancy of his friendship...this brave Pole encountered difficulty and sought danger.

Lee sums up Pulaski's standing in the Continental Army: "Nor do I have the smallest doubt if he had been conversant in our language, and better acquainted with our customs and country, but that he would have been one of our most conspicuous and useful officers."[10]

No doubt, if Pulaski knew English well, he could have removed many misunderstandings. Nevertheless, bravery in battle cuts through language differences and sparks admiration. General Washington told Henry Laurens, President of Congress: "The Count's valor and active zeal on all occasions have done him great honor." When Governor William Livingston of New Jersey praised the model behavior of Pulaski's cavalry during the winter

OPPOSITE PHOTO: *The equestrian statue of Pulaski on Pennsylvania Avenue at 13th Street was sculpted by Kazimierz Chodzinski and erected by the United States Government belatedly in 1910 to carry out the resolution of the Continental Congress of 22 November 1779 to honor Pulaski with a monument.*

GENERAL CASIMIR PULASKI IN WASHINGTON, D. C.
(Photo from the Library of Congress through the courtesy of Myra Lenard, Executive Director of the Polish American Congress, Washington Office).

of 1777-78, Washington wrote in reply: "I am pleased with the favourable account which you give of Count Pulaski's Conduct while at Trenton. He is a Gentleman of great activity and unquestionable bravery." Acknowledging Pulaski's intention of resigning from his post of Commander of the Horse, Washington again stressed his bravery: "I can only say, therefore, that it will always give me pleasure to bear testimony to the zeal and bravery which you displayed on every occasion."[11]

Americans who have studied General Pulaski's record of twenty-six months in the American Revolution invariably point to his bravery. William W. Gordon writes: "In all the military engagements of which we have record, he was distinguished for his extraordinary personal bravery and for his handling of cavalry, employing surprise tactics by virtue of which he almost invariably met with success despite the use of small numbers against greater forces." Gordon quotes how a comrade of Pulaski saw his commander perform in combat: "The Count in battle—how he seemed to fight as if enjoying a banquet; how, again and again, he would dash into the midst of the enemy, cutting his way on the right hand and on the left, as if the strength of ten men lay in his single arm; and then wheeling, cutting his way back again, and often without loss." Pulaski's enlisted dragoons also admired their commander. Following Pulaski's death at Savannah, a Hessian Legionnaire abandoned the remnant of the Legion to join his fellow Hessians in the British Army near Charleston. Captain Johann Ewald asked the dragoon what sort of man the deceased Count Pulaski had been. "He was a young and noble gentleman," the dragoon answered, "a very daring horseman, and feared nothing in the world." Surprised and impressed, Ewald exclaimed, "What a splendid eulogy for an officer after his death from the mouth of one of his subordinates!" And Ewald added, "What esteem does this count not merit in the eyes of every soldier?"[12]

Pulaski passionately embraced liberty as his goal in life. Gordon sums up this noble impulse:

The leading motive of General Pulaski's life was the love of liberty. For this he fought valiantly in behalf of his native land, and although in that struggle he lost his relatives, his home and all his property, and finally was driven from his country as an outlaw, his thirst for liberty could not be quenched, and he dedicated his talents and finally his life to the cause of American liberty.

Casimir Pulaski's great love of liberty is immortalized in the design of his monument at Savannah, Georgia. The eminent New York sculptor Robert Eberhardt Launitz not only designed the beautiful Thaddeus Kosciuszko Monument at West Point, New York, in 1828 but also the graceful Casimir Pulaski Monument at Savannah in 1854. The sculptor explained the reason why he surmounted the Pulaski Monument with a statue of liberty:

> The love of liberty brought Pulaski to America; for love of liberty he fought; and for liberty he lost his life. Thus, I thought that Liberty should crown his monument, and share with him the homage of the free.[13]

The opposition of some Americans to foreigners in the Continental Army and the lack of understanding of the effective employment of cavalry of most others did not deter Casimir Pulaski. He persisted in educating and convincing Americans of the great value of cavalry in military operations. His role as cavalry commander in the American Revolution justify the title "Father of American Cavalry."

• APPENDIX A •

Balancing the Books

Accounts of the Pulaski Legion

❧

GENERAL CASIMIR PULASKI RECRUITED, organized, and equipped his Legion in the remarkably short period of three months. His senior officers, Colonels Michael Kovatch and Baron Carl von Bose, Major Julius de Montford, Captain De Segond and others, set up recruiting stations in the Middle Atlantic area where they recruited soldiers for the novel legionary organization. In Baltimore, De Segond was so persuasive that twelve men who had enlisted in Continental Army units of Maryland switched their enlistments to the Legion. The episode demonstrated the enthusiasm of Pulaski's officers. At the same time, however, General William Smallwood of Maryland became outraged, protested loudly to Washington, and the Commander-in-Chief tempered the Legion's enthusiasm.

Congress agreed to advance $50,000 in Continental currency for the enlistment bounties and the purchase of clothing, horses, arms, accoutrements, and other necessary items. The money was advanced to Pulaski in three stages. When he ran out of money, he used his own rather than wait for the next advance from Congress and thereby slow down the momentum of the organizing effort. In his letter to Congress, 17 September 1778, he said he had expended $16,000 of his own money for the Legion. The expenditure of personal funds increased to a total of about $50,000. The Legion's paymaster, Captain Joseph Baldesqui, told Congress on 28 July 1779: "I am furthermore certain that Count Pulaski has laid out for the Legion at least fifty thousand dollars of his own money, which are not mentioned in his accounts." Baldesqui admitted frankly that some vouchers were lost or the Legion's officers failed to turn them over to him. The paymaster tried to allay the fears of Congress over the unaccounted deficiency. Relying on Pulaski's high sense of honor, Baldesqui confidently stated: "I know Count Pulaski well enough to be certain that he will pay it as soon as he will be informed."[1]

The auditors of Congress were unusually severe with Pulaski. They demanded signed receipts for the smallest purchases and even from individual soldiers for money advanced to them, for example, their monthly pay. "This might have been done very easily," Baldesqui said, "but I did not think it was necessary nor very regular, because the greater part of them could not write their names." He said he chose to keep their accounts "as we are accustomed to do it in France." He explained that the troops were paid in the presence of the captain of each company. The captains certified the pay rolls for their companies, together with the colonel and the general. He stressed that the French method was strictly followed in the Legion. Baldesqui asked for some understanding of cultural differences. "I hope, gentlemen, you will consider that a foreigner cannot be acquainted with the customs of your country as well as yourselves."[2]

Baldesqui wrestled with the paperwork and the auditors for eighteen months. Meanwhile, he could not assume his primary duty of command of the Legion's supernumerary company. Pulaski informed the Board of War that he needed the services of Baldesqui in the Legion. Richard Peters of the Board of War acknowledged Pulaski's request for Baldesqui in a letter to the Commissioners of Accounts: "He has written very pressingly for Capt. Baldesqui's joining him" Peters said, " but this cannot be done, as he is waiting for the settlement of his accounts which have been presented to you for that purpose." Before the arrears were settled, Baldesqui asked for more money for the Legion. Peters explained the reason to the auditors: "Gen. Pulaski says it was impossible for him, from the rapid rise of prices, to comply with his engagements to Congress; and therefore provided the articles enumerated at the current prices, and agreeably to this the accounts are made out." Nevertheless, Peters left the decision to the auditors. "You will judge the propriety of this," he concluded.[3]

At York, Pennsylvania, on the eve of his departure for the South, 27 March 1779, Pulaski again asked the auditors that Baldesqui be allowed to join the Legion. He also offered an explanation for some of the missing vouchers. "Some receipts were lost in the hands of Lieutenant-colonel Boze, who has been killed at Egg Harbor," he wrote, "but I hope also you will make no great difficulties, being persuaded you do depend enough on my honor to pass over such matter." However, the auditors did not relent, and they kept Baldesqui in Philadelphia. The next month, Baldesqui prepared a listing of payments made to Pulaski and himself amounting to $132,500. But the auditors countered with a higher figure. They claimed that Pulaski and Baldesqui received at sundry times the sum of $181,286.[4]

Prior to the departure of the Legion, Pulaski turned over to Baldesqui additional invoices and receipts that came into the possession of the Legion. Baldesqui prepared a revised accounting and attempted to meet with the auditors who informed him that they would be engaged in other work for the next three to four weeks. Baldesqui took advantage of the delay to visit Boston on personal matters. Before leaving, however, Baldesqui gave the auditors all the payments made by him to the officers and men, together with the papers from General Pulaski. He requested that the auditors and he review the accounts together upon his return from Boston. While there, Baldesqui took sick and was forced to delay his return to Philadelphia. To his consternation, he discovered that the auditors had examined the accounts of the Legion without waiting for him. They found discrepancies that they could not resolve and gave an unfavorable report to the

Treasury Board. What made matters worse, Congress rushed to publish the delinquent report in the newspapers. Thus, the people may have gained the impression that Baldesqui was incompetent and possibly a criminal. The paymaster felt injured and his honor impugned. Baldesqui did not react foolishly (perhaps challenging the President of Congress to a duel). Instead, he wrote a letter to Congress, 28 July 1779, in which he gave a reasonable explanation of the misunderstanding, and he closed his letter with a plea for justice: "I am in hopes, also, gentlemen, that a future resolve of Congress the effect of the former [publication of the unfavorable report] may be annulled. I mean that of the 10th of June, which I suppose was made through mistake, since it may induce the public to think I have misbehaved."[5]

The following month Pulaski wrote a long letter, and his final one, to Congress from South Carolina, 19 August 1779. Among the many subjects he presented, the Legion Commander informed the delegates that he had received a letter from his family, informing him that 100,000 French *livres* in hard money would be delivered to him. The sum was more than enough to pay for all expenditures that could not be substantiated with available invoices. The method of delivery of the money to America had to be established. Undoubtedly, in coordination with General Pulaski, the family selected the very resourceful Count Maurycy (Maurice) Benyowsky (also identified as Beniowski in Polish historical accounts). Casimir Pulaski knew Benyowsky well. They were brothers-in-arms. Benyowsky had joined Pulaski's Army of the Confederation of Bar where he demonstrated his ability and gained the rank of general. In 1769, he was at the side of Francis Pulaski, Casimir's brother, when the Russians captured them. The Russians knew little about Benyowsky, and he persuaded his captors to release him. He immediately rejoined Francis, but just as quickly the Russians captured him again. This time Catherine II decided to rid herself of Benyowsky for good by banishing him into the vastness of Siberia. To insure that he never returned to Europe, she ordered that Benyowsky be escorted to the Kamchatka Peninsula on the Pacific Ocean.

Banishment to Siberia became a favorite tactic of the tsars when they wished to eliminate troublesome subjects. Thousands of captured Poles from the Uprisings of 1830 and 1863 were cast into the wilds of Siberia. Exposed to the primitive and severe conditions of that inhospitable region, many Poles perished; others managed to survive. In time, the survivors formed communities where they organized societies, established churches and schools, and taught their offspring the Polish language, history, and culture. Remarkably, some communities continued into the twentieth century. In 1985, a group of Rice University alumni, accompanied by a faculty lecturer, made a long journey from Mongolia through Siberia to Moscow. The tour began in a village near Genghis Khan's old capital of Karakorum and proceeded north into Siberia. When the tour members reached Irkutsk, they were surprised to discover a former Roman Catholic church built by some 20,000 Poles who were exiled there for engaging in the 1863 Uprising against the Russians. The church served them until November 1917 when the godless Bolsheviks seized power in Russia and closed down the church. The Communists converted the church to an office building and concert hall. Interestingly, almost everyone in Irkutsk still referred to the building as *Polskiy Kostyol* (Polish Church). Despite the oppressive rule of atheistic Communists for seventy-four years, God prevailed. The post-Communist Russian government returned the church to the Catholic community of Irkutsk. The building was renovated and consecrated as Immaculate Heart of Mary Cathedral. Jesuit Father Benjamin Fiore reported to the *Polish American Journal* (October 2000) that Polish Archbishop Jerzy Mazur and Papal envoy Jan Pieter Cardinal Schotte jointly conducted the consecration. Archbishop Mazur was serving as the Apostolic Administrator of Eastern Siberia, sharing the vast land of Siberia with Bishop Joseph Werth at Tobolsk and caring for the spiritual needs of one million Catholics in a population of twenty-five million. Father Fiore said: "Some 50,000 Catholics live in Irkutsk, mostly the descendants of exiles to Siberia after the failed rebellion in Poland in 1863."[6]

Benyowsky survived his banishment to Siberia. Catherine II underestimated the resourcefulness of Benyowsky. He secretly organized a band of fellow exiles who seized a sailing vessel and departed Kamchatka with sixty-three men and seven women. Benyowsky sailed along the Kurile Islands past Japan to Formosa. Continuing, he reached the Portuguese possession of Macao on the China mainland near Canton, 23 September 1771. Six months later he reached France. Benyowsky's dramatic escape brought him fame. He now entered the French Army in the rank of colonel. The government gave him a project of forming a colony on the Island of Madagascar in the Indian Ocean. When the attempt failed, he returned to Europe. He next served the Austrian Empire, 1778-79. Following his Austrian service, the Pulaski family contacted him about carrying out the role of an emissary to America.[7]

On 21 August 1779, Benyowsky was in Providence, Rhode Island, speaking with General Horatio Gates, then commanding a wing of Washington's army. Benyowsky told Gates a remarkable story of his attempts to reach America, and he disclosed for the first time Pulaski's plan of recruiting a cavalry force in Europe for service in America. As Gates wrote John Jay, President of Congress, Pulaski had asked his former comrade-in-arms to recruit 300 German hussars and equip them with arms and accoutrements, for which the Pulaski family paid Benyowsky £25,000 sterling. Securing passage for the corps of hussars, Benyowsky sailed from Hamburg. Unfortunately, a British man-of-war intercepted Benyowsky's ship on the high seas and turned the ship back to Europe. Benyowsky persuaded the British to release him as the hussars were dispersed. Benyowsky's second attempt to America also failed, but he did not give up. Learning that the newly-designated French minister to America, Le Chevalier de La Luzerne, was about to sail to his post in Philadelphia, Benyowsky obtained passage on a vessel in the minister's convoy. A French warship guarded the convoy, and it arrived safely at Boston. When Gates met Benyowsky, the American was impressed by the suave and courtly European. Benyowsky demanded nothing for himself, except a horse with which to get to Pulaski in South Carolina. He vowed to travel on foot, if necessary. Gates told Jay he felt honor-bound to help a brother of an American general. Gates provided Benyowsky with a horse, property of the Continental Army, and a warrant for four hundred dollars for travel expenses. President Jay referred Gates' letter to the Board of War.[8]

In Philadelphia, members of the Board of War had a long talk with Benyowsky, who said he carried a letter for Pulaski and claimed the general to be his natural brother (Benyowsky was only a brother-in-arms). The Board recommended to Congress, 3 September 1779, under the signature of Richard Peters, that Benyowsky be provided with a horse and a thousand dollars for travel expenses. Congress concurred. Benyowsky reached Pulaski at Savannah a few days before the fateful day of 9 October 1779. He disclosed this fact to Congress in his letter of 9 May 1780. Historian Joseph Johnson also confirms Benyowsky presence at Savannah. He writes that Dr. P. Fayssoux, surgeon-general of South Carolina, told him "that Pulaski had the consolation of being attended, in his last hours, by a countryman—a relative, a friend—a brother confederate in the cause of their native country." If Benyowsky brought the 100,00 *livres,* as this author believes, Pulaski had the consoling thought of the Legion's accounts finally being settled. After Pulaski's death, Benyowsky returned to Philadelphia.[9]

Meanwhile, Baldesqui received some good news. He had objected to an earlier unfavorable report of his handling of the accounts and had asked Congress to correct that injury. On 24 August 1779, auditors James Johnson and David Howell, the same ones who had released the earlier report, reversed themselves. They now stated that "Captain Baldesqui had duly and regularly settled his accounts, as paymaster to Count Pulaski's Legion, to the first day of March last." Baldesqui was not aware of the Johnson-Howell certificate immediately. Moreover, with the news of Pulaski's death reaching Philadelphia, the auditors and Congress seem to have softened their attitude toward Pulaski's delinquent accounts. In addition, Benyowsky was ready with the Pulaski family money to deal with the auditors. Quietly and unofficially, it is believed, Benyowsky and Baldesqui made good on all outstanding accounts. Armed with the Johnson-Howell certificate, Baldesqui asked Congress to bring the matter of the Pulaski Legion accounts to a close. On 28 December 1779, Congress noted:

> The Board of Treasury, to whom was referred a memorial of Captain Joseph Baldesqui, paymaster of Brigadier Count Pulaski's legion, report,
> That by a certificate of Messrs. Johnson and Howell, auditors of the main army, dated at West Point, the 24 August 1779, accompanying the said memorial, it appears that Captain Baldesqui has duly and regularly settled his accounts, as pay master to Count Pulaski's legion, to the first of March last; and that on the whole of the evidence before the Board, they are of opinion he has discharged his duty with strict integrity and honor.

Congress concurred in the report.[10]

The very next day Baldesqui submitted his resignation. He had come to America to fight for independence. Instead he became immersed in a frustrating exercise of paperwork for eighteen months. Having finally settled the accounts of the Legion, he felt free to leave. Congress accepted his resignation the same day, 29 December 1779. Baldesqui settled in Germantown, Pennsylvania.[11]

ADDENDUM

FOLLOWING THE DEATH of General Casimir Pulaski, Count Benyowsky applied to Congress for an appointment in the Continental Army. However, Congress declined his offer. He tried again in a memorial to Congress of 26 June 1780. He said he would be willing to serve as a volunteer on George Washington's staff, but nothing came of his second offer. He made no further attempts for more than a year. Meanwhile, he developed the organization of a legion of three corps of 3483 soldiers. Specifically, his plan called for each corps to consist of two cavalry squadrons, four companies of infantry, one of grenadiers, one of sharpshooters, an artillery brigade, and a brigade train of wagons. Benyowsky pledged to recruit, equip, and arm the legion, and bring it to America for the sum of 518,000 *livres* (about $100,000). If Congress accepted the plan, it would repay Benyowsky in stages of one-third, as each of the three components of the legion joined the Continental Army. Benyowsky had crafted a well-thoughtout plan. He listed fifteen conditions that would affect the employment of the legion. Of course, Benyowsky expected to be appointed commanding general of the legion. In forwarding the plan to Congress, he first reviewed it with General Von Steuben, Inspector General, who favored and passed it on to General Washington. Benyowsky also obtained the endorsement of French Minister to America, De La Luzerne. Washington suggested several changes in the conditions and then approved it. Benyowsky presented the plan to Congress on 6 May 1782. A committee of the Board of War, consisting of Abraham Clark, John Rutledge, and Theodorick Bland, found the plan worthwhile and the conditions acceptable. The committee recommended that Congress approve Benyowsky's project. Suddenly, just four days later, another committee was appointed to review the plan again. The three committee members, James Madison, John Scott, and David Ramsay, recommended this time that the plan not be accepted. The abrupt change was caused by Congress receiving advance information that the British opposition parties persuaded King George III and his government to initiate preliminary peace negotiations. Benyowsky had proposed an excellent military unit for the Americans, but he was too late. Benyowsky returned to France temporarily. He decided to return to Madagascar where, again, he would become the leader of the natives. The French in Madagascar opposed him, and his support among the natives had dwindled. In a fight with the French, Benyowsky was killed, 23 May 1786, and was buried there.[12]

Count Maurycy Benyowsky's adventurous life attracted the interest of Romantic writers. The renowned Polish poet Juljusz Slowacki (1809-1849) composed a poem *Beniowski* in 1841.

Nobel Laureate Czeslaw Milosz wrote that "*Beniowski* is a poem of digressions, obviously competing with Byron's *Don Juan*. The plot traces the vicissitudes undergone by a Hungarian-Polish nobleman." On 15 June 2000, the Library of Congress hosted a seminar "Count Maurice Benyowsky: Citizen of the World." The event was organized by the Washington embassies of the Slovak Republic, Austria, France, Hungary, Madagascar, and Poland, in cooperation with the American Philosophical Society and the Library of Congress.[13]

• APPENDIX B •

PULASKI'S MILITARY EXPERIENCE

⚜

CASIMIR PULASKI was an experienced military commander when he met General George Washington in August 1777. Benjamin Franklin wrote Washington on 29 May 1777 that Pulaski was "an Officer famous throughout Europe for his Bravery and Conduct in Defense of Liberties of his Country." Pulaski gained that experience while fighting Russian-occupying forces in Poland over a period of four years, 1768-1772. At age 23, he took command of the military arm of the Confederation of Bar, a patriotic movement that sought to evict the Russians from Poland and restore sovereignty to the country.

The political conditions that gave rise to the Confederation of Bar date back to the death of the last hereditary king of the Jagiellonian dynasty, Zygmunt August, in 1572. The Polish magnates seized the occasion of a lack of an heir to make the kingship elective in order to gain more political power for themselves. They formed the "Nobles Republic" (representing about ten percent of the population). European monarchs also took advantage of the periodic elections to promote their own candidates and meddle in Poland's internal affairs. At the election in 1764, the Polish magnates in all their splendor gathered on the open field of Mokotow, just south of Warsaw, for the purpose of casting their votes for a new king. Several factions competed with each other. Russia, Austria, Prussia also backed their candidates through the control of factions. Tsarina Catherine II strongly supported Stanislaw August Poniatowski. To intimidate other candidates and their supporters, she ordered Russian army units to Warsaw. Poniatowski was elected. Years earlier, young Poniatowski was Princess Catherine's lover in St. Petersburg when he served as secretary to the British minister to Russia. She now did not allow any residual emotional feelings cloud her evil design for the destruction of Poland. She influenced the new king through her personal representative in Warsaw, Nikolay Repnin, and kept a large army in Poland, ostensibly to support the rule of Poniatowski.

Count Jozef Pulaski and other patriotic Polish magnates were deeply troubled at the erosion of Poland's sovereignty. They, therefore, organized the Confederation of Bar. Pulaski was a wealthy and respected member of the gentry and a renowned lawyer. His estate of Winiary was located south of Warsaw. He served as *Starosta* (Administrator) of the Warka region. In 1736, he married the wealthy Marianna Zielinska of Lomza (hence Casimir's kinship with Captain Jan Zielinski of the Pulaski Legion). She bore Jozef eight children—three sons: Franciszek, Kazimierz, and Antoni, and five daughters: Anna, Jozefa, Joanna, Paulina, and Malgorzata. The whole family, parents, sons, daughters and their husbands, formed a closely-knit group. Casimir was born at the family residence in Warsaw, 6 March 1745. The Pulaski boys attended school in Warsaw. When Casimir turned fifteen, father Jozef decided that his son should receive some polished training and sent Casimir to the court of Prince Karl of Courland at Mitawa (Mitau). (Courland was a fiefdom of Poland and extended over a part of present-day Latvia.) Karl was the son of Augustus III, King of Poland and Elector of Saxony. Prince Karl was a frivolous person, yet he convinced a large group of anti-Russian Poles that he would succeed to the throne of Poland and as king would reform Poland and bring the country to a dignified place among nations. Karl married the beautiful Franciszka

Krasinska without the King's consent. Augustus III, therefore, considered the marriage morganatic. Nevertheless, Princess Franciszka remained loyal to her husband, and she never lost hope that he would become King and she Queen of Poland. The fifteen-year-old Kazimierz fell in love with the nineteen-year-old Princess. But the attraction was worship at a distance. Biographer Clarence A. Manning writes: "It was the nearest to a love affair that he was ever to know." Franciszka admired the lad. She became strongly attached to him and loyally supported him in all his future trials and tribulations.

Rather than develop into a pleasure-seeking courtier in Mitawa, Casimir became a wiser and more ardent patriot. He studied the Machiavellian tactics of Russian diplomatic and military personnel in Courland that undermined Polish sovereignty at every turn. Thus, when Jozef Pulaski proposed a movement of patriotic gentry to oppose the ever-encroaching Russians, Casimir joined wholeheartedly. His brothers, Franciszek and Antoni, stood with the father, too, as did brother-in-law Antoni Suffczynski, husband of Casimir's sister, Paulina. The Pulaski family members traveled about the country, contacting friendly gentry and laying the groundwork for the movement. On 29 February 1768, Jozef Pulaski called an organizational meeting at the nondescript town of Bar, deep in the Polish Ukraine and near the border with Turkey. He selected the remote town to avoid attracting the attention of the King or the Russians. To give the movement a crusading fervor, Jozef established the Military Order of the Knights of the Holy Cross. The history of Poland has always been intimately associated with the Roman Catholic church. Therefore, the first rule of eleven for the Order reads: "To defend the Roman Catholic faith." This rule placed the Order in direct opposition to the Russian Orthodoxy of the enemy. Naturally, the first members of the order were Jozef Pulaski and his three sons. The Confederates voted to establish a military arm, a regiment of knights consisting of thirteen troops of hussars and heavy cavalry, and six companies of light troops. The leading force of the Confederation, Jozef Pulaski, was made commander. His three

POLAND IN 1768
When the Confederation of Bar was formed, 29 February 1768

sons and son-in-law Antoni also commanded units in the regiment. It was not long before Casimir developed into a bold and imaginative leader and rose to command the entire military force of the Confederation, numbering at times as high as 4000 soldiers. The Confederation consisted of a civilian as well as a military division. The civilian side engaged in national and diplomatic matters.

The Russians ignored the Confederates at first. During the lull, Casimir and the other leaders rode about the country, visiting nobles, collecting supplies, and recruiting men. However, the activities of the Confederates began to worry Repnin. He ordered

General Peter Krechetnikov with 8000 soldiers to march against the Confederates. About 20 April 1768, Casimir clashed with a detachment of carabineers, hussars, and Don Cossacks near the town of Staro-Konstantynow. The detachment was Krechetnikov's advance guard, and Casimir forced it to retreat. He withdrew to the town of Staro-Konstantynow and prepared to defend it. On the morning of 24 April 1768, the Russians attacked the town with more than 4000 soldiers. The twenty-three year old Casimir defended his position with fewer than 2,000 men. The Russians reported waging the attack for four hours without being able to defeat the Poles. Casimir said his smaller force successfully defended the town for more than ten hours. Due to Russian superiority, Casimir did not wait for a resumption of the attack the next day. Under cover of darkness, he slipped away with his soldiers, the wounded, and supplies to the neighboring town of Chmielnik. The Russian immediate commander, Podgorychanin, followed Pulaski to Chmielnik. For three days the Russians attacked the Poles in five separate attacks, but all assaults were repulsed. Learning that a relief force under Wawrzyniec Potocki and Antoni Pulaski, Casimir's younger brother, were marching to aid Casimir, Podgorychanin abandoned his fight with Casimir and marched to engage the new threat. He surprised and decisively defeated the Poles at Ulanow. Meanwhile, as Podgorychanin withdrew from Chmielnik, Casimir followed and arrived in time to save the remnants of the relief expedition.

Jozef Pulaski became encouraged by the action of Prince Joachim Potocki, one of the most powerful magnates possessing a private army. Potocki threw in his lot with the Confederates. In his first encounter with the Russians, however, he was annihilated. He showed gross carelessness when he took no precautions and allowed the Russians to infiltrate the town where his army rested. During the night the Russians attacked unexpectedly from all sides and smashed his force in one engagement. Potocki's fiasco severely damaged the cause of the Confederates. Other magnates who may have wanted to join Pulaski were intimidated and remained neutral.

Meanwhile, Casimir continued to lead the Confederate army and gain experience with each battle and skirmish. Although he lost some, he always managed to extricate his unit and carry on. At the fortified monastery at Berdyczow, 5000 Russians attacked Pulaski's 1400 soldiers. After a siege of two weeks, the Russians captured the monastery as well as Pulaski and his garrison. The Russians next seized Bar, the cradle of the Confederation. Jozef Pulaski and two sons, with some 2000 Confederate soldiers, escaped across the Dniester River into Turkey at Chocim. After holding Casimir a captive for one month, the Russians released him, and he joined the father. Nevertheless, the Bar Confederates soon reentered Poland and continued the struggle for three more years on their own. The Confederation could not induce France or Turkey to help their cause. The other Polish magnates remained cowed, fearful of losing their vast land holdings. Becoming desperate, a group of Confederates hatched a plot to abduct King Stanislaw August and persuade him to turn against the Russians. They also believed they could use the King as a bargaining chip, but none entertained the thought of harming the King. The plan was very risky. Capture of the abductors in case of failure could mean execution by the firing squad. Casimir did not take part in the actual abduction. To what extent he was aware of the plot is not known. On the evening of 3 November 1771, the plotters abducted the King from his carriage in Warsaw. As they led the prisoner out of Warsaw, the Confederates became fearful of being pursued and captured. They gave up the attempt and dispersed. The most well known and feared Confederate, Casimir Pulaski, was blamed for the attempt and smeared as a regicide. He was tried in absentia and condemned to death. Casimir felt compelled to leave Poland. The Confederation of Bar collapsed for good. His father, Jozef, died in Turkish captivity, and his brother Franciszek was killed in action. Casimir would never return to Poland again. He wandered around Europe. In France, he incurred heavy debt and was thrown into a debtor's prison. Friends, however, bailed him out. When news reached France of the outbreak of the American Revolution, Pulaski's spirits were revived. Perhaps he could fight for a people who sought freedom from oppression. Influential friends in France interceded in his behalf with American commissioners Benjamin Franklin and Silas Deane. Obtaining letters of recommendation to General Washington, he sailed to the New World to continue his life as a freedom fighter.

APPENDIX C

PULASKI'S BURIAL SITE

THE BELIEF THAT CASIMIR PULASKI was buried at sea remained strong for more than 200 years, despite the contradictory accounts of several Southerners. Historian Edward Pinkowski conducted a determined research for several decades in an attempt to confirm the claim of the early Southerners who maintained that Pulaski died of his battle wound aboard the American privateer *Wasp* and was buried on the Greenwich Plantation of widow Jane Bowen, located on the Wilmington River near Savannah. Pinkowski uncovered letters that speak of Poles visiting Pulaski's gravesite in the nineteenth century. William P. Bowen, Jane Bowen's grandson, said that a 66-year-old Jewish cotton dealer, Jacob Clavius Levy of Charleston, met Captain Jacob Ferdinand Boguslawski, who visited the gravesite in 1803 or 1804. Levy was a lad of fourteen or fifteen at the time. He told Bowen that Boguslawski said he was a nephew of Pulaski. The Polish visitor also said he was a survivor of a Polish legion that Napoleon had ordered to Haiti to suppress the Negro rebellion led by Toussaint L'Ouverture. General Kazimierz Malachowski, commander of a demibrigade in the ill-fated French expedition to Haiti, also wrote that Boguslawski and other Polish legionnaires visited Savannah. After the Pulaski Monument was erected in 1855, Bowen escorted a Polish visitor to Pulaski's former

CASIMIR PULASKI

Author Francis C. Kajencki stands on the bank of the Wilmington River at the former Greenwich Plantation of Jane Bowen, three miles east of Savannah, Georgia.

In October 1779, the American privateer Wasp, *Captain Samuel Bulfinch commanding, anchored near here to load American cannon following the disastrous defeat of the French and Americans at the Battle of Savannah, 9 October 1779. The mortally wounded Pulaski was brought aboard the* Wasp *where he died 15 October 1779 and was buried on land near the river in a torchlight ceremony the same day. (Photo by Anthony A. Kajencki II, 31 May 2000)*

gravesite. He was Henryk Dmochowski, a sculptor, who came to Savannah to exhibit his marble bust of Pulaski at the Georgia Historical Society. Writing from Savannah on 2 June 1859, Dmochowski said the location of the former gravesite is four miles from the city on the bank of a little river that empties into the Savannah River. Although the plantation belonged to the Bowen family for many years, the owner during Dmochowski's visit was a Mrs. Gilbert, a widow. She maintained the house beautifully, Dmochowski wrote. Bowen showed the visitor the trunk of a palmetto tree and an English holly bush that had marked Pulaski's

Pulaski's Burial Site

grave. Dmochowski was impressed by the beauty of the place, abounding with magnolia trees and hanging moss, a heavy carpet of bulrushes and bushes, and lying close to the river. (In May 2000, the author and son Anthony visited Pulaski's former gravesite. The area looked serenely beautiful. The Bowen family residence that had been built close to the Wilmington River was demolished and cleared, and the plantation had become the Greenwich Cemetery).

Pinkowski seemed to be convinced the historical data substantiated his claim that the remains in the metal box are those of Casimir Pulaski. Pinkowski found another piece of evidence when an X-ray of the right hand of the remains revealed it had suffered a break. Indeed, Pulaski had broken his right hand during a clash with the Russians at Grab, Poland, 13 January 1770. Pulaski's broken hand is documented in correspondence. Still Savannah officials undertook DNA testing to prove the claim beyond a doubt. The effort was led by Dr. James C. Metts, coroner of Savannah, and strongly supported by Pinkowski. Dr. Karen R. Burns, forensic anthropologist at the University of Georgia, joined the task force. A search for a female family ancestor took place in Poland and led to the tomb of Pulaski's grandniece, Teresa Witkowska, in the village of Promna. A delegation of Americans, whose flight to Poland was paid for by Pinkowski, arrived in Promna in September 1998. The group included Dr. Metts, Dr. Burns, Charles Powell, and Pinkowski. From Poland were Paul Barford, British-born archeologist in Warsaw, Witold Bujakowski, monument conservator in Radom, and Father Jan Gorny, pastor of St. Mary Magdalene Church in Promna. On 23 September 1998, soil was dug up and a few rows of bricks were removed from the ceiling of an underground crypt. Through the exposed opening, Dr. Burns stepped down a ladder with a flashlight and obtained samples of bones and teeth that were subjected to DNA testing in the United States. The tests were found to be inconclusive. More samples were needed, perhaps from another ancestor. As a result, Savannah officials postponed for two years the reinterment of Pulaski's remains, scheduled originally for 15 October 2000.

Other considerations also influenced the decision. Tentative plans of the City of Savannah call for international ceremonies to begin three days before the reinterment when the remains of General Pulaski will lie in state in the Rotunda of the Savannah City Hall. Because Phillips' original coffin had been made of wood, the coffin for the reburial was likewise made of wood. Ryszard Liebchen of the firm of Liebchen & Company of Warsaw and his wife furnished a ceremonial casket as a gift to the memory of General Pulaski. On 15 October, anniversary of Pulaski's death, the funeral cortege will leave City Hall and move to the Cathedral of St. John where the Bishop Military Ordinary of Poland and the Catholic Bishop of Savannah will concelebrate the funeral Mass. The casket will then be moved to the site of the renovated Pulaski Monument in Monterey Square and placed in a vault alongside the monument and sealed.

On 9 October 2001, the 222nd anniversary of the Battle of Savannah, the restored Pulaski Monument will be dedicated. Dr. Don Gardner, former Director of the Savannah Park Commission, actively participated in the restoration project. During the ceremony, Savannah Mayor Floyd Adams and Lee Meyer, Chairman of the Pulaski Jubilee Celebration Committee, will take leading roles. A replica of the Pulaski Legion banner may be presented to representatives of the Polish Army who are expected to place it in the Military Museum in Warsaw. This banner will be a replacement for the one that had been presented to the Polish Government in 1936 but disappeared in the chaos of World War II. A second replica will be presented to the City of Savannah and intended for display at Fort Pulaski National Monument where other artifacts about Pulaski can be seen. Citizens of the United States, Poland, and other countries will be invited to participate in the historic events in Savannah. Special invitations are expected to be extended to the Presidents of the United States and Poland.

Plans are also being considered for the celebration of the 225th anniversary of the Battle of Savannah and the death of Casimir Pulaski in October 2004.

APPENDIX D

ACKNOWLEDGEMENTS

※

THE AUTHOR IS GRATEFUL to the following individuals and institutions in Poland:

- Dr. Jadwiga Wroblewska
  Gdansk Library
  Polish Academy of Sciences

- Marek Skorupski
  Editor-in-Chief of Photography
  Polska Agencja Informacyjna, SA
  Warsaw

- Interpress Publishers
  Warsaw

The author is likewise grateful to the following individuals, libraries, and archival agencies in the United States:

- Jeffrey M. Flannery
  Manuscript Reference Librarian
  Library of Congress
  Washington, D. C.

- National Archives
  Photographic Service
  Washington, D. C.

- W. Todd Groce, Executive Director
  Valerie Frey, Manuscript Archivist
  Mandi D. Johnson
  Jewell Anderson
  Coby Linton
  Georgia Historical Society
  Savannah, Georgia

- Stanley A. Ciesielski
  President, Polish Heritage Association of Maryland
  Baltimore, Maryland

- Michael Ciesielski Photography
  Baltimore, Maryland

- Jan Lorys, Curator
  Polish Museum of America
  Chicago, Illinois

- Joseph and Della Kane
  Erie, Pennsylvania

- Beth Rorke
  Brandywine Battlefield Park
  Chadd's Ford, Pennsylvania

- Thaddeus V. Gromada, Executive Director
  Janina Kedron
  Polish Institute of Arts and Sciences in America
  New York, New York

- Mary E. Herbert
  Maryland Historical Society
  Baltimore, Maryland

Acknowledgements

- Myra Lenard, Executive Director
  Polish American Congress
  Washington, D. C.

- Frank Milewski, President
  New York Downstate Division
  Polish American Congress
  New York, New York

- Ron D. Jamro
  Naples, Florida

- Edward Dybicz
  Swedesburg, Pennsylvania

- Edward Pinkowski
  The Pinkowski Institute
  Cooper City, Florida

- Rev. Vernon Nelson, Curator
  The Moravian Museum
  Bethlehem, Pennsylvania

- Jonathan A. Teed
  Executive Assistant Manager
  Hotel Bethlehem
  Bethlehem, Pennsylvania

- Kathy Roscoe
  Valley Forge Historical Society
  Valley Forge, Pennsylvania

- Wendy Nesmith
  Document Express, The General Libraries
  The University of Texas at Austin

- Andrea Ashby
  Independence National Historical Park
  Philadelphia, Pennsylvania

- Patricia Polo
  Rebecca Preece
  New Jersey State Library
  Trenton

- Thomas Burdette
  Military History Division
  Special Collections
  University of Texas at El Paso

- Estella Reyes
  Intra Library Loan
  University of Texas at El Paso

- Sandra Ragonese
  Pennsylvania Historical Society
  Philadelphia

- Joyce N. Baker
  Gibbes Museum of Art/
    Carolina Art Association
  Charleston, South Carolina

- Barbara De Wolfe
  Curator of Manuscripts
  William L. Clements Library
  University of Michigan
  Ann Arbor, Michigan

- Dr. Ewa M. Thompson
  Rice University
  Houston, Texas

- Sharen Lee
  Reference Librarian
  Chatham. Effingham. Liberty Counties
    Regional Library
  Savannah, Georgia

· Notes ·

Chapter 1. Soldier of Liberty in America

1. Clarence A. Manning, *Soldier of Liberty, Casimir Pulaski* (New York: Philosophical Library, 1945), pp. 198-204; and William B. Willcox, ed. *The Papers of Benjamin Franklin* (New Haven and London: Yale University Press, 1984), XXIV: 98, 111-12, 120, 133.
2. William Heath, *Memoirs of Major-General Heath...during the American War* (Boston: I. Thomas and E.T. Andrews, 1798; reprint ed., Freeport, New York: Books for Libraries Press, 1970), p. 134.
3. Francois Pulaski, ed., *Correspondance du General Casimir Pulaski avec Claude de Rulhiere, 1774-1778* (Paris: Societe Historique et Litteraire Polonaise, 1948), pp. 31-33.
4. Stanley J. Idzerda, ed., *Lafayette in the Age of the American Revolution* (Ithaca and London: Cornell University Press, 1977), p. 107n; "Diary of Surgeon Albigence Waldo," *The Pennsylvania Magazine of History and Biography,* Vol. XXI, 1897, p. 320; and *Polish Armies 1569-1696 (1), Men-at-Arms Series,* Martin Windrow, ed., and text by Richard Brzezinski (London: Osprey Publishing, Ltd., 1987), p. 15.
5. Rupert Hughes, *George Washington: The Savior of the States. 1777-1781* (New York: William Morrow & Company, 1930), p. 96; Francis Casimir Kajencki, *Thaddeus Kosciuszko: Military Engineer of the American Revolution* (El Paso, Texas: Southwest Polonia Press, 1998), pp. 70-71; and R. Ernest Dupuy and Trevor N. Dupuy, *The Compact History of the Revolutionary War* (New York: Hawthorn Books, Inc., 1963), p. 116.
6. Washington to President of Congress, Bucks County, 21 August 1777, John C. Fitzpatrick, ed., *The Writings of George Washington, from the Original Manuscript Sources* (Washington: Government Printing Office, 1931-1944), V:112.
7. Marquis de la Fayette to James Lovell, 21 August 1777, in Senate Executive Document, No. 120, 2 March 1887, 49th Congress, 2nd Session, Item No. 5, p. 9.
8. Pulaski to Congress, Philadelphia, 24 August 1777, *Papers of the Continental Congress,* MF 247, 204 Reels (Washington, D.C.: Government Printing Office, 1959), Roll 51, I 41, V8, p. 22.

9. Worthington C. Ford, et al, eds. *Journals of the Continental Congress, 1774-1789* (Washington: Government Printing Office, 1904-1937), VIII: 673.
10. Washington to President of Congress, Wilmington, 28 August 1777, Fitzpatrick, *Writings of Washington,* IX: 143-44.
11. Christopher Ward, *The War of the Revolution,* 2 Vols.(New York: The Macmillan Company, 1952), I: 331, 336.
12. Martin I. J. Griffin, *Catholics and the American Revolution* (Philadelphia: Griffin, 1911), III: 8.
13. Paul Bentalou, *Pulaski Vindicated from an Unsubstantiated Charge* (Baltimore: Printed by John D. Toy, 1824; reprint ed., New York: William Abbatt, 1909), pp. 26-27.
14. Washington to President of Congress, Wilmington, Delaware, 28 August 1777, Fitzpatrick, *Writings of Washington,* IX: 143-44. Judge William Johnson of Charleston, South Carolina, stated wrongly that Washington never recommended Casimir Pulaski for promotion to brigadier general. Johnson writes: "Nor do I believe that it was on Washington's recommendation that Congress first created Pulaski a Chief of Cavalry," in Johnson's article "Remarks Critical and Historical Relating to Count Pulaski," *The North American Review,* No. 47 (Charleston: Printed by C. C. Sebring, 1825), p. 36.
15. Ward, *War of the Revolution,* I: 336-37, 342-43; and Joseph Townsend, *The Battle of Brandywine* (Philadelphia: Townsend War, Publisher, 1846; reprint ed., New York: The New York Times & Arno Press, 1969), pp. 9-10.
16. Lt. Col. Joseph B. Mitchell, *The Decisive Battles of the American Revolution* (New York: G. P. Putnam's Sons, 1962), pp. 110-11.
17. Jared Sparks, *The Writings of George Washington* (New York: Harper & Brothers, 1847), V: 459-60; and Ward, *War of the Revolution,* I: 346.
18. Ward, *War of the Revolution,* I: 348; and John F. Reed, *Campaign to Valley Forge, July 1, 1777-December 19, 1777* (Philadelphia: University of Pennsylvania Press, 1965), pp. 126-27.
19. Ward, *War of the Revolution,* I: 351-52; and Willard Sterne Randall, *George Washington, A Life* (New York: Henry Holt and Company, 1997), pp. 332-35.
20. Ward, *War of the Revolution,* I: 353; and Charlemagne Tower, *The Marquis de La Fayette in the American Revolution* (Philadelphia: J. B. Lippincott Company, 1901; reprint ed., New York: Da Capo Press, 1970), I: 232.
21. Bentalou, *Pulaski Vindicated,* p. 27.
22. Hughes, *George Washington,* p. 172.
23. Randall, *George Washington,* p. 335.
24. Bentalou, *Pulaski Vindicated,* p. 27.
25. Randall, *George Washington,* p. 335; David Ramsay, M. D., *The History of the American Revolution,* edited by Lester H. Cohen, 2 Vols. (Indianapolis, Indiana: Liberty Fund, Inc., 1990), II: 347; and Jared Sparks, *The Library of American Biography* (Boston: Charles C. Little and James Brown, 1845), XIV: 418.

Notes

26. Sparks, *Writings of Washington,* V: 458; and Mark Mayo Boatner III, *Encyclopedia of the American Revolution* (New York: David McKay Company, Inc., 1966), p. 888.
27. *Journals of Congress,* 15 September 1777, VIII: 745; "Bulletin," *Pennsylvania Historical Society,* 1845, VII: 44; and General Orders, Headquarters, 21 September 1777, Fitzpatrick, *Writings of Washington,* V: 244.

Chapter 2. Commander of the Horse

1. Charles Francis Adams, *Studies Military and Diplomatic 1775-1865* (New York: The Macmillan Company, 1911), p. 68.
2. Charles Lee to General Washington, Charleston, 1 July 1776, *The Lee Papers,* II: 102 (New York: Collections of the New-York Historical Society for the Year, 1872); and Miecislaus Haiman, *Kosciuszko in the American Revolution* (New York: Polish Institute of Arts and Sciences in America, 1943), p. 9n10.
3. *The Bland Papers,* Charles Campbell, ed., 2 Vols. (Petersburg, Virginia: Edmund & Julian Ruffin, 1840), I: xxx; Octavius Pickering, *The Life of Timothy Pickering* (Boston: Little, Brown, and Company, 1867), I: 118; and Boatner, *Encyclopedia of the American Revolution*, pp. 751-52.
4. Ward, *War of the Revolution,* I: 355-56; Bentalou, *Pulaski Vindicated,* p. 28; and William W. Gordon, "Count Casimir Pulaski,"*The Georgia Historical Quarterly,* Vol. XIII, No. 3 (September 1929), p. 184; and Hughes, *George Washington,* p. 181.
5. Bentalou, *Pulaski Vindicated,* p. 29; Ward, *War of the Revolution,* I: 356-60; and "Letters of Major Baurmeister during the Philadelphia Campaign, 1777-1778," *The Pennsylvania Magazine of History and Biography,* Vol. LIX (1935), pp. 410, 413.

    A private historical group in Philadelphia, Independence Hall Association, presents some details of the "rained out" battle on the internet. Their essay "The Battle of the Clouds" includes the part played by General Pulaski, but in a negative way. Historians of the Association assert, "Around 9 A.M. Washington learned of Howe's advance," but they do not provide any information that explains how Washington learned of General Howe's advance. They omit Pulaski's scouting the British on his own initiative and galloping to headquarters to alert the Commander-in-Chief. The essay of the Association continues:

    > The Battle of the Clouds commenced at about 1 P.M. when Washington ordered **Count Casimir Pulaski**, the recently appointed "Commander of the Horse," (Cavalry), to scout the British position and delay their advance. Cornwallis espied Pulaski and the 300 militia he was leading and sent his 1st Light Infantry charging at the Americans. The Americans "shamefully fled at the first fire" and delayed the enemy not at all.

    No, Washington did not order Pulaski to scout the British position.

Casimir Pulaski

Pulaski had scouted the British earlier and brought that intelligence to Washington. The Association makes a misleading statement that Pulaski led the 300 militia. On the contrary, Washington assigned the command of the militia to Brigadier General Charles Scott. When the militia came face to face with the British soldiers, they fled. This author quotes the same respected historian, Christopher Ward, as does the Association, but Ward writes: "The foot soldiers shamefully fled at the first fire and delayed the enemy not al all." The Association "improved" on Ward. They changed "foot soldiers" to read "Americans" and thereby included Pulaski's American cavalry and made a coward of Pulaski, too. Cowardly behavior was totally uncharacteristic of Pulaski. As Jared Sparks writes: "It is proved by the whole course of his life that Pulaski's military fault, if he had one, was rushing with too much impetuosity upon the enemy." It seems that Independence Hall Association seized an opportunity to denigrate Pulaski.

The derogation of Pulaski does not stop with the essay "The Battle of the Clouds." Independence Hall Association has another feature article on the web site entitled "Pulaski in the Clouds." The title insinuates that Pulaski was some kind of Don Quixote, although Douglas Heller, internet webmaster of the Association, defends the choice of title because of its relationship to "The Battle of the Clouds." Heller's defense is weak, at best. Undoubtedly the majority of readers do not make the connection and thereby gain a negative image of Pulaski. The title is unfair to Pulaski. He was an experienced and accomplished soldier when he came to America. The Association's "Pulaski in the Clouds" is a short biographical sketch, as shown below:

> Pulaski, a Polish nobleman, was received by Benjamin Franklin in Paris in 1776. He arrived in Boston, in July 1777, after being lent passage money by American Ambassador Silas Deane. Pulaski saw his first action as a volunteer aide-de-camp to Washington at Brandywine on September 11. Even before that battle, Pulaski had informed Washington of his cavalry experience in Poland. Thus, Washington had written Congress on August 27th asking that Pulaski be put in charge of four regiments of dragoons which had recently been created. Congress instead created the post "Commander of the Horse," made Pulaski a Brigadier General, and elected him to the new position.
>
> Naturally many American officers were incensed by Pulaski's new position. Even before the Pole had arrived, many battle-tested Continental officers were already disgusted with Congress for giving foreign adventurers ranks over theirs.
>
> To make matters worse, this Pulaski spoke no English and reported directly to Congress. Initially, the new "Commander of the Horse" was loath to take orders even from General Washington.

This author covers fully the subject of the resentment of American officers to foreigners and also explains Pulaski's handicap of not able to speak English. Nevertheless, the Association implies that Pulaski violated the chain of command by reporting directly to Congress. Of course, Pulaski reported to Congress on many occasions, as did other American generals. Pulaski addressed his letters to Congress primarily on matters that rested on the authority of Congress, like the appointment of officers and the allocation of money, especially during the organization of the Pulaski Legion. The final statement in the essay is false: "Initially, the new 'Commander of the Horse' was loath to take orders even from General Washington." This author challenges Independence Hall Association to prove the statement with **primary source** data. In view of the negative, misleading, and false statements about Pulaski, Independence Hall Association's promotion of the American Revolution appears erroneous and suspect.

6. Ward, *War of the Revolution,* I: 361, 363; Bentalou, *Pulaski Vindicated,* p. 29; and Hughes, *George Washington,* p. 192.

7. Benson J. Lossing, *Pictorial Field-Book of the Revolution,* 2 Vols. (New York: Harper, 1851-52), I: 112; William Johnson, *Sketches of the Life and Correspondence of Nathanael Greene,* 2 Vols. (Charleston, South Carolina: A.E. Miller, 1822); reprint ed., New York: Da Capo Press, 1973), I: 83; Griffin, *Catholics and the American Revolution,* III: 20, Bentalou, *Pulaski Vindicated,* pp. 20- 21; Washington to President of Congress, Camp near Pennibackers Mill, 5 and 7 October 1777, in Fitzpatrick, *Writings of Washington,* IX: 308, 319; and Hughes, *George Washington,* p. 192.

8. George Washington Parke Custis, *Recollections and Private Memories of Washington* (New York: Derby & Jackson, 1860), p. 195; and Griffin, *Catholics,* III: 22.

9. J. Bennett Nolan, *Lafayette in America Day by Day* (Baltimore: The John Hopkins University Press, 1934), pp. 253, 278, 299; Paul Bentalou, *A Reply to Judge Johnson's Remarks on an Article in the North American Review Relating to Count Pulaski* (Baltimore: J. D. Toy, 1826), pp. 10-11; Griffin, *Catholics,* III: 19, 22; and Sparks, *Library of American Biography,* XIV: 421. For a more detailed examination of the Johnson-Bentalou polemic, see Leszek Szymanski, *Casimir Pulaski: A Hero of the American Revolution* (New York: Hippocrene Books, 1979), pp. 52-61; and William Johnson, "Remarks Critical and Historical, on An Article in the Forty-Seventh Number of *The North American Review* Relating to Count Pulaski" (Charleston, South Carolina: Printed by C. C. Sebring, 1825), pp. 1-37.

10. Andre Lasseray, *Les Francais sous Treize Etoiles* (Paris: Protat Freres, 1935), I:81; Boatner, *Encyclopedia,* p. 1092; and "General Orders," Headquarters, October 3, 1777, Fitzpatrick, V: 305.

11. Burt Garfield Loescher, *Washington's Eyes, The Continental Light Dragoons* (Fort Collins, Colorado: The Old Army Press, 1977), pp. 107-08.

12. Page Smith, *A New Age Now Begins* (New York: McGraw-Hill Book Company, 1976), 2 Vols., II: 998; Longin Pastusiak, *Kosciuszko, Pulaski, i Inni* (Warszawa: Krajowa Agencja Wydawnicza[National Publishing Agency], 1977) p. 47; "Tadeusz Kosciuszko: Hero of Polish and American Independence," *The Polish Review,* July 5, 1943, p. 4; and Henry Williams,

An Address on Laying the Corner Stone of a Monument to Pulaski (Savannah, Georgia: W. Thorne Williams, 1855), p. 10. (At the Georgia Historical Society).
13. General Orders, Headquarters, Whitpain Township, 31 October 1777, Fitzpatrick, *Writings of Washington,* V: 472.
14. Louis Gottschalk, *The Letters of Lafayette to Washington* (New York: Hubbard, 1949), p. 22; and Haiman, *Kosciuszko in the American Revolution,* p. 197.
15. Griffin, *Catholics,* III: 24-25.
16. Pulaski's "Memorial Relative to the Cavalry" to Washington, 23 November 1777, *George Washington Papers,* 204 Reels, National Archives, Reel 45, p.39.
17. John Laurens, *The Correspondence of Colonel John Laurens in the Years 1777-8,* reprint ed., New York: New York Times & Arno Press, 1969), p. 141.
18. Washington's Circular to Dragoon Commanders, 25 October 1777, in Fitzpatrick, *Writings of Washington,* V: 432-33.
19. George Washington Greene, *The Life of General Nathanael Greene,* 3 Vols. (New York: D. Appleton and Company, 1893), III: 288; and William Paca to Governor William Johnson, Wye Island, Maryland, 11 June 1778, *Archives of Maryland,* p. 131.
20. Lossing, *Pictorial Field-Book,* I: 310n; Griffin, *Catholics,* III: 10; and A Brief on Brigadier-General Casimir Pulaski, compiled by Wm. R. Richardson, *The Pulaski Sesqui-Centennial, Jersey City, New Jersey, October 20th, 1929,* p. 29.
21. Worthington Chauncey Ford, "Defences of Philadelphia in 1777," (containing the opinion of Count Pulaski), *The Pennsylvania Magazine of History and Biography,* Vol. XX, No. 3, 1896, pp. 400-01; Richard Wheeler, *Voices of 1776,* (New York: Thomas Crowell Company, 1972), p. 254; and Gilbert S. Jones, "Pulaski Campaigned Valley Forge Area," *The Picket Post,* January 1948, p. 52.
22. Allen Bowman, *The Morale of the American Revolutionary Army* (Port Washington, New York: Kennikat Press, Inc., 1964), pp. 18, 24, 29, 55-56.

Chapter 3. Pulaski Attacks British at Haddonfield

1. Washington to President of Congress, Valley Forge, 23 December 1777, Fitzpatrick, X: 192; and Friederick Kapp, *Life of John Kalb, Major General in the Revolutionary Army* (New York: Henry Holt and Company, 1884), pp. 137-41.
2. Pulaski to Washington, 23 November 1777, *George Washington Papers,* National Archives, MF Series 4, Reel 45.
3. Pulaski to Washington, Valley Forge, 29 December 1777, *George Washington Papers,* MF Series 4, Reel 46.
4. Washington to Major James Jameson, 24 December 1777, and Washing-

Notes

ton to Pulaski, 31 December 1777, Fitzpatrick, X: 199, 234-35; and John F. Reed, *Valley Forge, Crucible of Victory* (Monmouth Beach, New Jersey: Philip Freneau Press, 1969), p. 18.

5. Pulaski to Washington, Trenton, 9 January 1778, *George Washington Papers,* MF Reel 46.
6. Washington to Count Pulaski, 14 January 1778, Fitzpatrick, X: 304-05; Griffin, *Catholics,* III: 33; and Emil Lengyel, *Americans from Hungary* (Philadelphia: J. B. Lippincott, 1948), pp. 26-28.
7. Washington to Pulaski, Valley Forge, 14 January 1778, Fitzpatrick, X: 304; *New Jersey Gazette,* 21 January 1778, p. 3; and Griffin, *Catholics,,* III: 34-35.
8. Pulaski to Washington, Trenton, 20 January 1778, *George Washington Papers,* MF Reel 46; and Washington to Pulaski, 26 January 1778, Fitzpatrick,*Writings of Washington,* X: 352-53.
9. Philip Katcher, *Armies of the American Wars, 1753-1815* (New York: Hastings House Publishers, 1975), p. 96.
10. Washington to Count Pulaski, Valley Forge, 26 January 1778, Fitzpatrick, *Writings of Washington,* X: 353; and Pulaski to Washington, Trenton, 10 February 1778, *George Washington Papers,* MF Reel 47; and Griffin, *Catholics,* III: 45.
11. Washington to Count Pulaski, Valley Forge, 26 January 1778, Fitzpatrick, *Writings of Washington,* X: 352-53.
12. Pulaski to Washington, Trenton, 8 February 1778, *George Washington Papers,* MF Reel 47; Griffin, *Catholics,* III: 44.
13. Pulaski's "Regulations of Cavalry" in Pulaski to Washington, *George Washington Papers,* MF Reel 47; and Griffin, *Catholics,* III: 40-41.
14. Pulaski to sister Anna Walewska, Trenton, 24 February 1778, in Leonard Chodzko, *Zywot Kazimierza na Pulaziu Pulaskiego, (Life of Casimir on the Pulaski Estate)* (Lwow, 1869), pp. 215-16; Pulaski to Rulhiere, *Correspondance,* pp. 34-37.
15. Pulaski to Washington, Burlington, New Jersey, 28 February 1778, *George Washington Papers,* MF Reel 47; and Griffin, *Catholics,* III: 49-50.
16. Jared Sparks, *The Library of American Biography,* XIV: 424-25.
17. Washington to Brigadier General Wayne, Valley Forge, 9 and 28 February and 2 March 1778, Fitzpatrick, *Writings of Washington,* X: 232-33, 524, XI: 13-14; Wheeler, *Voices of 1776,* p. 254; Wildes, *Anthony Wayne,* pp. 155; Paul David Nelson, *Anthony Wayne: Soldier of the Early Republic* (Bloomington: Indiana University Press, 1985), p. 74; and *New Jersey Gazette.* 11 March 1778.
18. Wildes, *Anthony Wayne,* p. 156.
19. Pulaski to Washington, Haddonfield, 3 March 1778, *George Washington Papers,* Reel 47; General Wayne to General Washington, Haddonfield, 4th March 1778, in Charles J. Stille, *Major-General Anthony Wayne and the Pennsylvania Line in the Continental Army* (Port Washington: New York: Kennikat Press, Inc., 1968), pp. 131-32; and Wildes, *Anthony Wayne,* p. 155.

20. Washington to Count Pulaski, 1 and 3 March 1778, and to Brigadier General Anthony Wayne, 2 March 1778, Fitzpatrick, *Writings of Washington*, XI: 6-7, 13, 20.
21. Washington to Governor William Livingston, Valley Forge, 14 March 1778, Fitzpatrick, XI: 80.
22. Kapp. *Life of John Kalb,* pp. 145, 166-67, 172, 184-85; Ward, *War of the Revolution,* II: 730; and Pulaski to Ruhliere, *Correspondance,* p. 35.
23. Washington to Colonel Stephen Moylan, Valley Forge, 20 March 1778, Fitzpatrick, XI: 114-15.
24. Washington to Colonel Stephen Moylan, Valley Forge, 11 April 1778, Fitzpatrick, XI: 244-45; Washington to Moylan, Valley Forge, 13 May 1778, and Washington to President of Congress, White Plains, 3 August 1778, Fitzpatrick, *Writings of Washington,* XI: 384-85, XII: 276; and Boatner, *Encyclopedia,* p. 751.
25. Washington to Colonel Stephen Moylan, 14 April 1778, and to Major Tallmadge, Valley Forge, 14 April 1778, Fitzpatrick, *Writings of Washington,* XI: 259, 384-85.
26. Washington to President of Congress, 29 September and 3 October 1778, Fitzpatrick, *Writings of Washington,* XII: 515, XIII: 14; Washington to Governor William Livingston, 22 October 1778, Fitzpatrick, XIII: 125; and Boatner, *Encyclopedia of the American Revolution,* pp. 1085-86.
27. Washington to Brigadier General Charles Scott, 8 October 1778, Fitzpatrick, *Writings of Washington,* XIII: 47.

Chapter 4. The Pulaski Legion

1. Casimir Pulaski to Congress, Charleston, 19 August 1779, Senate Executive Document No. 120, Item No. 31, 49th Congress, 2nd Session (Washington: Government Printing Office, 1887), pp. 27-29.
2. Washington to President of Congress, 14 March 1778, Fitzpatrick, *Writings of Washington,* XI: 80-82; and Laurens, *Army Correspondence,* pp. 141-43.
3. General Charles Lee's "Proposal for the Formation of a Body of Light Troops," *The Lee Papers* (New York: Collections of the New-York Historical Society, 1873), III: 286-87.
4. Report of the Board of War, York, 19 March 1778, *Papers of Congress,* M247, R157, I 147, V1, p. 557; and *Journals of Congress,* 28 March 1778, X: 291.
5. Gordon, "Count Casimir Pulaski," p. 186; Washington to Colonel Stephen Moylan, 9 April 1778, Sparks, *Writings of Washington,* XI: 230; and William Hand Browne, ed., *Archives of Maryland, Records of Maryland Troops in the Continental Service during the War of the American Revolution, 1775-83* (Baltimore: Maryland Historical Society, 1900), XVIII: 591.

The headquarters and recruiting office of General Pulaski in Baltimore were located at Baltimore and Grant Streets. According to *The Minute*

Man, Official Bulletin of the National Society of the Sons of the American Revolution, the site was known as the "Dr. John Stevenson House" during the American Revolution. In 1929, the Sons of the American Revolution, in coordination with the State of Maryland and the City of Baltimore, held several Pulaski sesquicentennial observances, of which one was the unveiling of a tablet at Baltimore and Grant Streets. At the unveiling ceremony, addresses were delivered by Governor Albert C. Ritchie, Mayor William F. Broening, and Monsignor Stanislaus Wachowiak, Rector of the Holy Rosary Church, the largest Polish church in Baltimore.

Another observance took place in Patterson Park at the selected site for a monument to General Pulaski. James Henry Preston presided at the ceremony. He was a Past President General of the National Society of the Sons of the American Revolution. Again Governor Ritchie and Mayor Broening addressed the audience. In addition, addresses were also made by Count Francis Pulaski, kinsman of the General, and by Professor Roman Dyboski of the Jagiellonian University of Krakow. ("The Pulaski Sesquicentennails," *The Minute Man* (1929), pp. 323-29, provided the author through the courtesy of Stanley A. Ciesielski, President of The Polish Heritage Association of Maryland)

6. *Journals of Congress,* 6 April 1778, X: 312-13; *The New Jersey Gazette,* 23 April 1778; and Washington to Count Pulaski, 13 June 1778, Fitzpatrick, *Writings of Washington,* XII: 55.

7. Washington to Count Pulaski, 1 May 1778, Fitzpatrick, *Writings of Washington,* XI:337; and Edmund C. Burnett, *Letters of Members of the Continental Congress* (Washington: Carnegie Institution of Washington, 1926; reprint ed., Gloucester, Massachusetts: Peter Smith, 1963), III: 279; and Edward J. Lowell, *The Hessians and Other German Auxiliaries of Great Britain in the Revolutionary War* (1884, reprint ed., Port Washington, New York: Kennikat Press, Inc., 1965), p. 290.

8. Washington to Count Pulaski, 1 May 1778, Fitzpatrick, XI: 337.

9. Washington to the Committee for the Affairs of the Army, 9 April 1778, *Papers of Congress,* M247, R168, I 152, V5, p. 435.

10. *Journals of Congress,* 18 April 1778, X: 364; Capitaine Gilbert Bodinier, *Dictionnaire des officiers de l'armee royale qui ont combattu aux Etats-Unis pendant la guerre d'Independance, 1776-1783* (Chateau De Vincennes, France: 1983), p. 430; A.S. Salley, ed., "Letters from the Marquis de Lafayette to Hon. Henry Laurens," *South Carolina Historical and Genealogical Magazine,* Vol. VIII, April 1907, p. 59; Louis Gottschalk, *Lafayette Joins the American Army,* Book II of *Lafayette in America, 1777-1783* (Arveyres, France: L'Esprit de Lafayette Society, 1975), p. 169; Franklin W. Kemp, *A Nest of Rebel Pirates* (Egg Harbor City, New Jersey: The Laureate Press, 1993), p. 46; Bentalou, *Pulaski Vindicated,* p. 5; "List of All Officers belonging to General Count Pulaski's Legion,"*Papers of Congress,* M247, R181, I 164, p. 13; Francis B. Heitman, *Historical Register of Officers of the Continental Army during the War of the Revolution* (Washington, 1914; reprint ed., Baltimore: Genealogical Publishing

Company, 1967), pp. 96, 100, 148, 191, 193, 195, 336, 344, 424, 428, 454, 475, 488, 517, 527, 560, and 611; Richard Henry Spencer, "Pulaski's Legion," *Maryland Historical Magazine,* Vol. XIII (1918), pp. 220-25; Donald W. Holst and Marko Zlatich, "Dress and Equipment of Pulaski's Independent Legion," *Military Collector & Historian,* Winter 1964, Washington, D. C., pp. 97-103; and Gordon, "Count Casimir Pulaski," p. 182.

11. For each cavalryman and light infantry soldier, one stock, one cap, a pair of breeches, one comb, two pair of stockings, two pair gaiters, three pair shoes, one pair buckles, a spear, and cartouch box (cartridge box).

For each trooper, a pair of boots, a saddle, halters, curry-comb and brush portmantle, picket cord, and pack saddle. The leather for the portmantle and pack saddle to be furnished out of public stores by order of the Board of War, *Journals of Congress,* X: 300, 312, XI: 489, 538.

12. Pulaski to President of Congress, 17 September 1778, *Papers of Congress,* M247, R126, I 164, p, 13; Davis, *George Washington,* p. 297; and *New Jersey Gazette,* 18 November 1778.

13. Pulaski to Congress, Philadelphia, 17 September 1778, *Papers of Congress,* M247, R181, I 164, p. 13; *Journals of Congress,* 20 August 1778, XI: 824; and Davis, *George Washington,* p. 297.

14. William Hand Browne, ed. *Archives of Maryland, Journal and Correspondence of the Council of Maryland,* XXI: 48, 90, 112, 127, 152, 185; and *Military Collector & Historian* (Winter 1964), p. 98.

15. Harold L. Peterson, *The Book of The Continental Soldier* (Harrisburg, Pennsylvania: The Stackpole Books, 1968), pp. 45, 104, 195, 237; and Lt. Charles M. Lefferts, *Uniforms of the American, British, French, and German Armies in the War of the American Revolution, 1775-1783* (Old Greenwich, Connecticut: WE Inc., 1926), p. 87.

16. "Moravian Records," in William W. Gordon, "Count Casimir Pulaski," *The Georgia Historical Quarterly,* Vol. XIII, No. 3 (September 1929), p. 190.

17. Joseph Mortimer Levering, *A History of Bethlehem, Pennsylvania, 1741-1892* (Bethlehem: Times Publishing Company, 1903), pp. 485-88; John Hill Martin, *Historical Sketch of Bethlehem in Pennsylvania and the Moravian Church* (Philadelphia, 1872); reprint ed., New York: AMS Press, 1971), p. 31; Gordon, "Count Casimir Pulaski," p. 191; and Henry Wadsworth Longfellow, *The Poetical Works of Henry Wadsworth Longfellow* (Boston: Houghton, Mifflin Company, 1893), p. 9.

18. Lossing, *Pictorial Field-Book,* I: 392; and author's notes.

The photo of the Pulaski Banner shown in this book is a replica of the original banner that over a period of nearly two hundred years became tattered and faded. In 1974, the General Joseph Haller Post of the American Legion of Baltimore donated an air proof glass case to the Maryland Historical Society for the purpose of saving the banner. In 1976, the Polish Heritage Association of Maryland commissioned Sister Irene Olkowska of the Sister Servants of Mary Immaculate to make two copies of the Pulaski Banner. An expert seamstress, Sister Olkowska crafted two replicas of impeccable similarity.

The Polish Heritage Association presented one of the replicas to the Maryland Historical Society and the second to the Sons of the American Revolution, Maryland Chapter, which added the banner to its Color Guard and displays it at all patriotic functions, in Stanley Ciesielski, "Maryland Historical Society is Home to Authentic Pulaski Banner," *Polish American Journal* (Buffalo), January 2000, p. 8.
19. Pulaski to Henry Laurens, 5 July 1778, in Joseph Johnson, *Traditions and Reminiscences of the American Revolution* (Charleston, South Carolina: Walker & James, 1851), p. 243-44; and Ward, *War of the Revolution*, II: 808.
20. *The Maryland Journal and Baltimore Advertiser,* 4 August 1778
21. Richard H. Lee (grandson), *Memoir of the Life of Richard Henry Lee and His Correspondence,* 2 Vols. (Philadelphia: H. C. Carey and L. Lea, 1825), I: 296.
22. Gerard to the French Foreign Minister, Comte de Vergennes, Philadelphia, 12 and 25 September 1778, in John J. Meng, ed., *Despatches and Instructions of Conrad Alexandre Gerard, 1778-1780* (Baltimore: Johns Hopkins University Press, 1938), pp. 214-15, 234.

Chapter 5. Betrayal at Little Egg Harbor

1. Pulaski to Congress, 17 September 1778, *Papers of Congress,* M247, R181, I 164, p. 13; and Wladyslaw Konopczynski, *Casimir Pulaski,* Translated from the Polish by Irena Makarewicz (Chicago: Polish Roman Catholic Union of America, 1947), p. 56.
2. Joseph Reed, Committee of Arrangement, to George Washington, Philadelphia, 30 September 1778, in Burnett, *Letters of Members of Congress,* III: 432; Washington to Committee of Arrangement from Congress, Fishkill, 6 October 1778, Fitzpatrick, XIII: 41-43; and William B. Reed, *Life and Correspondence of Joseph Reed* (Philadelphia: Lindsay and Blakiston, 1847), I: 133-34, 368. In his letter to the Committee of Arrangement, Washington revealed some private thinking on encouraging the organization of Pulaski's Independent Legion. He wrote: "The principal motive for authorizing the Count to raise his corps, was to induce him voluntarily to relinquish command of the cavalry, with which the officers under him were in general dissatisfied; and it was thought better to submit to the defect in its composition, than either to leave the cavalry in a state, which occasioned a total relaxation of discipline, and destroyed its usefulness, or to force the Count out of it, whose zeal and bravery entitled him to regard, without compensating in some way that might reconcile him to the sacrifice, he was required to make."
3. Chief Justice Thomas McKean to Congress, 1 and 3 October 1778, *Journals of Congress,,* XII: 974, 979; and Samuel Adams to James Warren, Philadelphia, 20 October 1778, Burnett, *Letters of Members of Congress,* III: 458.

4. Washington to Major Henry Lee, Fishkill, November 29, 1778, Fitzpatrick, XIII: 357.
5. Washington to the Board of War, West Point, 19 September 1778, Fitzpatrick, *Writings of Washington,* XII: 470; Washington to Council of War, Fredericksburg, 29 September 1778, Fitzpatrick, XII: 523; and Washington to Gates, Fredericksburg, 30 September 1778, Fitzpatrick, XII: 528.
6. *Journals of Congress,* 30 September and 5 October 1778, XII: 969, 981, 983-84.
7. Kemp, *A Nest of Rebel Pirates,* p. 9; and Richard K. Showman, ed., *The Papers of General Nathanael Greene* (Chapel Hill: The University of North Carolina Press, 1983), III: 356n.
8. William B. Willcox, ed., *The American Rebellion: Sir Henry Clinton's Narrative of His Campaigns, 1775-1782* (New Haven, Connecticut: Yale University Press, 1954), p. 105.
9. Kemp, *A Nest of Rebel Pirates,* pp. 10-16.
10. Charles Stedman, *The History of the Origin, Progress, and Termination of the American War,* 2 Vols. (London: J. Murray, J. Debrett, and J. Kerby, 1794), II: 41-44; and Kemp, *A Nest of Rebel Pirates,* p. 36.
11. William S. Stryker, *The Affair at Egg Harbor, New Jersey, October 15, 1778* (Trenton: Naar, Day & Naar, 1894), pp. 10-14.
12. Bentalou, *A Reply to Judge Johnson's Remarks on an Article in the North American Review relating to Count Pulaski* (Baltimore: J. D. Toy, 1826), pp. 36-37.
13. *Journals of Congress,* War Office, 2 September 1778, XII: 867-68; and Rodney Atwood, *The Hessians: Mercenaries from Hessen-Kassel in the American Revolution* (Cambridge, England: Cambridge University Press, 1980), p. 203.
14. Stedman, *History of the American War,* II: 44.
15. Bentalou, "Reply to Judge Johnson's Remarks," p. 37; Stedman, *History of the American War,* II: 44-45; and Dupuy and Dupuy, *The Compact History,* pp. 292-93.
16. Stryker, *Affair at Egg Harbor,* pp. 23, 31; and Stedman, *History of the American War,* p. 45.
17. Pulaski to the President of Congress, Little Egg Harbor, 16 October 1778, *Papers of Congress,* M247, R181, I 164, p. 17; and Stryker, *Affair at Egg Harbor,* p. 32.
18. Ward, *War of the Revolution,* I: 236-37, II: 500-01; Fitzpatrick, *Writings of Washington,* VI: 4-7; and Lowell, *The Hessians,* p. 291.
19. *Journals of Congress,* 13 February 1779, XIII: 182-83: and Heitman, *Historical Record of Officers,* p. 517.
20. Dunlap's *Pennsylvania Packet,* Philadelphia, 20 October 1778; and *Journals of Congress,* 30 October 1778, XII: 1080-82.
21. Pulaski to Congress, Trenton, 27 October 1778, *Papers of Congress,* M247. R181, I 164, p. 55.
22. Boatner, *Encyclopedia of the American Revolution,* p. 638; Bentalou, *A Reply to Judge Johnson's Remarks,* p. 36; Lewis, "Casimir Pulaski,"

Pennsylvania Magazine, p. 17; and Kajencki, *Thaddeus Kosciuszko,* pp. 158, 160.

Chapter 6. Mis-Assignment to Minisink

1. Gerard de St. Elme to President of Congress, Stafford, 19 October 1778, *Papers of Congress,* M247, R181, I 164, p. 34.
2. Pulaski to President of Congress, Little Egg Harbor, 21 October 1778, *Papers of Congress,* M247, R181, I 164, p. 25; and *Journals of Congress,* October 23, 1778, XII: 1056.
3. Pulaski to Congress, Trenton, 24 October 1778, M247, R181, I 164, p. 46; *Journals of Congress,* 1 March 1779, XIII: 263; and Pulaski to Congress, Philadelphia, 3 November 1778, M247, R181, I 164, p. 58.
4. *Journals of Congress,* 1 December 1778, XII: 1180, and 23 January 1779, XIII: 107; Willcox, *Benjamin Franklin,* XXIII: 39-40; *Journals of Congress,* 10 December 1778, XII: 1210, and 23 February 1779, XIII: 238-39; and Charles Bedaulx to Congress, 13 November 1778, *Papers of Congress,* M247, R91, I 78, pp. 213, 217.
5. Pulaski to Congress, Trenton, 26 October 1778, *Papers of Congress,* M247, R181, I 164, p. 52; and *Journals of Congress,* 27 October 1778, XII: 1065.
6. *Journals of Congress,* 26 October 1778, XII: 1061-62; and Pulaski to Washington, Sussex County Courthouse, 6 November 1778, *George Washington Papers,* MF 54; and Washington to Count Pulaski, Poughkeepsie, 10 November 1778, Fitzpatrick, *Writings of Washington,* XIII: 220-21.
7. Ward, *War of the Revolution,* II: 630; Smith, *A New Age Now Begins,* II: 1155-56; Pulaski to Washington, 15 November 1778, *George Washington Papers,* MF Reel 54; Washington to Pulaski, Fredericksburg, 24 November 1778, Fitzpatrick, XIII: 322-23; Washington to President of Congress, and Washington to Lord Stirling, Fredericksburg, both letters dated 16 November 1778, Fitzpatrick, XIII: 264, 266; and Pulaski to Congress, 3 December 1778, *Papers of Congress,* M247, R181, I 164, p. 76.
8. Pulaski to President of Congress, Minisink, 25 November 1778, *Papers of Congress,* M247, R181, I 164, p. 68.
9. Pulaski to Washington, Rosencrantz, 15 November 1778, *George Washington Papers,* MF Reel 54; Fitzpatrick, XIII; 221n33; and *Journals of Congress,* 10 December 1778, XII: 1210.
10. General Edward Hand to Washington, Minisink, 15 January 1779, *George Washington Papers,* MF Reel 55; and Washington to Hand, Middle Brook, 7 February 1779, Fitzpatrick, XIV: 75.
11. Washington to Pulaski, Fredericksburg, 24 November 1778, Fitzpatrick, XIII: 322-23.
12. Pulaski to President of Congress, Minisink, 3 December 1778, M247, R181, I 164, p. 76.
13. James McHenry to General Greene, Headquarters, 15 December 1778, Fitzpatrick XIII: 397-98; Colonel Tench Tilghman to General Greene,

Middlebrook, N.J., 15 December 1778, Showman, *Papers of General Nathanael Greene*, III: 113-14; Washington to Officer Commanding Pulaski's Corps, Middle Brook,16 December 1778, and Washington to Brigadier General Edward Hand, Philadelphia, 1 January 1779, Fitzpatrick, XIII: 402, 475.
14. Greene to Colonel Clement Biddle, Philadelphia, 20 January 1779, *Papers of General Greene,* III: 172.
15. Gerard to Vergennes, Philadelphia, 20 September 1778. in Meng, *Despatches and Instructions,* p. 379; and Pulaski to President of Congress, Minisink, 4 December 1778, M247, R181, I 164, p. 80.
16. Washington to President Caesar Rodney, Philadelphia, and Washington to Count Pulaski, both letters dated 19 January 1779, Fitzpatrick, XIV: 24, 26; and George F. Scheer and Hugh F. Rankin, *Rebels and Redcoats* (Cleveland: The World Publishing Company, 1957), p. 390.
17. *Journals of Congress,* 2 February 1779, XIII: 132.

Chapter 7. The Long March to Savannah

1. Pulaski to Congress, Philadelphia, February 4, 1779, *Papers of Congress,* M247, R181, I 164, p. 84; Heitman, *Register of Officers,* pp. 95, 330, 560; *Journals of Congress,* February 12, 1779, XIII: 179n4; Washington to Count Pulaski, Middlebrook, February 8, 1779, Fitzpatrick, XIV: 79; and the Board of War to General Benjamin Lincoln, 6 February 1779, in Burnette, *Letters of Members of the Continental Congress,* IV: 58-59.
2. Alexander O'Neil to Congress, January 1779, *Papers of Congress,* M247, R51, I 41, V7, p. 216; Pulaski to Congress, Philadelphia, 4 February 1779, *Papers of Congress,* M247, R181, I 164, p. 84; and *Journals of Congress,* 1 March 1779, and 21 June 1779, XIII: 263, XIV: 754-55.
3. *Journals of Congress,* 20 February 1779, XII: 215; and Heitman, *Register of Officers,* p. 148.
4. Baron D'Ugglaa to Board of War, Philadelphia, 24 February 1779, *Papers of Congress,* M247, R158, I 147, V3, p. 95; *Journals of Congress,* 2 March 1779, XIII: 269; and John Jay to Mons. George Gustave D'Ugglaa, Philadelphia, 5 March 1779, *Papers of Congress,* M247, R24, I 14, p. 63.
5. *Journals of Congress,* 12 August 1778, XI: 778-79; Baron de Knoblauch to Congress, Philadelphia, 4 May, 7 June, and 9 July 1779, *Papers of Congress,* M247, R97, I 78, V13, pp. 507, 511, 517; and Washington to Baron de Knobelauch [sic], Middle Brook, 7 March 1779, Fitzpatrick, XIV: 209-10.
6. *Journals of Congress,* 4 February 1779, XIII: 143; Washington to Count Pulaski, Middlebrook, 8 February 1779, Fitzpatrick, XIV: 78-79; Pulaski to General Hand, Philadelphia, 7 February 1779, Mss. at Polish Museum of America, Chicago; and Robert L. Hooper, Jr., Deputy Quartermaster General, to General Nathanael Greene, Quartermaster General, Easton, Pennsylvania, 18 February 1779, Showman, *Papers of General Greene,* III: 275.

Notes

7. Samuel Hazard, ed. *Pennsylvania Archives* (Philadelphia: Joseph Severns & Co., 1853), Vol. VII, Series 1, pp. 230-34; and Henry Laurens to the President of South Carolina (Rawlins Lowndes), 12 February 1779, in Burnett, *Letters of Members of Congress*, IV: 67.

    Joseph Reed complained frequently about various issues. A controversial political figure, he had some powerful enemies. Historian George Bancroft calls Reed a "trimmer," one who changes his political loyalty to suit his personal interests.

    Colonel Charles Pettit, Assistant Quartermaster General, advised General Nathanael Greene to talk to Joseph Reed about the Pennsylvanian's activities relating to the army and to inform him also of the responsibilities of the Quartermaster General. Pettit believed that both would gain a better understanding of each other. Pettit described Reed as a "Man of Wisdom" and one possessing "a good deal of Knowledge of Mankind and the Affairs of Government." However, he added that "he is not entirely exempted from the Passions and Prejudices which designate the Frailty of Man." (*Papers of General Greene,* III: 358.)

8. *Journals of Congress,* 13 February 1779, XIII: 181; and Pulaski to Congress, Philadelphia, 12 and 16 February 1779, *Papers of Congress*, M247, R181, I 164, pp. 88, 90.

9. Showman, *Papers of General Greene,* III: 234, 237, 249, 259; and Griffin, *Catholics,* III: 85-86.

10. Pettit to Greene, Philadelphia, 20 March 1779, *Papers of General Greene,* III: 357.

11. Greene to Washington, Camp [Middlebrook, New Jersey], 19 April 1779, *Papers of General Greene,* III: 417-19; and R. D. Jamro, *Pulaski, A Portrait of Freedom* (Savannah, Georgia: The Printcraft Press, Inc., 1970), p. 144.

12. Pulaski to Congress, York Town, 28 March, 1779, *Papers of Congress,* M247, R181, I 164, p. 98.

13. Count Pulaski to Council, Annapolis, 10 April 1779, and Council to the Chevalier De Segond de la Place, 20 April 1779, in William Hand Browne, *Archives of Maryland, Journals and Correspondence of the Council of Maryland, 1778-1789,* (Baltimore: Maryland Historical Society, 1901), XXI: 341, 354-55.

14. Baron D'Ugglaa to Congress, 2 June 1780, *Papers of Congress,* M247, R104, I 78, V23, p.1.

15. Hugh F. Rankin, *The North Carolina Continentals,* (Chapel Hill: The University of North Carolina Press, 1971), p. 208.

16. Thomas Bee to Henry Drayton, Charles Town, 5 April 1779, *Papers of Congress,* M247, R86, I 72, p. 485.

17. Ward, *War of the Revolution,* II: 684-85.

Chapter 8. Pulaski Saves Charleston

1. Richard Barry, *Mr. Rutledge of South Carolina* (New York: Duell, Sloan and Pierce, 1942), pp. 252, 270, 279; and Henry Steele Commager and

Richard B. Morris, *The Spirit of 'Seventy-Six* (Indianapolis: Bobbs-Merrill Company, Inc., 1958), p. 1085.
2. Barry, *Mr. Rutledge,* pp. 253-54.
3. Barry, *Mr. Rutledge,* pp. 260-61; Bentalou, *Pulaski Vindicated,* p. 31; Lengyel, *Americans from Hungary,* p. 28; Joseph Johnson, *Traditions and Reminiscences,* p. 244; Haiman, *Kosciuszko in the American Revolution,* pp. 197-98; and Maciej Rogowski, *Reszty Pamietnikow Macieja Rogowskiego* [The Remainder of Matthew Rogowski's Memoirs] (Paryz: W Ksiegarni Katolickiej Polskiej [Paris: Polish Catholic Bookstore], 1847), pp. 110-111. Rogowski writes that Pulaski, seeing that the infantry had prematurely left its screened ambush position, burst out angrily: *"A niech kaczki zdepca francuza!"*
4. Moultrie, *Memoirs,* pp. 441-42; Griffin, *Catholics,* III: 98; and Bentalou, *Reply to Johnson's Remarks,* p. 31.
5. Moultrie, *Memoirs,* pp. 423-24.
6. William Gordon, *The History of the Rise, Progress, and Establishment of the Independence of the United States of America,* 4 Vols., (1788); reprint ed., Freeport, New York: Books for Libraries Press, 1969), III: 256-57; and Meng, *Despatches of Gerard,* pp. 772-75.
7. Major F. Skelly, "Journal," *The Magazine of American History,* (July-December 1891), XXVI: 153.
8. Sparks, *Library of American Biography,* XIV: 433; and John Frederick Lewis, "Casimir Pulaski," *Pennsylvania Magazine of History, 1931,* LV: 19-21.
9. Barry, *Mr. Rutledge,* p. 262; and Moultrie, *Memoirs,* pp. 439, 441.
10. Moultrie, *Memoirs,* p. 435.
11. Smith, *A New Age Now Begins,* II: 1326; and Lewis, "Casimir Pulaski," *Pennsylvania Magazine of History,* pp. 19-21.
12. Moultrie, *Memoirs,* I: 435-36.
13. Willcox, *The American Rebellion: Sir Henry Clinton's Narrative,* p. 134.
14. Page, *A New Age Now Begins,* II: 1321-22; Washington to President of Congress, White Plains, August 3, 1778, Fitzpatrick, XII: 276; and Kemp, *A Nest of Rebel Pirates,* p. 39.
15. Colonel Frederic Gilbert Bauer, "Notes on the Use of the Cavalry in the American Revolution," *The Cavalry Journal,* Vol. 47, No. 2 (March-April, 1938), p. 141; and Roger Bruns, *George Washington* (New York: Chelsea House Publishers, 1987), p. 69.

Chapter 9. The Siege of Savannah

1. Moultrie, *Memoirs,* I: 442-43, 466-67.
2. Pulaski to John Jay, President of Congress, Jacksonborough Road, 4 June 1779, *Papers of Congress,* M247, R181, I 164, p. 106; and Governor Rutledge to Delegates of South Carolina, Charles Town, 22 July 1779, *Papers of Congress,* M247, R86, I 72, p. 520.
3. Moultrie, *Memoirs,* I: 479, 481, 489.
4. Moultrie, *Memoirs,* I: 490-93; and Ward, *War of the Revolution,* II: 686.

5. Moultrie, *Memoirs,* I: 495-96; and Lewis, "Casimir Pulaski," *Pennsylvania Magazine of History,* LV: 20.
6. Moultrie, *Memoirs,* II: 23, 27.
7. Count Pulaski to Congress, Charleston, 19 August 1779, Senate Executive Document No. 120, 49th Congress, 2nd Session, pp. 27-29; and *Papers of Congress,* M247, R181, I 164, p. 108.

COMMENTARY ON THE CAPTAIN BEDKIN FIASCO

When General Pulaski learned that Captain Henry Bedkin's company of dragoons, left behind temporarily to recruit Legionnaires, was pulled from the Legion, he was devastated by the incomprehensible action. What was so compelling in the North that required the immediate services of Captain Bedkin?

This author made an intensive search of primary and secondary sources for the answer. He found the first clue in the *George Washington Papers.* From his headquarters at Middle Brook, New Jersey, on 3 June 1779, General Washington ordered Captain Bedkin to march his company to Morristown, New Jersey:

> You will be pleased immediately upon receipt of this letter to march the horse with your command to the army by the way of Morristown— you will make no delay and come as light and unencumbered of baggage as possible.[1]

At the time, Bedkin was in Virginia where Deputy Quartermaster General William Finnie of Williamsburg wrote President John Jay on 23 April 1779, telling Jay that Pulaski upon departing Williamsburg had asked him to purchase a number of horses. Finnie said that Pulaski left a captain to recruit cavalrymen, while he bought the horses. However, Finnie informed Jay he had no money. He asked Jay for advice and also requested that money be sent him as soon as possible.[2]

Pulaski provided Bedkin with $5000 for recruiting and for the purchase of horses and other required items. Finnie's letter, therefore, brings up several questions. Did Bedkin tell Finnie that he had expended the $5000 and suggested that Finnie ask Congress for more funds? If Bedkin had spend all the money, his recruiting effort was over, and he should have marched off to join Pulaski. Perhaps Bedkin had recruited a number of men, but having exhausted the money, he wished to mount them before departing for the South. Or, perhaps he lied to Finnie and kept the money for hmself.

When John Jay received Finnie's letter, the President forwarded it to the Board of War. This author closely reviewed the *Journals of the Continental Congress* for the period April-May 1779, searching for a response of the Board to Congress. He found none. Perhaps Pulaski's apparent request through Finnie for additional money struck the Board members the wrong way. As Washington always maintained, cavalry units were expensive and taxed the limited funds of Congress for the prosecution of the war. The best answer to Finnie's letter, it is believed, was for Congress to ignore Finnie's request. If money was of great concern, let Pulaski get along with the cavalry he had on hand. However, it appears that the Board of War may have indulged in vindictive action. It also appears that neither Congress nor Washington informed Pulaski of Bedkin's removal from the Legion. Pulaski probably got the bad news from Bedkin himself. It was Bedkin's responsibility to inform his commander of Washington's overriding order.

Undoubtedly Bedkin was not neutral in Pulaski's loss. For reasons of his own, Bedkin may have wanted to remain in the North and so informed Washington's staff. Some misunderstanding may also have developed between Pulaski and Bedkin. In his letter to Congress, 19 August 1779, Pulaski had some harsh words for Bedkin:

> Capt. Bedkin who was Left, with a detachment of Light horse, to collect men remaining behind sick or on furlough with horses belonging to the Legion, and entrusted with the sum of 5,000 dollars for the recruiting Service, has found protection with the Same board [Board of War], who have rendered him independent altho he has failed in the Duty of an honest man.[3]

On the same day that Washington ordered Bedkin to Morristown, 3 June 1779, he also directed Major Henry Lee, Jr. likewise to Morristown. "You will make no delay at this place" Washington said, "but continue your march to Pompton [location of General Lord Stirling's division] by way of Morris Town, with as much dispatch as you can without injuring your horse." In neither letter did Washington disclose the reason for his order. Evidently he was planning some sensitive operation against the British.[4]

Because Washington could not spare any military forces, except Pulaski's Legion (by order of Congress), to counter the British strategy of conquering Georgia and South Carolina and then rolling north, it seems that Congress should have refrained from reducing the capability of that minimal assistance. Notwithstanding, Washington's order to Bedkin did exactly that. Perhaps the military situation in the summer of 1779 can provide clues to Washington's urgent orders to Lee and Bedkin. At New York, General Sir Henry Clinton sent a force of 6000 soldiers up the Hudson River to capture Stony Point and Verplanck's Point. Both fortified sites faced each other across the river. Having seized the two strongholds on 1 June 1779, the British threatened West Point, some fifteen miles further up river. However, Clinton felt content to simply hold the two positions. Washington, therefore, decided to recapture Stony Point. He assigned the mission to General Anthony Wayne who accomplished the task successfully in a dawn attack on 16 July 1779. In this operation, Major Lee's dragoons performed excellent reconnaissance for Wayne, but reports do not mention Bedkin's cavalry. Wayne's capture of Stony Point served only as a psychological boost for the Americans because Washington abandoned Stony Point as untenable.[5]

Bedkin is not mentioned again until 24 July 1779 when Washington writes General Lord Stirling: "I have ordered Captn. Bedkin with his Troop to join your division perswaded(sic) that your Lordship will not suffer them to be used improperly."[6] At this time Washington contemplated a quick strike at Paulus Hook, New Jersey, a British strong point on the Hudson River opposite New York. He assigned the command of the strike force to Major Lee and politely ordered Lord Stirling to furnish the attacking units. On 19 August 1779, Lee executed a daring attack on Paulus Hook, capturing some 150 British soldiers. Stirling supported Lee's attack additionally with a 300-man force holding a key bridge across the Hackensack River over which Lee made good his escape. Several company-size units are singled out in this psychological strike. Bedkin is not, although his company formed an element of Stirling's division since 24 July 1779. It appears that after reaching Morristown, Bedkin remained idle.[7]

On 23 August 1779, Washington finally gave Bedkin a documented task. He informed Lord Stirling to levy Bedkin for six troopers for the purpose of escorting a shipment of money to Philadelphia![8]

Pulaski needed Bedkin's company for the fighting in the South. The company had trained with the Legion and formed an integral part. The sum of $5000, any recruits gained by Bedkin, and troopers rounded up on leave with their expensive horses, belonged to the Legion. However, Bedkin kept it all for himself. The actions of Congress, Washington, and Bedkin, therefore, weakened Pulaski's Legion for its important mission in the South. Fortunately, Pulaski made up the loss of Bedkin with Georgia and South Carolina cavalry over which he assumed command, including Colonel Daniel Horry's South Carolina Light Dragoons. Nevertheless, when Washington took away Bedkin's dragoons, the Commander-in-Chief frittered away the capability of a trained cavalry unit. As for Congress, it damaged Pulaski's Legion unnecessarily and crippled Pulaski's fighting capability. Pulaski felt injured and expressed keen disappointment in the capricious and destructive behavior of the Continental Congress.

1. *George Washington Papers,* MF, Reel 59.
2. William Finnie, Williamsburg, 23 April 1779, to President John Jay, *Papers of Continental Congress,* M247, R95, I 98, V9, p. 253.
3. Pulaski to Congress, Charles Town, 19 August 1779, *Papers of Congress,* M247, R181, I 164, p. 108.
4. Fitzpatrick, *Writings of Washington,* XV: 220.
5. Ward, *War of the Revolution,* II: 596-601; and Nelson, *Anthony Wayne,* pp.100-01.
6. Fitzpatrick, *Writings of Washington,* XV: 473.
7. Ward, *War of the Revolution,* II: 604-10; Alan Valentine, *Lord Stirling* (New York: Oxford University Press, 1969), p. 243; and Major Henry Lee to Washington, Paramus, 22 August 1779 (Report of the Raid on Paulus Hook, 12 pages), *Papers of Congress,* M247, R187, I 169, V6, p. 97.
8. Fitzpatrick, *Writings of Washington,* XVI: 157.

8. David B. Mattern, *Benjamin Lincoln and the American Revolution* (Columbia: University of South Carolina Press, 1995), p. 76.
9. Mattern, *Benjamin Lincoln*, p. 80; and David Ramsay, *The History of the Revolution of South Carolina*, 2 Vols. (Trenton, New Jersey: Isaac Collins, 1785), II: 36.
10. Commager and Morris, eds., *The Spirit of Seventy-Six*, p. 1096; and Moultrie, *Memoirs*, II: 33.
11. Mattern, *Benjamin Lincoln*, p. 81; and Bentalou, *Reply to Johnson's Remarks*, pp. 32-33.
12. Charles C. Jones, Jr., ed., *The Siege of Savannah in 1779: As Described in Two Contemporaneous Journals of French Officers of the Fleet of Count D'Estaing* (Albany, New York: Joel Munsell, 1874; reprint ed., New York: The New York Times & Arno Press, 1968), pp. 13-15, 17; and Bentalou, *Reply to Johnson's Remarks,* p. 33.
13. Alexander A. Lawrence, *Storm over Savannah: The Story of Count D'Estaing and the Siege of the Town in 1779* (Athens: The University of Georgia Press, 1951), pp. 21-22; and Henry B. Carrington, *Battles of the American Revolution, 1775-1781* (New York: A. S. Barnes & Company, 1877 reprint ed., New York: The New York Times &Arno Press, 1968), p. 478; and Bentalou, *Reply to Johnson's Remarks*, p. 33.
14. Mattern, *Benjamin Lincoln*, pp. 84-85; and Sparks, "Count Pulaski," *Library of American Biography*, XIV: 439.
15. Lawrence, *Storm over Savannah*, pp. 86, 88; Mattern, *Benjamin Lincoln*, p. 85; and Carrington, *Battles of the American Revolution*, p. 480.
16. Lawrence, *Storm over Savannah*, pp. 43, 57-60, 65.

Chapter 10. The French-American Assault on Savannah

1. Jones, *Siege of Savannah*, p. 30; and Lawrence, *Storm over Savannah*, pp. 88-90.
2. Lawrence, *Storm over Savannah*, pp. 96-98; and Charles C. Jones, ed., *Extract from the Journal of a Naval Officer in the Fleet of Count D'Estaing, 1782*, p. 66.
3. Bentalou, *Pulaski Vindicated*, p. 32; Lawrence, *Storm over Savannah*, p. 109; Joseph Johnson, *Traditions and Reminiscences*, pp. 245-46; A. S. Salley, "Dr. James Lynah, A Surgeon of the Revolution," *South Carolina Historical Magazine*, Vol. XL (July 1939), pp. 87-90; Gordon, *Georgia Historical Quarterly*, XIII: 222; Jones, *Siege of Savannah*, pp. 34, 36; and Lee, *Memoirs*, p. 142.
4. Bentalou, *Pulaski Vindicated*, p. 33; Mabel L. Webber, ed., "Extracts from the Journal of Mrs. Ann Manigault," *South Carolina Historical and Genealogical Magazine*, Vol, XXI (July 1920), p. 119; *The South Carolina and American General Gazette*, Charlestown, 29 October 1779; Manning, *Casimir Pulaski*, pp. 303-04; Czeslaw Milosz, *The History of*

Notes

     Polish Literature (Berkely: University of California Press, 1983), pp. 208-32; and Adam Mickiewicz, "Ode to Youth," *Poems of Adam Mickiewicz,* Czeslaw Zgorzelski, ed. (Warsaw: Warsaw Reader, 1979), I: 15.

5. Joseph Johnson, *Traditions and Reminiscences,* p. 245n; Edward Pinkowski, "Pulaski's Tomb in Monterey Square," *Polish Heritage,* Vol. XLVII, No. 4 (Winter 1996), pp. 1, 4; Sam Bulfinch, Captain of the *Wasp,* to General Benjamin Lincoln, 15 October 1779, in *Benjamin Lincoln Papers,* Massachusetts Historical Society, Boston, Film 1673, Roll 4, Frame 743; and Edward Pinkowski, *General Pulaski's Body,* p. 6, (Cooper City, Florida: Pinkowski Institute, 1997).
6. Gordon, *Georgia Historical Quarterly,* XIII: 220.
7. Dupuy and Dupuy, *Compact History of Revolutionary War,* pp. 327-28; Commager and Morris, *Spirit of Seventy-Six*. p. 1096; Griffin, *Catholics,* III: 106-07; and Henry Williams, *An Address Delivered on Laying the Corner Stone of a Monument to Pulaski....,* 11 October 1855 (Savannah, Georgia: W. Thorne Williams, 1855), p. 31 (At Georgia Historical Society).
8. Joseph Johnson, *Traditions and Reminiscences,* p. 245; Lee. *Memoirs,* p. 141; and Carrington, *Battles of the American Revolution,* p. 481.
9. Jones, *Siege of Savannah,* pp. 35, 38.
10. Gaszynski, *Memoirs,* pp. 91-92, 95-97; and Jones, *Siege of Savannah,* p. 38.
11. Benson Bobrick, *Angel in the Whirlwind: The Triumph of the American Revolution* (New York: Simon & Schuster, 1997), p. 379; William Johnson, *Remarks, Critical and Historical,* pp. 34-35; Bentalou, *Reply to Johnson's Remarks,* pp. 34-35; *The South Carolina and American General Gazette,* Charlestown, 29 October 1779; and Robert Wernich and Editors, *Blitzkrieg* (Alexandria, Virginia: Time-Life Books, 1977), p. 21.

Chapter 11. Demise of the Pulaski Legion

1. Jones, *Siege of Savannah,* p. 37; Frank Moore, *Diary of the American Revolution* (New York: Charles Scribner, 1858), p. 222; Ward, *War of the Revolution,* II: 694; and "The Siege of Savannah, 1779, as Related by Colonel John Harris Cruger," *The Magazine of American History,* Vol. II, No. 8 (August 1878), p. 489.
2. Lawrence, *Storm over Savannah,* pp. 107, 113-22.
3. Scheer and Rankin, *Rebels and Redcoats,* p. 395; Willcox, *The American Rebellion,* p. 151; and Ward, *War of the Revolution,* II: 696, 703.
4. Bedaulx to President of Congress, Charlestown, 25 October 1779, *Papers of Congress,* M247, R177, I 158, p. 293.
5. Lincoln to Samuel Huntington, Charlestown, 22 October 1779, *Papers of Congress,* M247, R177, I 158, V6, p. 279; *Journals of Congress,* 29 November 1779, XV: 1324; Thomas McKean to William Augustus Atlee, delegate from Pennsylvania, 13 November 1779, in Burnett, *Letters of Members of Congress,* IV: 518. McKean writes, "Our disappointment in

247

Georgia has somewhat deranged us...Count Pulaski is killed and Count D'Estaing had two balls thro' him...; Gordon, *History of the Revolution*, III: 332; and Fitzpatrick, *Writings of Washington*, "General Orders," 17 November 1779, XVII: 121.

6. *The Savannah Georgian*, Savannah, 1 February 1825; Gordon, "Count Pulaski," *Georgia Historical Quarterly*, pp. 224-26; Williams, *An Address on Laying the Corner Stone*, p. 5; and biographical sketch of Launitz in *American National Biography*, John A. Garraty and Mark C. Carnes, eds. (New York: Oxford University Press, 1999), XIII: 254-55.

Robert Eberhardt Launitz has been called a Pole, Russian-born, and a Latvian. William R. Gordon in his essay "Count Casimir Pulaski" refers to him as "a Polish sculptor." The Georgia Historical Commission called him "Russian-born" on the historic marker at the Pulaski Monument in Savannah. The editors of *American National Biography* say he was born in Riga, Latvia on 4 November 1806. The three terms all fit. In the 17th and 18th centuries, Latvia was a part of the Kingdom of Poland. Hence, the natives of Latvia were citizens of Poland, including the ancestors of Launitz. At the end of the 18th century, Russia seized Latvia, the Baltic area, and large slices of Poland during the infamous Partitions. Hence, Launitz was born when Russia ruled Latvia. At the end of World War I in 1918, Latvia emerged independent, only to be swallowed up again by predatory Russia in 1939. Notwithstanding, with the collapse of the Soviet Union in 1991, Latvia emerged free once again. Sculptor Launitz displayed admiration for the Polish heroes of the American Revolution with his beautiful monument to Thaddeus Kosciuszko at West Point in 1828 and the one to Casimir Pulaski at Savannah in 1854.

The completed Pulaski Monument was formally turned over to the City of Savannah on 8 January 1855. On this memorable day in Monterey Square, Mayor Edward C. Anderson and the Savannah aldermen accepted the beautiful monument that has since adorned the square for the past 145 years. Mayor Anderson pledged that he and his associates would protect and preserve the monument. Following the ceremonies, the commissioners, city officials, and invited guests adjourned to the Pulaski House "where a sumptuous collation had been prepared."

The Monument Committee thoughtfully invited nearly 500 school children and their teachers to the ceremony. The *Savannah Daily News* reported the next day: "It was a beautiful sight to see the neatly dressed scholars, with their white satin badges, and silk banners of various designs, marching with their several teachers at their head around the square, into the places assigned them by the order of the ceremonies." The newspaper called the invitation to the school children "a most happy idea, and the scene was one which will be long and fondly remembered in maturer years by the little participants." The school children were rewarded by an ample meal of sweetmeats, cakes, fruit "and all those things most likely to tempt the appetite of the juveniles." The food was quickly consumed or "annihilated" as the newspaper said. (Williams, *An Address on the*

Notes

   Laying the Corner Stone, pp. 27-28).
7. Bedaulx to Congress, Charleston, 25 October 1779, and Lincoln to President of Congress, Charles Town, 31 October 1779, *Papers of Congress,* M247, R177, I 158, pp. 285, 289, 293.
8. "Records Kept by Colonel Isaac Hayne," *South Carolina Historical and Genealogical Magazine,* Vol. X (October 1909), p. 229; Edward Pinkowski, *General Pulaski's Body"* (Cooper City, Florida: Pinkowski Institute, 1997), p. 5; Ward, *War of the Revolution,* II: 701-02; Scheer and Rankin, *Rebels and Redcoats,* pp. 397-98; *Journals of Congress,* 14 November 1780, XVIII: 1051; and Bernhard A. Uhlenberg, *The Siege of Charleston* (Ann Arbor: University of Michigan Press, 1938), p. 61.
9. *Journals of Congress,* XXVI: 43-44, XVII: 643-64, XIX: 182-83, XXII: 363; and Lasseray, *Les Francais sous Les Treize Etoils,* I: 410-12.
10. *Journals of Congress,* XIX: 181; and Bentalou, *Pulaski Vindicated* and *A Reply to Judge Johnson's Remarks.*
11. *Journals of Congress,* 6 September 1780, XVII: 804-05.
12. Showman, ed., *Papers of General Greene,* III: 360n; Paschke to President of Congress, 22 January 1781, and Paschke to Congress, Philadelphia, 2 April 1781, *Papers of Congress,* M247, I 78, V18, pp. 345, 369; Testimonial of Edward Carrington, Charles Town, 7 August 1783, *Papers of Congress,* M247, R51, I 41, V8, p. 201; Paschke to Congress, Annapolis, 11 January 1784, *Papers of Congress,* M247, R55, I 42, V6, p. 282; Paschke to Congress, Philadelphia, 30 October 1784, *Papers of Congress,* M247, R51, I 41, V18, p. 194; *Journals of Congress,* 2 February 1781, XIX: 106-07, and 22 January 1784, XXVI: 42; and *South Carolina Gazette,* Charles Town, 16 June 1788.
13. Williams, *An Address on Laying the Corner Stone,* p. 9.

Chapter 12. Evaluating General Pulaski's Service

1. Gordon, *History of the United States,* III: 256-57.
2. Sparks, "Count Pulaski," *The Library of American Biography,* XIV: 444-46.
3. Pulaski to Congress, Philadelphia, 17 September 1778, and 19 August 1779, Charles Town, *Papers of Congress,* M247, R181, I 164, pp. 13, 108.
4. "William Washington Gordon," *Dictionary of American Biography,* Allen Johnson and Dumas Malone, eds. (New York: Charles Scribner's Sons, 1931), IV: 427-28; "William Washington Gordon, *"The National Cyclopedia of American Biography, Being the History of the United States* (Ann Arbor, Michigan: University Microfilms, 1967), XV: 217-18; and "Who's Who in This Issue," *Georgia Historical Quarterly* (September 1929), p. 342.
5. Gordon, "Count Casimir Pulaski," p. 226.
6. Washington to President of Congress, White Plains, 3 August 1778, Fitzpatrick, *Writings of Washington,* XII: 276; and *Journals of Congress,*

24 November 1778. XII: 1158.
7. Noel B. Poirier, "Young General Lafayette," *MHQ: The Quarterly Journal of Military History,* Vol. 12, No. 2 (Winter 2000), p. 39.
8. Adams, *Studies Military and Diplomatic,* pp. 59, 68, 72.
9. Adams, *Studies Military and Diplomatic,* p. 64.
10. Lee, *Memoirs,* p. 141.
11. Washington to Count Pulaski, 3 March 1778, to Governor Livingston, 14 March 1778, and to President of Congress, 14 March 1778, Valley Forge, Fitzpatrick, XI: 20, 80-82.
12. Gordon, "Count Casimir Pulaski," p. 226; and Captain Johann Ewald, *Diary of the American War: A Hessian Journal,* Joseph P. Tustin, trans. and ed. (New Haven: Yale University Press, 1979), p. 209.
13. Gordon, "Count Casimir Pulaski." p. 227; and Williams, *An Address on Laying a Corner Stone,* pp. 17-18.

Appendix A. Balancing the Books
Accounts of the Pulaski Legion

1. Pulaski to President of Congress, Philadelphia, 17 September 1778, *Papers of Congress,* M247, R181, I 164, p. 13; and W.T.R. Saffell, *Records of the Revolutionary War: Containing the Military and Financial Correspondence of Distinguished Officers* (New York: Pudney & Russell Publishers, 1858), pp. 35-36.
2. Saffell, *Records of the Revolutionary War,* p. 36.
3. Saffell, *Records of the Revolutionary War,* p. 32.
4. Pulaski to Auditors of the Army, Yorktown, March 27, 1779; and James Johnson, auditor, to Board of Treasury, May 15, 1779, in Saffell, *Records of the Revolutionary War,* pp. 33-34.
5. Baldesqui to Congress, Philadelphia, July 28, 1779, printed in Saffell, *Records of the Revolutionary War,* pp. 35-36.
6. Pulaski to Congress, Charlestown, August 19, 1779, *Papers of Congress,* M247, R181, I 164, p. 108; Biographical Sketch of Maurycy Beniowski, *Polski Slownik Biograficzny* [Polish Biographical Dictionary] (Krakow, 1935), I: 429-32; Ewa M. Thompson, "Letter from Mongolia, "*Chronicles of Culture,* February 1986(Rockford, Illinois: Rockford Institute), pp. 41-44 [Name of publication later changed to *Chronicles: A Magazine of American Culture*]; and *Polish American Journal,* October 2000, p. 5.
7. *Polish Biographical Dictionary,* I: 430
8. General Gates to John Jay, President of Congress, Providence, Rhode Island, August 21, 1779, *Papers of Congress,* M247, R190, I 171, p. 252.
9. Richard Peters, "Report of the Board of War," 3 September 1779, in W. M. Kozlowski,"Beniowski w Ameryce," (Rozmaitosci) [Beniowski in America, Miscellanea], II: 157-58, *Biblioteku Warszawska [Warsaw Library],* 1903; Benyowsky to Congress, Philadelphia, May 9, 1780, *Papers of Congress,* M247, R91, I 78, V3, p. 461; and Joseph Johnson, *Traditions and Remi-*

niscences, p. 246.
10. *Journals of Congress,* December 28, 1779, XV: 1414.
11. *Journals of Congress,* December 29, 1779, XV: 1417-18; Giovanni Schiavo, *Four Centuries of Italian-American History* (New York: The Vigo Press, 1957), p. 139; and *Collections of the Massachusetts Historical Society,* Sixth Series—Vol. VII (Boston: Published by the Society, 1896), containing *Historical Index to The Pickering Papers* (Microfilm edition), p. 33.
12. Benyowsky to Congress, June 26, 1780, and Benyowsky to President of Congress, May 6, 1782, *Papers of Congress,* M247, R48, I 41, V1, p. 291 and R92, I 78, V4. p. 299; Washington to Comte de Beniowski, Philadelphia, March 18, 1782, and Washington to Baron Steuben, Newburgh, April 12, 1782, and Washington to Comte de Beniowski, Newburgh, April 27, 1782, Fitzpatrick, *Writings of Washington,* XXIV: 77-78. 112-15, 175; *Journals of Congress,* May 10, 24, and 29, 1782, XXII: 261, 196-98, 309; Kozlowski, "Beniowski w Ameryce," II: 155-70; and Polish Biographical Dictionary, I: 431.
13. Milosz, *The History of Polish Literature,* p. 239; "News from Poland," Newsletter of the Embassy of the Republic of Poland, Washington, D. C., Vol. VI, May-June 2000, p. 6.

Appendix B. Pulaski's Military Experience in Poland

The following documents are the sources for this Appendix: Clarence A. Manning, *Soldier of Liberty, Casimir Pulaski;* Jan Stanislaw Kopczewski, *Kosciuszko and Pulaski:* and Jared Sparks, "Count Pulaski," *The Library of American Biography,* Vol. XIV.

Appendix C. Pulaski's Burial Site

The information comes from the research data of the Pinkowski Institute, Cooper City, Florida. (http://www.poles.org/)

· BIBLIOGRAPHY ·

I. PRIMARY SOURCES

1. Government Documents.

Archives of Maryland:
>William Paca to Governor William Johnson, Wye Island, Maryland, 11 June 1778.
>*Records of Maryland Troops in the Continental Service during the War of the American Revolution, 1775-83.* Vol. XVIII.
>*Journal and Correspondence of the Council of Maryland,* Vol. XXI.

Casimir Pulaski, 1747-1779, A Selective List of Reading Materials in English, Janina W. Hoskins, comp. Library of Congress, European Division, Washington, D. C., 1979.

George Washington Papers, 1741-1799, MF, 124 Reels, 1964, National Archives

Journals of the Continental Congress, 1774-1789, Worthington C. Ford et al, eds., 34 Vols. Washington: Government Printing Office, 1904-1937.

Pennsylvania Archives, Samuel Hazard, ed., Vol. VII, Series 1. Philadelphia: Joseph Severns & Co., 1853.

Secret Journals of the Acts and Proceedings of Congress, 4 Vols. Boston: Thomas B. Wait, 1820.

Senate Executive Document No. 120, Item 31, 49th Congress, 2nd Session, Washington: Government Printing Office, 1887.

The Papers of the Continental Congress, 1774-1789, M247, Reels 1-204, 1904, National Archives.

The Writings of George Washington, from the Original Manuscript Sources, John C. Fitzpatrick, ed., 39 Vols. Washington: Government Printing Office, 1931-1944.

2. Books.

Bentalou, Paul. *Pulaski Vindicated from an Unsupported Charge.* Baltimore: John D. Toy, 1824; reprint ed., New York: William Abbatt, 1909.

──────────. *A Reply to Judge Johnson's Remarks on an Article in the North American Review relating to Count Pulaski.* Baltimore: J. D. Toy, 1826. (Both publications at Maryland Historical Society).

Bodinier, Capitaine Gilbert. *Dictionnaire des officiers de l'armee royale qui ont combattu aux Etats-Unis pendant la guerre d'independance, 1776-1783.* Chateau des Vincennes, France: 1983.

Burnett, Edmund C. *Letters of Members of the Continental Congress,* Vol. III. Washington, D. C.: Carnegie Institution of Washington, 1926; reprint ed., Gloucester, Massachusetts: Peter Smith, 1963.

Campbell, Charles, ed. *The Bland Papers: Being a Selection from the Manuscripts of Colonel Theodorick Bland, Jr.,* 2 Vols. Petersburg, Virginia: Edmund & Julian C. Ruffin, 1840, 1843.

Custis, George Washington Parke. *Recollections and Private Memories of Washington.* New York: Derby & Jackson, 1860.

Ewald, Captain Johann. *Diary of the American War: A Hessian Journal.* Joseph P. Tustin, trans. and ed. New Haven: Yale University Press, 1979.

Gordon, William, D. D. *The History of the Rise, Progress, and Establishment of the Independence of the United States of America,* 4 Vols. London: 1788; reprint ed., Freeport, New York: Books for Libraries Press, 1969.

Gottschalk, Louis. *The Letters of Lafayette to Washington.* New York: Hubbard, 1949.

Heath, William. *Memoirs of Major-General Heath...during the American War.* Boston: I. Thomas and E.T. Andrews, 1798; reprint ed., Freeport, New York: Books for Libraries Press, 1970.

Heitman, Francis B. *Historical Register of the Officers of the Continental Army during the War of the Revolution.* Baltimore: Genealogical Publishing Company, 1967.

Bibliography

Idzerda, Stanley J., ed. *Lafayette in the Age of the American Revolution.* Ithaca, New York: Cornell University Press, 1977.

Jones, Charles C., Jr., ed. *The Siege of Savannah in 1779: As Described in Two Contemporaneous Journals of French Officers of the Fleet of Count D'Estaing.* Albany, New York: Joel Munsell, 1874; reprint ed., New York: The New York Times & Arno Press, 1968.

Laurens, John. *The Army Correspondence of John Laurens in the Years 1778-1780.* New York: The New York Times and Arno Press, 1969.

Lee, Henry. *Memoirs of the War in the Southern Department of the United States.* New York: University Publishing Company, 1869; reprint ed., New York: Arno Press, 1969.

Lee, Richard H. *Memoir of the Life of Richard Henry Lee and His Correspondence,* 2 Vols. Philadelphia: H. C. Cary and L. Lea, 1825.

Lefferts, Lt. Charles M. *Uniforms of the American, British, French, and German Armies in the War of the American Revolution, 1775-1783.* Old Greenwich, Connecticut: WE, Inc., 1926.

Longfellow, Henry Wadsworth. *The Poetical Works of Henry Wadsworth Longfellow.* Boston: Houghton, Mifflin Company, 1893.

Meng, John J. *Despatches and Instructions of Conrad Alexander Gerard, 1778-1780.* Baltimore: The Johns Hopkins Press, 1939.

Mollo, John. *Uniforms of the American Revolution, in Color.* New York: Sterling Publishing Company, Inc., 1991.

Moultrie, William. *Memoirs of the American Revolution,* New York: Printed by David Longworth, 1802; reprint ed., New York: The New York Times & Arno Press, 1968.

Polski Slownik Biograficzny [Polish Biographical Dictionary]. Krakow, 1935. (Count Maurycy Beniowski)

Pulaski, Francois, ed. *Correspondance du General Casimir Pulaski avec Claude de Rulhiere, 1774-1778.* Paris: Societe Historique et Litteraire Polonaise, 1948.

Ramsay, David. *History of the Revolution in South Carolina,* 2 Vols. Trenton: New Jersey: I. Collins, 1785.

_____. *History of the Revolution in South Carolina,* 2 Vols., edited by Lester H. Cohen. Indianapolis, Indiana: Liberty Fund, 1990.

Saffell, W.T.R., ed. *Records of the Revolutionary War.* New York: Pudney & Russell, Publishers, 1858.

Showman, Richard K. *The Papers of Nathanael Greene,* Vol. III.

Chapel Hill: The University of North Carolina Press, 1983.
Sparks, Jared. *The Writings of George Washington,* 12 Vols. New York: Harper & Brothers, 1847.
Stedman, Charles. *The History of the Origin, Progress, and Termination of the American War,* 2 Vols. London: J. Murray, J. Debrett, and J. Kerby, 1794.
Stryker, William S. *The Affair at Egg Harbor, New Jersey, October 15, 1778.* Trenton: Naar, Day & Naar, 1894.
Townsend, Joseph. *The Battle of Brandywine.* Philadelphia: Townsend War, Publisher, 1846; reprint ed., New York: The New York Times and Arno Press, 1969.
Uhlendorf, Bernhard A., tran. and ed. The *Siege of Charleston.* Ann Arbor: University of Michigan Press, 1938.
Willcox, William B., ed. The *American Revolution: Sir Henry Clinton's Narrative of His Campaigns, 1775-1782.* New Haven: Yale University Press, 1954.
_____. *The Papers of Benjamin Franklin,* Vol. XXIV. New Haven, Connecticut: Yale University Press, 1984.
Windrow, Martin, ed. *Polish Armies, 1569-1696 (1), Men-at-Arms Series.* Text by Richard Brzezinski. London: Osprey Publishing, Ltd., 1987.
_____. *The British Army in North America*, Text by Robin May. London: Osprey Publishing, Ltd., 1974.

3. Benjamin Lincoln Papers:

Samuel Bulfinch, Captain of the *Wasp,* to General Benjamin Lincoln, 15 October 1779, Film 1673, Roll 4, Frame 743, Massachusetts Historical Society.

4. Newspapers.

Dunlap's *Pennsylvania Packet* (Philadelphia)
New Jersey Gazette (Trenton)
Polish American Journal (Buffalo, New York)
The Maryland Journal and Baltimore Advertiser
The Savannah Daily News
The Savannah Georgian
The South Carolina and American General Gazette (Charleston)

5. Periodicals and Magazines.
(Both Primary and Secondary Sources)

Bauer, Frederic Gilbert, "Notes on the Use of the Cavalry in the American Revolution," *The Cavalry Journal,* Vol. 47, No. 2 (March-April, 1938).

Collections of the Massachusetts Historical Society, Sixth Series—Vol. VIII. Boston: Published by the Society, 1896, containing the *Historical Index to The Pickering Papers* (Microfilm edition).

Collection of the New-York Historical Society:
    1872: Vol. II, Charles Lee to General Washington, Charleston, 1 July 1776.
    1873: Vol. III, General Charles Lee's "Proposal for the Formation of a Body of Light Troops."

Colonel John Harris Cruger, "The Siege of Savannah," *The Magazine of American History,* Vol. II, No. 8 (August 1878).

Dictionary of American Biography, Allen Johnson and Dumas Malone, eds. New York: Charles Scribner's Sons, 1931. (William Washington Gordon).

Eastby, Allen G., "Setback for the Continental Army," *Military History,* Vol. 15, No. 5 (December 1998).

Gaszynski, Konstanty, ed., *Reszty Pamietnikow Macieja Rogowskiego* (The Rest of the Memoirs of Maciej Rogowski), Paryz: W Ksiegarni Katolickiej Polskiej, 1847 (Paris: Polish Catholic Bookstore).

Gordon, William W., "Count Casimir Pulaski," *The Georgia Historical Quarterly,* Vol. XIII, No. 3 (September 1929).

Holst, Donald W., and Zlatich, Marko. "Dress and Equipment of Pulaski's Independent Legion," *Military Collector & Historian,* Winter 1964, Washington, D.C.

Johnson, William, "Remarks Critical and Historical Relating to Count Pulaski," *The North American Review,* No. 47. Charleston: C.C. Sebring, 1825.

Jones, Gilbert S., "Pulaski Campaigned Valley Forge Area," *The Picket Post,* January 1948.

Kozlowski, W.M., "Beniowski w Ameryce" (Rozmaitosci) [Beniowski in America, Miscellanea], Vol. II, *Biblioteka Warszawska* [Warsaw Library], 1903.

Lewis, John Frederick, "Casimir Pulaski," *The Pennsylvania Magazine of History and Biography,* Vol. LV, No. 1 (1931).

"News from Poland," Newsletter of the Embassy of the Republic of Poland, Washington, D.C., Vol. VI (May-June 2000).

Pinkowski, Edward, "Pulaski's Tomb in Monterey Square," *Polish Heritage,* Vol. XLVII, No. 4 (Winter 1996).

_____, "General Pulaski's Body," Cooper City, Florida: Pinkowski Institute, 1997.

Poirier, Noel B., "Young General Lafayette," *MHQ: The Quarterly Journal of Military History,* Vol. 12, No. 2 (Winter 2000).

Pennsylvania Historical Society, "Bulletin," Vol. VII (1845).

Skelly, Major F., "Journal," *The Magazine of American History,* Vol. XXVI (July-August 1891).

Spencer, Richard Henry, "Pulaski's Legion," *Maryland Historical Magazine,* Vol. XIII, 1918.

The National Cyclopedia of American Biography Being the History of the United States, Vol. XIV. Ann Arbor, Michigan: University Microfilms, 1967 (William Washington Gordon)

The Polish Review, "Tadeusz Kosciuszko: Hero of Polish and American Independence," 5 July 1943,

The Pennsylvania Magazine of History and Biography:
"Diary of Surgeon Albigence Waldo," Vol. XXI, 1897.
"Letters of Major Baurmeister during the Philadelphia Campaign, 1777- 1778," Vol. LIX, 1935.
"Defences of Philadelphia in 1777," (Worthington Chauncey Ford), Vol. XX, No. 3, 1896

The South Carolina Historical and Genealogical Magazine:
A.S. Salley, ed., "Letters from the Marquis de Lafayette to Hon. Henry Laurens," Vol. VIII, April 1907.
A.S. Salley, ed. "Dr. James Lynah, A Surgeon of the Revolution," Vol. XL (July 1939).
Mabel L. Webber, ed., "Extracts from Journal of Mrs. Ann Manigault," Vol. XXI (July 1920).

Thompson, Ewa M., "Letter from Mongolia," *Chronicles of Culture,* February 1986 (Rockford Institute, Rockford, Illinois) [Name of publication later changed to *Chronicles: A Magazine of American Culture.*]

Winton, Harold R., "Toward an American Philosophy of Command," *The Journal of Military History,* Vol. 64, No. 4, October 2000.

Zabecki, David T., "Kazimierz Pulaski and the Birth of American Cavalry," *Military History,* Vol. 13, No. 7 (March 1997).

II. SECONDARY SOURCES

1. Books:

Adams, Charles Francis. *Studies Military and Diplomatic, 1775-1865*. New York: The Macmillan Company, 1911.

Alden, John R. *A History of the American Revolution*. New York: Alfred A. Knopf, 1969.

Atwood, Rodney. *The Hessians: Mercenaries from Hessen-Kassel in the American Revolution*. Cambridge: Cambridge University Press, 1980.

Barry, Richard. *Mr. Rutledge of South Carolina*. New York: Duell, Sloan & Pearce, 1942.

Bill, Alfred H. *Valley Forge: The Making of an Army*. New York: Harper & Brothers, 1952

Boatner, Mark Mayo III. *Encyclopedia of the American Revolution*. New York: David McKay Company, Inc., 1966.

Bobrick, Benson. *Angel in the Whirlwind: The Triumph of the American Revolution*. New York: Simon & Schuster, 1997.

Bowman, Allen. *The Morale of the American Revolutionary Army*. Port Washington, New York: Kennikat Press, Inc., 1944.

Bruns, Roger. *George Washington*. New York: Chelsea House Publishers, 1987.

Carrington, Henry B. *Battles of the American Revolution, 1775-1781*. New York: A.S. Barnes & Company, 1877; reprint ed., New York: The New York Times & Arno Press, 1968.

Chidsey, Donald Barr. *Valley Forge; a day-by-day chronicle from December 17, 1777 to June 18, 1778, compiled from the sources*. Philadelphia: University of Pennsylvania Press, 1963.

Chodzko, Leonard. *Zywot Kazimierza na Pulaziu Pulaskiego* (Life of Casimir on the Pulaski Estate). Lwow, 1869.

Davis, Burke. *George Washington and the American Revolution*. New York: Random House, 1975.

Dupuy, R. Ernest, and Dupuy, Trevor N. *The Compact History of the Revolutionary War*. New York: Hawthorn Books, Inc., 1963.

Gottschalk, Louis. *Lafayette Joins the American Army,* Book II of *Lafayette in America, 1777-1783*. Arveyres, France: L'Esprit de Lafayette Society, 1975.

Griffin, Martin I.J. *Catholics and the American Revolution*. Philadelphia: Published by the author, 1911.

Greene, George Washington. *The Life of General Nathanael Greene,* 3 Vols. New York: D. Appleton and Company, 1893.

Haiman, Miecislaus. *Kosciuszko in the American Revolution.* New York: Polish Institute of Arts and Sciences in America, 1943.

Hughes, Rupert. *George Washington: The Savior of the States, 1777-1781.* New York: William Morrow & Company, 1930.

Jamro, R.D. *Pulaski, A Portrait of Freedom.* Savannah, Georgia: The Printcraft Press, Inc., 1979.

Johnson, Dr. Joseph. *Traditions and Reminiscences of the American Revolution in the South.* Charleston: Walker & James, 1851.

Johnson, William. *Sketches of the Life and Correspondence of Nathanael Greene, Major General of the Armies of the United States,* 2 Vols. Charleston: A.E. Miller, 1822; reprint ed., New York: De Capo Press, 1973.

Kajencki, Francis Casimir. *Thaddeus Kosciuszko: Military Engineer of the American Revolution.* El Paso, Texas: Southwest Polonia Press, 1998.

Kapp. Friederick, *Life of John Kalb. Major General of the Revolutionary Army.* New York: Henry Holt and Company, 1884.

Katcher, Philip R.N. *Armies of the American Wars, 1753-1815.* New York: Hastings House, 1975.

Kemp, Franklin W. *A Nest of Rebel Pirates.* Egg Harbor City, New Jersey: The Laureate Press, 1993.

Konopczynski, Wladyslaw. *Casimir Pulaski,* translated from the Polish by Irena Makarewicz. Chicago: Polish Roman Catholic Union of America, 1947.

Lasseray, Andre. *Les Francais sous Treize Etoiles.* Paris: Protat Freres, 1935.

Lawrence, Alexander A. *Storm over Savannah: The Story of Count D'Estaing and the Siege of the Town in 1779.* Athens, Georgia: The University of Georgia Press, 1951; reprint ed., 1968.

Lengyel, Emil. *Americans from Hungary.* Philadelphia: J.B. Lippincott, 1948.

Levering, Joseph Mortimer. *A History of Bethlehem, Pennsylvania, 1741-1892.* Bethlehem: Times publishing company, 1903; reprint ed., New York: AMS Press, 1971.

Loescher, Burt Garfield. *Washington's Eyes, The Continental Light Dragoons.* Fort Collins, Colorado: The Old Army Press, 1977.

Lossing, Benson J. *Pictorial Field-Book of the Revolution,* 2 Vols. New York: Harper, 1851-52.

Manning, Clarence A. *Soldier of Liberty, Casimir Pulaski.* New York: Philosophical Library, 1945.

Martin, John Hill. *Historical Sketch of Bethlehem in Pennsylvania and the Moravian Church.* Philadelphia; 1872; reprint ed., New York: AMS Press, 1971.

Mattern, David B. *Benjamin Lincoln and the American Revolution.* Columbia: University of South Columbia Press, 1995.

Milosz, Czeslaw. *The History of Polish Literature.* Berkeley: University of California Press, 1983.

Mitchell, Lt. Col. Joseph B. *The Decisive Battles of the American Revolution.* New York: G.P. Putnam's Sons, 1962.

Moore, Frank. *Diary of the American Revolution.* New York: Charles Scribner, 1858.

Nelson, Paul David. *Anthony Wayne: Soldier of the Early Republic.* Bloomington: Indiana University Press, 1985.

Nolan, J. Bennett. *Lafayette in America Day by Day.* Baltimore: The John Hopkins University Press, 1934.

Pastusiak, Longin. *Kosciuszko, Pulaski, i Inni.* Warszawa: Krajowa Agencja Wydawnicza, 1977 [National Publishing Agency].

Peterson, Harold L. *The Book of the Continental Soldier.* Harrisburg: The Stackpole Company, 1968.

Pickering, Octavius (Son), *The Life of Timothy Pickering,* Vol. I. Boston: Little, Brown, and Company, 1867.

(Upham, Charles W. *The Life of Timothy Pickering,* Vols. II-IV. Boston: Little, Brown, and Company, 1873.)

Randall, Willard Sterne. *George Washington, A Life.* New York: Henry Holt and Company, 1997.

Rankin, Hugh F. *The North Carolina Continentals.* Chapel Hill: The University of North Carolina Press, 1971.

Reed, John Ford. *Valley Forge, Crucible of Victory.* Monmouth Beach, New Jersey: Philip Freneau Press, 1969.

Reed, William. *Life and Correspondence of Joseph Reed,* 2 Vols. Philadelphia: Lindsay and Blakiston, 1847.

Schiavo, Giovanni. *Four Centuries of Italian-American History.* New York: The Vigo Press, 1957.

Scheer, George F., and Rankin, Hugh F. *Rebels and Redcoats.* Cleveland: The World Publishing Company, 1957.

Smith, Page. *A New Age Now Begins,* 2 Vols. New York: McGraw-Hill Book Company, 1976.

Sparks, Jared. "Count Pulaski," *The Library of American Biography,* Vol. XIV. Boston: Charles C. Little and James Brown, 1845.

Stille, Charles J. *Major-General Anthony Wayne and the Pennsylvania Line in the Continental Army.* Port Washington, New York: Kennikat Press, Inc., 1968.

Stoudt, John Joseph. *Ordeal at Valley Forge; a day-by-day chronicle from December 17, 1777 to June 18, 1778 compiled from the sources.* Philadelphia: University of Pennsylvania Press, 1959.

Szymanski, Leszek. *Casimir Pulaski: A Hero of the American Revolution.* New York: Hippocrene Books, 1994.

Tower, Charlemagne. *The Marquis de Lafayette in the American Revolution,* Philadelphia: J.B. Lippincott Company, 1901; reprint ed., New York: De Capo Press, 1970.

Ward, Christopher. *The War of the Revolution,* 2 Vols. New York: The Macmillan Company, 1952.

Waring, Charles Ellis, and Waring, Elizabeth Stewart. *Savannah and Its Environs, 1733-1903.* Savannah: The Georgia Historical Society, 1974.

Wernich, Robert et al, eds. *Blitzkrieg.* Alexandria, Virginia: Time-Life Books, 1977.

Wheeler, Richard. *Voices of 1776.* New York: Thomas Y. Crowell Company, 1972.

Wildes, Harry Emerson. *Valley Forge.* New York: Macmillan, 1938.

Index

Abbreviations of military rank:
Sgt. Sergeant
Sgt. Maj., Sergeant Major
Lt., Lieutenant
Capt., Captain
Maj., Major
Lt. Col., Lieutenant Colonel
Col., Colonel
Gen., General

Adams, Charles Francis, xii, 19, 194-195
Adams, Floyd, 222
Adams, Samuel, 72, 81
Albany, New York, 29, 93
America, xi, xii, 1, 3-4, 6, 13, 20, 25, 28, 33, 44, 51, 58, 64, 66, 72, 79, 93, 106, 115-116, 129, 138, 141, 148-150, 163, 168, 176, 204, 206
Americans, xi, xii, xiii, 1, 3, 20, 25, 42, 58, 63, 75, 101, 126, 140
American Army, 63
American Continental Army, xiii, 3-9. 11, 13, 16, 19-22, 28, 34, 37, 40, 45, 49-50, 57- 58, 64, 66, 76-77, 83, 88, 93, 106, 108, 111, 113, 115, 117, 122, 131, 148, 168, 180-181, 185, 189, 192, 195
American Continental Army Units:
    1st Cavalry Regiment (Bland), 41-42, 46, 123, 180, 191-192, 195
    2nd Cavalry Regiment (Sheldon), 41, 51-54, 62, 123, 180, 191
    3rd Cavalry Regiment (Baylor), 41, 54, 84, 94, 123, 180, 191
    4th Cavalry Regiment (Moylan), 21, 30, 41-42, 66, 123, 180, 191
    Captain John Schott's Infantry Company, 114, 129
    Colonel Chariot's Regiment, 115
    Colonel Oliver Spencer's Infantry Regiment, 105
    Colonel Proctor's Pennsylvania Artillery Regiment, 67, 86, 92, 101
    South Carolina Cavalry Regiment (Horry), 143, 163, 173
    2nd South Carolina Regiment, 164
    3rd South Carolina Regiment, 147
    Colonel Thomas Hartley's Infantry Regiment , 66
    Armand's Legion, 105, 108-109, 115, 118, 120, 180, 182
    Lee's Legion, 31, 82, 110
    Pulaski's Legion, 68, 124, 180 (and throughout)
American Militia Units:
    Charleston Militia, 147, 158, 162
    Georgia Militia, 153, 171
    New Hampshire Brigade (Gen. John Stark), 93
    North Carolina Militia, 147
    New Jersey Militia, 86, 92
    Virginia Militia, 147, 171
American Independence, 25, 30, 57, 66, 99, 108, 129-130, 148, 184, 187
American Philosophical Society, 210
American Revolution, xii, xiii, 21, 38, 63, 72, 84, 110, 113, 133, 180-181, 185, 188-190, 193, 195, 198, 216

American Southern Army, 42, 113, 136, 146-147, 153, 171, 173, 180, 182-183
Anderson, Jewell, 224
Anderson, Mayor Edward C., 248
Annapolis, Maryland, 125
Anzio Beachhead, Italy, 195
Armstrong, Gen. John, 9
Army of the Confederation of Bar (Poland), xi, 27, 32, 41, 106, 115, 168, 204
Arnold, Dr. Richard D., 175, 177
Ashby, Andrea, 225
Ashley's Ferry, South Carolina, 132, 143
Ashley River, South Carolina, 139, 143, 147, 180
Atlantic City, New Jersey, 96
Atlantic Ocean, 1, 83, 96
Augusta, Georgia, 153
Augustus III, King of Poland, 212-213 (and Elector of Saxony),
Austria, 2, 181, 296, 210, 212
Avery, Attorney General ———, 121

Bader, Julia, 71
Baker, Joyce N., 226
Baldesqui, Capt. Joseph, 67, 77, 79, 114, 122, 125, 189, 202-204, 208
Baltimore, Maryland, 25-26, 62, 72, 125-126, 181, 201
Bar, Poland, 213, 216
Barford, Paul, 221
Barney, John, 26
Barnegat, New Jersey, 101
Barry, Richard, 131
Batsto, New Jersey, 83, 86, 96
Battle of Bennington, 93
Battle of Brandywine, xi, 8, 10, 12-13, 15-17, 27, 66, 71, 75, 148
Battle of Bunker Hill, 172
Battle of Camden, 57, 75
"Battle of the Clouds," 229
Battle of Germantown, xi, 21, 24-27, 66, 75
Battle of Guilford Court House, 76
Battle of King's Mountain, 91
Battle of Long Island, xi, 19, 75, 92, 195
Battle of Monmouth, 75-76
Battle of Saratoga, 61, 93

Battle of Savannah, xiii, 166, 169, 172, 176, 181, 184, 190, 198, 222
Bauer, Col. Frederic Gilbert, 141
Baylor, Col. George, 6, 31, 51-52, 84, 140, 192
Baurmeister, Maj. (Hessian), 23
Beaufort, South Carolina, 146, 151, 155, 159
Beaver, John, 38
Beaulieu, Georgia, 153, 155
Beaulieu, Lt. Louis de, 101, 114, 181
Bedaulx, Lt. Col. Charles Frederick, 102, 118, 133-134, 168, 173, 176
Bedkin, Capt. Henry, 30, 66, 68, 149, 180, 191
"Bedkin Fiasco," 243
Bee, Thomas, 130
Bellcour, Capt. Jerome Le Brun, 66, 68, 181
Belleville, Dr. Nicholas Jacques Emanuel de, 67-68
Benjamin Lincoln Papers, 165
Bentalou, Capt. Paul, 8, 13-14, 22-26, 66, 69, 90-91, 98, 152-153, 155, 163-167, 169-170, 181
Benyowsky (Beniowski), Count Maurycy, 204, 206-209
Beniowski (poem), 209-210
Berdyczow, Poland, 216
Bethisy, Col. de, 162
Bethlehem, Pennsylvania, 71
Biddle, Col. Clements, 40, 109-110, 121
Birmingham-Lafayette Cemetery (Brandywine), 15
Birmingham Meeting House (Brandywine), 11, 13
Bismarck State College, North Dakota, xv
Bland, Col. Theodorick, 6, 9, 11, 20-21, 29, 31, 42, 44, 51-52, 140, 191, 195, 209
Blitzkrieg (book), 170
Blum, Anna, 71
Board of War, Continental Congress, 21, 61, 63, 69-70, 81-82, 88, 91, 102, 107, 114-117, 119, 122-123, 149, 173, 182, 202, 207
Boatner, Mark Mayo III, 96, 98
Bobrick, Benson, 169

Index

Bogulawski, Capt. Jacob Ferdinand, 219
Bordeaux, France, 102
Borderie, Lt. Joseph de la, 67, 87-88, 91, 95, 184
Borre, Gen. Prudhomme de, 16
Boston, Massachusettsm 2, 116, 130, 203, 206
Bowen, Jane, 165, 167, 219
Bowen, Col. William P., 167, 175, 219-220
Bowman, Allen, 35
Braddock, Gen. Edward, 193
Brandywine Battlefield Park, Pennsylvania, 15
Brandywine Creek, Pennsylvania, 9, 11
Brenton's Ford (Brandywine), 16
British, 13, 54, 60, 76
British Army, xi, 2, 7-8, 11-13, 19, 22-23, 27, 30, 33, 38-39, 46, 49, 51, 61, 75-76, 79-80. 86, 103, 108, 110, 131, 133, 136, 143, 145-146, 152, 187, 193, 198
British cavalry, 133, 180
British units:
    5th Regiment of Foot, 84
    70th Regiment of Foot, 84
    3rd Battalion of New Jersey Loyalists, 84
Broening, Mayor William F., 235
Broglie, Comte de, 37
Bronville, Lt. James de, 67, 100-101
"Brown Bess," (British musket), 84
Bronx, New York, 103
Bruns, Roger, 141
Buffington's Ford (Brandywine), 9, 15
Bujakowski, Witold, 221
Bulfinch, Samuel, 165
Burdette, Thomas, 226
Burgoyne, Gen. John, 2, 61, 93, 115
Burlington, New Jersey, 45-46
Burns, Dr. Karen R., 221
Butler, Col. John, 105

Cadwallader, John, 53
Canada, 93, 115
Canton, China, 206
Caribbean Sea, 66
Carnes, Lt. Patrick, 82

Carrington. Lt. Col. Edward, 183
Carrington, Henry, 155, 158, 167
Caswell, Governor Richard, 129
Cathedral of St. John, Savannah, Georgia, 222
Catherine II, Russian Tsarina, 204, 206, 212
Celeron, Capt. Lewis, 115-116, 134, 136, 181
Chad's Ford, Pennsylvania, 9, 11, 13-14, 22
Chariot, Col, ____, 115
Charleston, South Carolina, 19, 24, 30, 130-132, 134, 137-141, 143-146, 148, 163-166, 168, 173, 180, 184, 187-189, 198, 219
Chesapeake Bay, Maryland, 7
Chester, Pennsylvania, 9, 13-14
Chestnut Neck, New Jersey, 83
Chippewa Square, Savannah, Georgia, 26, 175
Chmielnik, Poland, 215
Chocim, Turkey, 216
Chodzinski, Kazimierz, 196
Ciesielski, Stanley A., 224, (Color Insert)
City Hall, Savannah, Georgia, 222
Civil War, American, xii, 1, 190, 193-194
Clap Tavern Road, New Jersey, 54
Clark, Abraham, 209
Clark, Gen. Mark, 195
Clinton, Governor George, 82, 104
Clinton, General Sir Henry, 75, 83-84, 91, 126, 139, 172
Clough, Maj. Alexander, 54
Cockspur Island, Georgia, 194
Cole's Fort, New York, 104-105
Colins, Commander Henry, 84, 86, 88, 91, 98-99
Commager, Henry Steele, 131, 152, 167
Commander of the Horse (cavalry), xii, xiii, 7, 17, 21, 38, 42-43, 50, 53, 108, 191-192, 198
Commissary Department, 37
Committee of Congress for the Affairs of the Army, 64-65
Committee of Arrangements, 80
Committee on Foreign Applications, 5-6
Concord, Massachusetts, 28

265

Cooper's Ferry, Philadelphia, 46
Cooper River, South Carolina, 130, 132, 187
Confederate cavalry, 1, 193
Confederation of Bar (Poland), 32, 67, 211-212, 214
Confederate States of America, xii
Connecticut, 6, 195
Constitution of 1789, United States, 187
Continental Congress, xi, xii, xiii, 3-5, 8, 15-17, 19-20, 24, 27, 31, 33, 35, 37, 44, 51-52, 57- 58, 62, 64, 66-67, 69-70, 76-77, 79-83, 88, 91-92, 94, 101-104, 106, 110-111, 113-123, 125-126, 129, 132, 134, 140, 144-145, 148-149, 168, 173, 176, 180-185, 191, 193-194, 201, 204
Cork, Ireland, 21
Cornwallis, General Charles Lord, 8-9, 11, 23, 75-76, 195
Coudray, Gen, Phillip du, 3
Cox, Cornelius, 122
Craig, Capt. John, 42, 52, 191
Cruger, Lt. Col. John Harris, 172
Curry, Sgt. Maj. James, 161
Custer, Gen. George, 193
Custis, George Washington Parke, 25

Dan River, Virginia, 185
Deane, Silas, xii, 2-3, 5, 20, 102, 106-107, 217
De Bretigny, Col. ____, 151
D'Estaing, Admiral Charles Comte, 72, 151, 153, 155, 157-159, 161-163, 167, 171-172, 179
De Fry, Capt. Baron, 107
De Grasse, Admiral Comte Francois, 76
D'Gugglaa, Baron George Gustave, 116-117, 125-126
De Kalb, Gen. Baron Johan, 3, 37-38, 50-51, 88, 102, 182, 185
Delaware River, 46, 104-105
De Segond, Capt. Maria Blaise Jacques, 66-67, 70, 125, 180, 201
De Wolfe, Barbara, 226
Diary of the American Revolution, 171
Dillon, Col. Arthur, 158, 161-162
Dilworth, Pennsylvania, 9, 11

Dmochowski, Henryk, 220-221
Dniester River, Poland, 216
Don Cossacks, 215
Don Juan (Byron), 210
Don Quixote, 230
Dorchester, South Carolina, 139
Drayton, Henry, 130
Duer, William, 88
Duff, Governor James, 34
Dunlap's *Pennsylvania Packet,* 94
Dupuy, R. Ernest and Trevor N., 3, 166
Dutch Army, 102, 116
Dybicz, Edward, 34, 225
Dyboski, Prof. Roman, 235

Easton, Pennsylvania, 62, 108-109
Elizabeth Town, New Jersey, 116
Elton, George, 67
Empress of Russia, 116
Encyclopedia of the American Revolution, 96
English people, 63
English language, xiii, 2-3, 20, 38, 191, 196
Europe, 2-3, 6, 20, 38, 41-42, 64, 106-108, 110, 119, 168-169, 176, 182, 191, 204, 206, 216
Europeans, 3, 64, 116
Ewald, Capt. Johann, 198

Faucet, Mr. (Quartermaster Corps), 121
Fayssoux, Dr. P., 207
Ferguson, Capt. Patrick, 84, 86, 88, 90-91, 93-94, 96, 98-99, 101, 134, 180
Ferguson rifle, 84
Finnie, William, 243-244
Fiore, Rev. Benjamin, S.J., 205
Fisk, Capt. John, 1
Fitzpatrick, John C., xv
Flanders, Belgium, 115
Flannery, Jeffrey M., 223
Flemington, New Jersey, 41
Fleury, Lt. Col. Marquis de, 3, 27, 168
Fontages, Gen. Viscount de, 151
Forks, New Jersey, 92
Formosa, 206
Forrest, Gen. Nathan Bedford, 193
Fort Nelson, Gosport, Virginia, 126

Index

Fort Pulaski National Monument, Georgia, 194, 222
Fort Ticonderoga, New York, 2, 115
Fortress West Point, New York, 75
Foster, Dr. (At Bethlehem), 72
France, 1, 3, 16, 28, 37, 44, 57, 66-67, 93, 106, 110, 181, 202, 206, 209-210, 216-217,
Franklin, Benjamin, xii, 1-3, 5, 28, 102, 106-107, 211, 217
Fraser, Charles, 60
French Army, 27, 51, 93, 110, 158, 171, 206
French Fleet, 151
French and Indian War, 193
French language, 2, 5, 20, 22, 26
French officers, 57, 67, 110, 158
Frey, Valerie, 224

Gambier, Admiral James, 86
Gardner, Dr. Don, 222
Gates, Gen. Horatio, 61, 75, 93, 182, 193, 206-207
General Joseph Haller Post, American Legion, Baltimore, 236
Genghis Khan, 205
George III, British monarch, 87, 111, 172, 209
George Washington Papers, 243
Georgia, 111, 120, 130, 139, 157, 159, 165, 172-173, 175
Gerogia Central Railroad, 190
Georgia Historical Commission, 177-179
Georgia Historical Quarterly, 163, 190
Georgia Historical Society, Savannah, 163, 174, 190, 194, 220
Georgia State Cavalry, 190
Gerard, Conrad Alexandre, 77, 110
Germain, Lord George, 83
Germans, 63, 88, 102, 115, 195
German Americans, 14
Germantown, Pennsylvania, 23, 26, 208
Germany, 115
Gersdorf, Eldress Susan von, 71
Gibbes Art Gallery/Carolina Art Association, Charleston, South Carolina, 60, 226

Gilbert, Mrs. ____, 220
Giles, Capt. ____, 170
Gordon, Rev. William, 130, 187-188
Gordon, William Washington I, 190
Gordon, William Washington II, 190,
Gordon, William Washington III, 22, 136, 166, 187, 190, 198
Gorny, Rev. Jan, 221
Gosport, Virginia, 126
Goteborg, Sweden, 129
Gottschalk, Louis, 67
Grab, Poland, 221
Granby (British ship), 84
Gray, George, 72, (Color Insert)
Great Valley Road (Brandywine), 9-11
Greene, Gen. Nathanael, 3, 9, 11, 13, 24, 31, 35, 42, 75-76, 109, 113, 121-123, 182-183, 185, 193
Greenwich (British ship), 84
Greenwich Cemetery, Savannah, Georgia, 221
Greenwich Plantation, Savannah, 165, 178, 219
Grey, Gen. Charles, 54, 84, 94
Grier, Col. David, 122
Grimke, Col. John F., 147
Groce, W. Todd, 224
Gromada, Thaddeus V., 224
Guadaloupe Island, 181

Hackensack River, New Jersey, 245
Haddonfield, New Jersey, 45-46, 57, 132, 192
Haiti, 219
Half-pay officers pension, 176, 182
Hamburg. Europe, 206
Hamilton, Alexander, 22, 209
Hancock, John, 5-8
Hand, Gen. Edward, 107-109, 111, 118, 192
Haussegger, Col. Nicholas, 66
Hayne, Maj. Isaac, 176
Hazen, Col. Moses, 9, 11, 16
Head of the Elk, Maryland, 7-8
Heath, Gen. William, 2
Heller, Douglas, 230
Herbert, Mary, E., 224
Hessians, xii, 13, 23, 58, 63, 75, 80, 87-

267

88, 91, 93, 140, 146, 198
Highlands of the Hudson, New York, 75, 82
Historical Society of Pennsylvania, 98
Holland, 181
Holy Rosary Catholic Church, Baltimore, 235
Hooper, Col. Robert, 109
Hornkohl, Anna, 72
Horry, Col. Daniel, 143, 163
Hotel Bethlehem, Bethlehem, Pennsylvania, 72
Howe, Gen. Sir William, 7, 9-11, 23, 45, 83
Howell, David, 176, 198
Hudson River, 54, 84, 93, 234
Huger, Gen. Isaac, 143-144, 158, 161, 180-181
Hughes, Rupert, 3, 14, 24
Hungary, 210
Huntington, Samuel, 173
Hussey, Anna, 71
"Hymn of the Moravian Nuns of Bethlehem" (poem), 72, 74

Immaculate Heart of Mary Cathedral, Irkutsk, Siberia, 205
Independence Hall, Philadelphia, 77, 229-231
Independence Hall Association, 23n
Independence National Historical Park, 4, 47, 59
Independence Square, Philadelphia, 77
Indian Ocean, 206
Indians, 105-108, 195
Interpress Publishers, Warsaw, 223
Irkutsk, Siberia, 205

Jacksonborough, South Carolina, 144
Jagiellonian dynasty (Poland), 211
Jagiellonian University, Krakow, Poland, 235
James Island, South Carolina, 138, 143, 145-147
Jameson, Maj. John, 39
Jamro, R. D., 72, 225
Japan, 206
Jasper, Sgt. William, 164, 179

Jay, John, 116-117, 206-207
Jeffries' Ford (Brandywine), 9
Johns Island, South Carolina, 138, 143, 145, 173
Johnson, Governor William, 32
Johnson, James, 207
Johnson, Dr. Joseph, 133, 165, 167, 207
Johnson, Judge William, 24-26, 169-170
Johnson, Mandi D., 224
Johnson, Sir Guy, 105
Jones, Charles C., Jr., 167
Jones' Ford (Brandywine), 16
Journals of the Continental Congress, 116
Juliat, Lt. Carl Wilhelm, 87-88, 90-91
Jupiter, Florida, xv

Kajencki, Anthony A. II, xv, 220-221
Kajencki, Dr. AnnMarie, xv
Kajencki, Francis C., 220-221
Kamchatka Peninsula, Siberia, 204, 206
Kane, Joseph and Della, 224
Kapp, Friederick, 51
Karakorum, Mongolia, 205
Kean, J., Esq., 147
Kedron, Janina, 224
Kemp, Franklin, 140
Kent County, Delaware, 110
Kerlevan, Lt. Andrew, 101, 114
Kings Bridge, New York, 103-104
Klein, Lt. Col. _____, 115
Knoblauch, Baron de, 117
Knox, Gen. Henry, 3
Knyphausen, Gen. Wilhelm von, 8-9, 11, 13-14
Konopczynski, Wladyslaw, 79
Kosciuszko, Col. Thaddeus, 3, 29, 61, 75. 98, 185
Kosciuszko Monument, West Point, New York, 199
Kotkowski, Capt. Stanislaw, 106-107, 140, 169
Kovatch, Col. Michael, 40, 42, 64, 66, 71. 77, 125, 134, 173, 184, 189, 201
Krasinska, Princess Franciszka, 213
Krechetnikov, Gen. Peter, 215
Kurile Islands, 206

Index

LaClose, Lt. Henry de, 101, 114, 134, 181
Lafayette, Adrienne de Noaille, 3-4
Lafayette, George Washington, 26
Lafayette, Marquis de, 3-6, 13, 25-29, 66-67, 71-72, 102, 141, 168, 175, 181. 185, 193
Lancaster, Pennsylvania, 117-119
Langley, Rebecca and Ermuth, 71
Latvia, 212
Launitz, Robert Eberhardt, 175-176, 199
Laurens, Henry, xi, 30, 58, 61, 66, 72, 94, 99, 104, 120, 196
Laurens, Lt. Col. John, 30, 58, 133, 158-159, 162
Lawrence, Alexander A., 72, 158-159
Lee, Arthur, 183
Lee, Gen. Charles, 19, 61, 193
Lee, Maj. Henry, Jr., 31, 61, 77, 82, 164, 191, 196
Lee, Richard Henry, 76
Lee, Lt. Robert E., 194
Lee, Sharen, 226
Lenard, Myra, 197, 225
Levasseur, A., 26
Levy, Jacob Clavius, 219
Lewis, John Frederick, 98, 138
Lexington, Massachusetts, 28
Library of Congress, 197, 210
Liebchen, Ryszard, 222
Lincoln, President Abraham, 193
Lincoln, Gen. Benjamin, 111, 114, 120, 122, 130, 132, 136, 138-139. 141. 143-144, 146-147, 151-153, 155, 157-159, 162, 165, 169, 171-173, 176, 180,
Linton, Coby, 224
Litomski, Lt. Charles, 165
Little Egg Harbor, New Jersey, 81, 83-85, 87-88, 93-94, 96, 98-99, 101, 103, 134, 149, 180, 184, 189, 203
Livingston, Governor William, 40, 50, 86, 196
Loescher, Burt Garfield, 27
Lomza, Poland 212
Longfellow, William Wadsworth, 72, 74,
Lord Byron, 210
Lord Stirling, Gen. (William Alexander), 9, 15, 82, 99, 103, 105
Lorys, Jan, 224
Lossing, Benson J., 24, 72
Lovell, James, 5-6, 17
L'Overture, Toussaint, 219
Lowell, Edward J., 63, 92
Lowndes, Rawlins, 120
Luzerne, Le Chevalier de la, 206, 209
Lynah, Edward, 163
Lynah, Dr. James, 163, 178

Macao, Asia (Portuguese colony), 206
Madagascar, 206, 209-210
Madison, James, 209
Maitland, Lt. Col. John, 146, 151, 155, 159, 161, 172
Malachowski, Gen. Kazimierz, 219
Maleszewski, Tytus, v
Maliszewski, Gen. Thaddeus W., xv
Manhattan, New York, 103
Manning, Clarence A., 213
Mannigault, Ann, 164
Marblehead, Massachusetts, 2
Marshall, Col. ____, 126
Martin, John Hill, 71
Maryland, 31, 62-63, 70-71, 125, 132, 201
Maryland Historical Society, 72, 236
Maryland Journal and Baltimore Advertiser, 76
"Maryland Legion," 125
Maryland State Council, 70, 125
Massachusetts, xii, 5
Massachusetts (ship), 1
Massachusetts Historical Society, 165
Mattern, David B., 158
Mauleon, Capt. Count de, 102-103
Maxwell, Gen. William, 11, 15, 82
Mazur, Most Rev. Jerzy, Apostolic Administrator of Eastern Siberia, 205
McHenry, James, 109
McIntosh, Gen. Lachlan, 153, 157
McKean, Thomas, 81
Melchior, Adam, 67
Metts, Dr. James C., 221
Meyer, Lee, 222
Michael Ciesielski Photography, Baltimore, 224, (Color Insert)

269

CASIMIR PULASKI

Mickiewicz, Adam, 165
Middle Brook, New Jersey, 109, 243
Middle of the Shore (Tuckerton), New Jersey, 87
Milewski, Frank, 225
Military Collector & Historian, 70
Military Museum, Warsaw, Poland, 222
Military Order of the Knights of the Holy Cross (Poland), 213
Milosz, Czeslaw, 210
Minisink, New York, 104-105, 107-111, 118, 192, 195
Mitawa, Poland, 212-213
Mokotow (Warsaw suburb), 211
Moncrief, Capt. James, 155
Monck's Corner, South Carolina, 180-181, 184
Moore, Frank, 171
Mongolia, 205
Monterey Square, Savannah, 175
Montford, Maj. Count Julius de, 62, 64, 66, 92, 102, 201
Moravian Records, 71
Moravian Sisters, Bethlehem, 71-72
Morgan, Col. Daniel, 105
Morris, Richard B., 126, 152, 167
Morristown, New Jersey, 211, 243
Moscow, Russia, 205
Moultrie, Gen. William, 131-134, 136, 138-139, 143, 145-147, 151
Mount Holly, New Jersey, 45-46
Moylan, Col. Stephen, 6, 20-21, 28-31, 41, 44, 51-53, 64, 81, 140, 192
Muhlenberg, Gen. Peter, 24
Mullica River, New Jersey, 83, 86
Mystic Island, New Jersey, 94

Nantes, France, 1
Napoleon Bonaparte, 193, 219
National Archives, 224
Nautilus (ship), 84, 88
Nazareth, Pennsylvania, 118
Nelson, Paul David, 46
Nelson, Rev. Vernon, 225, (Color Insert)
Neshaminy Creek, Pennsylvania, 2, 161
Nesmith, Wendy, 225
New Bern, North Carolina, 115
New Jersey, 45, 71, 82-84, 86, 101, 103

New Jersey Gazette, 46, 62
Newport, Rhode Island, 151, 155
New York State, 82, 104, 115
New York, New York, 7, 75, 83-84, 86, 113, 116, 126, 130, 139, 175, 195
New Windsor, New York, 126
Ninety-Six, South Carolina, 98
Nobles Republic (Poland), 211
North America, 83, 179
North Carolina, 111, 121, 125, 129-130
Nourse, Joseph, 70
Nova Scotia, Canada, 83

Ogeechee River, Georgia, 157
Ogeechee River Ferry, 154
Old Tappan, New Jersey, 54, 84, 94
Olkowska, Sister Irene, 236, (Color Insert)
O'Neil, Capt. Alexander, 114-115, 181
Osborn's Island, New Jersey, 87, 90
Osborn, Richard, 90
Osborn, Thomas, 90
Ossawbaw River, Georgia, 153
Ottendorf, Baron Nicholas Dietrich de, 114

Paca, William, 31-32
Pacific Ocean, 204
Painter's Ford (Brandywine), 9
Palmer, Lt. William, 67
Paoli, Pennsylvania, 54, 94
Paramus, New Jersey, 82
Paris, France, xii, 1, 3, 21, 67, 102
Paschke, Capt. Frederick, 67, 122, 182-183
Paulus Hook, New Jersey, 245
Peale, Charles Willson, 4, 59, 128
Peale, Edmund, 72
Peale's Museum, Baltimore, 72
Penn, John, 121
Pennington, New Jersey, 41
Pennsylvania, 6, 37, 45, 70-71, 81, 104, 111, 119-120, 144, 149
Pennsylvanians, 30-31, 66, 113, 129
Pennsylvania Historical and Museum Commission, 16, (Color Insert)
Peters, Richard, 61, 88, 102, 202, 207
Peterson, Harold L., 70

Index

Pettit, Col. Charles, 121-123
Philadelphia (Quaker City), Pennsylvania, xv, 2, 5, 7-9, 21-23, 27, 39, 45, 49, 53, 77, 79, 81-83, 101, 103, 106-108, 110, 113, 116, 118, 122, 125-126, 129-130, 148, 168-169, 173, 181-183, 203, 206-207
Philadelphia County, 81
Phillips, Eleazar, 165, 222
Piasecka, Marzena, xv
Pickering, Timothy, 21, 61, 88, 102, 114, 119-120, 183
Pinckney, Col. Charles Cotesworth, 24, 159
Pinkowski, Edward, 165-166, 219, 221, 225
Pleasonton, Gen. Alfred, 193
Plombard, French Consul, 151
Podgorychanin, Gen. (Russian), 215
Poirier, Noel B., 193
Poland, xi, xv, 2, 5, 8, 13, 20, 27, 32-33, 43, 67, 72, 103, 106, 114, 133, 137, 150, 163, 168, 175, 184, 188, 190, 193, 195, 210-213, 216, 221-222
Poles, xii, 17, 140, 205, 212, 219
Polish American Congress, 197
Polish American Journal. 205
Polish Army, 20, 222
Polish cavalry, 39
Polish freedom slogan, xiii, 28
Polish Heritage Association of Maryland, 235, (Color Insert)
Polish hussar, 3
Polish Ukraine, 213
Polish Uprising of 1831, 205
Polish Uprising of 1863, 205
Polo, Patricia, 226
Poniatowski, King Stanislaw August, 20, 212-213, 216
Poor, Gen. Enoch, 38
Port Royal Island, South Carolina, 146, 151
Portsmouth, Virginia, 126
Potocki, Prince Joachim, 215
Potocki, Wawrzyniec, 215
Powell. Charles, 221
Preece, Rebecca, 226
Preston, James Henry, 235

Prevost, Gen. Augustin, 130-133, 135-139, 141, 143, 146, 151-152, 155, 157, 161, 172
Prevost, Col. Mark, 144
Prince Karl of Courland, 212
Princeton, New Jersey, xii, 34, 75, 83
Promna, Poland, 221
Providence, Rhode Island, 206
Prussia, 2, 3, 110, 212
Prussian Army, 40, 117
Prussian cavalry, 38, 191
Pulaski family, 204, 206
Pulaska, Anna (Walewska), 43, 212
Pulaska, Joanna, 212
Pulaska, Jozefa, 212
Pulaska, Malgorzata, 212
Pulaska, Marianna Zielinska, 212
Pulaska, Paulina, 212-213
Pulaski, Antoni, 212-216
Pulaski, Count Francis, 235
Pulaski, Franciszek, 204, 212-214, 216
Pulaski, Count Jozef, 212-213, 216
Pulaski, Brig, Gen, Casimir,
  Polish Phase:
    Birth of Casimir and the Pulaski family, 212
    Serves at the court of Prince Karl of Courland, 212
    Meets Princess Franciszka Krasinska, 213
    Sees Russian Machiavellian tactics first hand, 213
    Joins father Jozef and brothers to oppose Russian domination of Poland, 213
    Confederation of Bar is established, 213
    Becomes military commander of the Confederation, 214
    Fights Russian forces, 215
    Repulses Russians at Staro-Konstantynow, 215
    Successfully defends Chmielnik, 215
    Russians defeat Polish relief force under Wawrzyniec Potocki, 215
    Russians defeat Pulaski ally, Prince Joachim Potocki, 215
    Pulaski is besieged at Berdyczow,

captured but released, 216
Confederation abandons Bar and
 escapes to Chocim, Turkey, 216
Confederation reenters Poland and
 continues losing struggle for three
 more years, 216
Confederates abduct the King but
 release him, 216
Casimir blamed for the abduction
 and smeared as a regicide, 216
Confederation of Bar collapses, 216
Casimir forced to leave Poland,
 wanders about Europe, comes to
 France, 216
News of the American Revolution
 revive his flagging spirit, 216-217
Decides to fight for American
 independence, 217
Sails for America with Franklin and
 Deane recommendations, 217

American Phase:
Pulaski arrives in Massachusetts,
 1777, 1
Meets Gen. Wm. Heath in Boston and
 obtains overview of war, 2
Writes Franch historian Rulhiere of
 his impressions, 2
Reports to Washington's headquarters, 2
Delivers letter to Lafayette, 2, 4
Finds American officers hostile to
 foreigners, 3
Has strong backing of Lafayette, 5
Washington recommends Pulaski's
 appointment to a position deemed
 proper by Congress, 5
Pulaski returns to Washington's
 Army as Battle of Brandywine
 approaches, 7
Washington now recommends Pulaski
 for commander of the cavalry, 8
At Brandywine, Pulaski strikes the
 British twice and helps the American Army escape, 13, 14
Historians praise Pulaski's
 performance at Brandywine, 14-15
Congress appoints Pulaski Brig. Gen.
 and command of the cavalry, 17
Faces serious problems, 19
Washington lacks understanding of
 cavalry operations, 19
Pulaski's ignorance of English proves
 a drawback, 20
Three of the four regimental commanders are hostile, 20
Col. Theodorick Bland behaves in
 friendly manner, 20
Col. Stephen Moylan proves a thorn
 in Pulaski's side, 21
Moylan undermines Pulaski's standing with Washington, 21
Pulaski alerts Washington to
 approaching BritishArmy, 21
Deluge of rain stops the expectant
 battle, 22
Washington denudes the cavalry and
 Pulaski is left with no fighting
 force at Germantown, 23
Pulaski accused of sleeping instead
 of patrolling, 24
Historians and Bentalou defend
 Pulaski, 24-26
Pulaski begins vigorous training of
 the cavalry, 27
Ably assisted by Marquis de Fleury
 and Jan Zielinski, 27
Moylan and Zielinski confront each
 other, 27
Pulaski court martials Moylan, but
 court acquits him, 28
Lafayette protests biased action of
 court martial board, 29
Zielinski unhorses Moylan during
 cavalry exercise, 29
Pulaski supports Capt. Bedkin,
 Moylan's adjutant, 30
Col. John Laurens defends Pulaski in
 letter to father, President Henry
 Laurens, 30
Washington admonishes Pulaski for
 seizing horses from loyalists and
 patriots alike, 31
Pulaski demonstrates consummate
 horsemanship at Washington's
 headquarters, 32

Index

Washington's generals advise against winter operations, 33-34
Only Pulaski recommends continuing operations during winter, 34
Pulaski trains cavalry according to Prussian regulations, 38
Pulaski's cavalry horses threatened with starvation at Valley Forge, 39
Washington orders cavalry to Trenton, 39
Tasks Michael Kovatch to serve as Master of Exercise, 40
Organizes a company of lancers, 42
American officers complain of Pulaski's rigorous training, 42
Object directly to Washington, 42
Washington asks Pulaski to let up, 43
Pulaski releases frustration in letters to sister Anna and Rulhiere, 43-44
Offers Washington his resignation, 44
Washington orders Pulaski to reinforce Gen. Wayne at Haddonfield, 45
Joins Wayne and attacks superior British force, 46
British give up the fight and escape to Philadelphia, 48-49
Wayne praises Pulaski's bravery, 49
Pulaski resigns from command of the cavalry, 50
Cautions Washington not to give the command to Moylan, 51
Moylan proves incompetent and cavalry corps deteriorates, 51-52
Col. Baylor's regiment is destroyed at Old Tappan, 54
Col. Sheldon's cavalry suffers losses, 54-55
Pulaski's rigorous training standards are vindicated, 55
Proposes an independent legion of cavalry and infantry, 57
Washington recommends that Congress approve the legion, 58
Gen. Charles Lee proposes an expanded legion, 61
Congress approves Pulaski's independent command, 61

Begins vigorous recruiting, equipping, and training, 62
Washington approves a cadre from the regular cavalry regiments, 62
Pulaski chooses experienced officers, 64-68
Officers of The Pulaski Legion, Figure 1, 68
Receives money for bounties from Congress, 69
Purchases and draws equipment, 70
Uniform of Pulaski Legionnaire, 70
Visits convalescing Lafayette at Bethlehem, 71
Receives crimson banner from Moravian Sisters, 72
Longfellow immortalizes banner in poetic verse, 72
Pulaski advises Congress to pursue a strategy of avoiding general battles, 72, 75
Pulaski Legion passes in review before Congress, 77
Chafes at delays in facing the enemy, 79-81
Washington orders Pulaski to join Gen. Lord Stirling, 82
Congress issues emergency orders to defend Little Egg Harbor, 83
British raiding force lands, quickly destroys American facilities, and reembarks, 84-86
Pulaski Legion reaches Little Egg Harbor and protects the American base of Batsto, 87
Hessian Lt. Juliat betrays Pulaski Legion, 87
British party lands at night and secretly attacks Pulaski's infantry outpost, 88-89
Pulaski's cavalry pursue the British who escape, 90
Reports the vicious attack to Congress, 91-92
Congress warns the British of retaliation for killing Americans without mercy, 94
Analysis of a misleading account of

273

Little Egg Harbor, 96, 98
British single out Pulaski for his passion for independence, 99
Pulaski asks Congress to commission several volunteer officers, 101
Replaces slain Von Bose with Lt. Col. Charles Bedaulx, 102
Selects Maj. Peter Verney to replace Maj. De Montford, 102-103
Proposes a "flying corps" to watch the British at Kings Bridge, New York, 103
Pulaski Legion ordered to Sussex County, Northern New Jersey, 104
Washington tasks Pulaski to guard Minisink against Indian raids, 104
Pulaski is reinforced with 250 soldiers of Armand's Legion and Col. Spencer's regiment, 105
Pulaski at Minisink is a mis-assignment of cavalry, 106
Capt. Kotkowski joins the Legion but soon is courtmartialed for misbehavior, 106-107
Discouraged by the misuse of cavalry, Pulaski considers resignation, 107-108
Decides to remain in America, 108
Orders his cavalry and that of Armand to Easton to keep horses from starving, 109
Washington mistakenly believes that Pulaski left the wild frontier for more comfortable quarters, 109
Influx of horses into Pennsylvania angers Governor Joseph Reed, 109-110
Confers with French minister Gerard about the numerous departures of French officers, 110
Washington orders Pulaski's cavalry to Southern Delaware, 111
Movement is overtaken by decision to assign the Pulaski Legion to the Southern Theater, 111
Pulaski is delighted with the new assignment, 113
Pulaski faces challenge of a 700-mile march to Savannah, 113
Asks Congress to place him directly under the Southern Commander, 114
Pulaski asks for the appontment of officers to fill vacancies, 114-115
Interesting case of Swedish baron George D'Gugglaa, 116-117
Congress plans logistical support during the march, 118
Some Legionnaires stir up trouble in Pennsylvania, 118-119
Congress grants $50,000 for recruiting Legion to strength, 120
Army Quartermaster plans excellent route to Savannah, 121, 124
Capt. Paschke appointed Legion quartermaster officer, 122
Problem of the sufficiency of wagons, 116
Muster of the Pulaski Legion on eve of march, 124
Infantry marches first; cavalry pauses in Annapolis, 125
The Baron D'Ugglaa Affair, 125, 129
Southerners welcome the Legion along the march, 129
South Carolinians are dubious of any help from the Legion, 129-130
Legion arrives at Charleston in good shape and in time to fight the British, 130
Governor Rutledge offers to surrender Charleston to the British, 131-133
Pulaski vigorously opposes surrender, 133
Decides to attack and lead British into an ambush, 133
Legion's infantry commander spoils the ambush, 134
Legion is mauled by superior enemy force, 134
Historian Gordon's account of ambuscade, 136
British account of ambuscade, 137
Pulaski's bold attack stops British seizure of Charleston, 138

Index

American historians credit Pulaski with saving Charleston, 141
Pulaski scouts movements of Prevost's British Army, 143
Calls off attack on British at Johns Island, 143-144
Tells Congress of his satisfaction of fighting the British, 144
Rutledge praises Pulaski to South Carolinian delegates of Congress, 144-145
Lincoln's attack on British at Stono River fails, 145-146
Pulaski returns to Charleston to recuperate from sickness, 146
Writes his last letter to Congress, 148-150
States his noble purpose of why he fights for American independence, 150
Tells Congress his family in Poland is sending money to pay off debts to Congress, 150
French Fleet enters the fight for Savannah, 151
Pulaski Legion leads Lincoln's Army to Savannah, 152
First American commander to meet Admiral D'Estaing, 153
Leads French soldiers to outskirts of Savannah, 155
D'Estaing demands Prevost surrender Savannah, 155
Prevost procratinates while fortifying his lines, 155
D'Estaing bombards Savannah but British refuse to yield, 156
D'Estaing, Lincoln, and Pulaski plan to assault Savannah, 157
Pulaski's cavalry positioned to penetrate into Savannah, 158
Pulaski's role to be the coup de grace, 162
Rides in search of the wounded D'Estaing, 163
Struck in the groin by British shell, 163
Dr. Lynah removes imbedded shell on the battlefield, 163
Pulaski asks to be moved out of reach of the British, 163-164
Mortally wounded, Pulaski is carried aboard the *Wasp,* 164
Dies on 15 October 1779 and according to Bentalou is buried at sea, 164
Impressive funeral service is held in Charleston, 164-165
Southerners believe that Pulaski was buried at Greenwich Plantation, 165
Historian Pinkowski uncovers evidence of Pulaski's burial on land, 165-166
Historians differ over the manner of Pulaski's wound, 166-167
Maj. Rogowski's account of Pulaski's death, 167-168
Wm. Johnson accuses Pulaski of a foolish charge at Savannah, 169
Johnson may have created a myth, 170
Congress votes a monument to Pulaski, 173
Pulaski's unselfish devotion to freedom earns the Southerners' respect, 175
Savannah plans a monument in Pulaski's honor, 175
Lafayette lays cornerstone of Pulaski Monument, 175
Reasons for the monument, 175
Early American historians favorably evaluate Pulaski's service, 187-188
Pulaski earned the title "Father of American Cavalry," 191, 193, 199

Appendix A:
Demonstrates remarkable recruiting ability, 201
Lays out $50,000 of his own money, 202
Follows French method of paying his soldiers, 202
Informs Congress that family is sending a substantial sum of money, 204-206

Count Benyowsky serves as emissary of Pulaski family, 204
Pulaski and Benyowsky meet prior to Battle of Savannah, 207
Pulaski's accounts with Congress are settled, 207-208
Pulaski Legion Banner, 181, (Color Insert)
Pulaski Monument, Savannah, 28, 166, 177, 184, 199, 219, 222
Pulaski Monument, Washington, D.C., 197
Pulaski Vindicated from an Unsupported Charge, 25
Purrysburg, South Carolina, 121, 152
Pyle's Ford (Brandywine), 9

Quakers, 30
Quartermaster General, 21, 31, 114, 121

"Raccoons" (mounted militia), 136, 188
Radom, Poland, 221
Ragonese, Sandra, 226
Ramsay, David, 15, 151, 209
Randall, Willard Sterne, 14
Rankin, Hugh F. 111, 172
Recollections and Private Memories of Washington, 25
Reed, Joseph, 7, 53, 80-81, 103, 109-111, 119, 144, 149
Regiment de la Martinique, 66
Remarks Relating to Count Pulaski, 169
Repnin, Nikolay, 212, 214
Reyes, Estella, 226
Rice University, Houston, Texas, 205
Ridgway, Jeremiah, 87, 90, 94
Riga, Latvia, 248
Ritchie, Gov. Albert C., 235
Robertson, William, 175
Rochambeau, Gen. Jean Comte de, 76
Rodney, Caesar, 111
Rogowski, Maj. Maciej, 134, 167-169
Roman Catholic Church, 213
Roman legions, 62, 132
Root, Jesse, 102
Rorke, Beth, 224
Roscoe, Kathy, 225
Rosenkrantz, New Jersey, 105
Ross, Lt. Col. James, 10

Ross, Mrs. (Baltimore), 62
Roth, Lt. Francois de, 67
Rudolph, Capt. Michael, 31-32
Rulhiere, Claude de, 2, 44, 50
Russia, 2, 181, 205, 212
Russian forces, 5, 13, 27, 32, 41, 72, 103, 106-107, 133, 138, 164, 168, 191, 204, 211-212
Russian Orthodoxy, 213
Russians, xii, 205, 214
Rutledge, Governor John, 131-134, 144-145, 151, 164, 209, 221

St. Clair, Gen. Arthur, 113, 115, 193
St. Elme, Lt. Gerard de, 93, 99, 104
St. Mary Magdalene Church, Promna, Poland, 221
St. Michael's Church, Charleston, South Carolina, 164
St. Petersburg, Russia, 212
St. Phillips Church, Charleston, South Carolina, 180, 184
Savannah, Georgia, xv, 26, 28, 72, 113, 121, 139, 146, 151-153, 155, 157, 159, 165-166, 168 -173, 175-176, 190, 199, 207, 219-222
Savannah Daily News, 248
Savannah River, 121, 151-153, 161-163, 194, 220
Saxons, 64, 87
Scheer, George F., 111, 172
Schotte, Cardinal Jan Pieter, 205
Schuykill River, 22, 39
Schultz, Maria Rosina, 71
Schuyler, Gen. Philip, 2
Sconneltown, Pennsylvania, 11
Scott, Gen. Charles, 22, 54
Scott, John, 209
Secret Journals of Congress, 129
Seneca Indians, 105
Seydelin, Lt. John, 67
Sharples (artist), 47
Sheldon, Col. Elisha, 6, 31, 51-53, 140, 192
Shelton, South Carolina, 151
Shenandoah Valley, Virginia, 121
Sheridan, Gen. Philip, 193
Siberia, 204-206

276

Index

Sister Servants of Mary Immaculate, 236, (Color Insert)
Six Nations of the Iroquois, 105
Skelly, Maj. F., 137, 167
Skorupski, Marek, v, 223
Slovak Republic, 210
Slowacki, Juljusz, 209
Smallwood, Gen. William, 63, 201
Smith, Page, 28, 105, 138-140, 191
Smith, Thomas, 70
Society of the Cincinnati, 94, 184
Society of the Cincinnati in France, 181
Sommers, South Carolina, 147
Sons of the American Revolution, 235, (Color Insert)
Sopot, Poland, xv
South Atlantic Ocean, 151
South Carolina, 111, 113, 120, 129-131, 139-140, 144, 149, 151, 172-173, 176, 181-182, 204, 207
South Carolina and American General Gazette, Charleston, 170, 184
South Carolina Historical and Genealogical Magazine, 165
South Carolina Privy Council, 131-132
South Carolinians, 130-131, 133, 136, 139, 141, 144
Southern Department, 55, 111, 114-115, 144
Southern Theater of Operations, xiii, 113, 120
Spanish-American War, 190
Sparks, Jared, xv, 26, 44-45, 138, 188-189
Spears, Maj. James, 11
Spring Hill Redoubt, Savannah, 158, 161-163, 166, 169-170
Spuyten Duyvil Creek, New York, 103
Stark, Gen. John, 93
Staro-Konstantynow, Poland, 215
Staten Island, New York, 103
Staunton, Virginia, 125
Stedman, Charles, 88
Stephen, Gen. Adam, 9, 15, 24
Stey, Lt. John, 67
Stirling, Col. (British), 45-46, 49, 99
Stono Ferry, South Carolina, 143-145
Stono River, 147

Stony Point, New York, 244
Stuart, Gen. Jeb, xii, 190, 193
Suffczynski, Antoni, 213-214
Sullivan, Gen. John, 3, 9-11, 13, 15-16, 108, 155
Sullivan, Capt. William, 68, 101
Sunbury, Georgia, 172
Sussex County, Delaware, 110
Sussex County, New Jersey, 104
Swedesburg, Pennsylvania, 34
Swedish, 116

Tarleton, Lt. Col. Banastre, 180-181
Tawes, Capt. (British), 133, 137, 171
Taylor, John G., 15
Teed, Jonathan A., 225
Tefft, I. K., 165
Texier, Dr. Felix, 181
Thacher, Dr. James, 35
Thaddeus Kosciuszko Monument, West Point, New York, 199
The Cavalry Journal, 141
The Library of American Biography, 188
The Minute Man, 234
The North American Review, 25
The Savannah Georgian, 175
The Writings of George Washington, xv
Thompson, Dr. Ewa M., 205, 226
Thomson, Charles, 100
Thunderbolt, Georgia, 171
Tilton, James, 183
Time-Life Books, 170
Tobolsk, Siberia, 205
Tories, 105, 107
Treasury Board, Congress, 57, 64, 77, 129, 183, 204, 208
Trenton, New Jersey, xii, 34, 39-48, 45-46, 50-51, 62, 75, 87-88, 98-99, 101, 104, 192, 198
Trimble's Ford (Brandywine), 9
Troye, Lt. Francois Antoine de, 67
Trumbull, Governor Jonathan, 195
Turkey, 213, 216
Tybee Island, Georgia, 153

Ulanow, Poland, 215
Unitarian Church, Baltimore, 26
United States, 25, 221-222

277

U. S. Military Academy, West Point, New York, 190
U. S. Military Journal, 190
University of Georgia, 221
Upper Dublin, Pennsylvania, 27

Valley Forge, Pennsylvania, 27, 35, 37-39, 45, 49-51, 53, 57-58, 66
Valley Forge National Historical Park, 32
Vauban, Marquis de, 155
Venus of London (ship), 83
Verdier, Lt. Baptiste, 114
Vergennes, Comte Charles de, 110
Verney, Maj. Peter, 102-103, 114, 126, 168, 180
Verplanck's Point, New York, 244
Village of the Forks, New Jersey, 83
Virginia, 6, 22, 75-76, 126
Von Bose, Lt. Col. Baron Carl, 64, 87-88, 91, 95, 102, 134, 184, 189, 201, 203
Von Steuben, Gen. Baron, 3, 35, 40, 117, 185, 191, 209

Wachowiak, Monsignor Stanislaw, 235
Wade, Frank, 111
Waldo, Surgeon Albigence, 2
Walewska, Anna, 43
Wappoo-cut, South Carolina, 147
War of 1812, 15
Ward, Christopher, 9, 22, 146, 172, 230
Warka, Poland, 212
Warren, James, 81
Warren and White Horse Taverns, Pennsylvania, 21
Warsaw, Poland, 211-212, 216, 221
Washington, D. C., 173
Washington, Gen. George, xi, xii, xiii, 1-11, 13-15, 17, 19-34, 37-45, 49, 52-58, 62-64, 69, 75-76, 80, 82-84, 104-111, 114, 117-118, 120, 123, 126, 129, 139-140, 150, 168, 173, 182, 184-185, 187, 189, 192-193, 195-196, 201, 209, 211, 217
Washington, Lt. Col. William, 42, 180
Wasp (ship), 164-166, 219
Wayne, Gen. Anthony, 9, 11-14, 45-46, 49, 54, 94, 132, 192
Weiss, Anna Maria, 71

Welch, Lt. William, 67
Werth, Bishop Joseph, 205
Westfall, David, 107
West Indies, 20, 131, 151, 158
West Point, New York, 173, 199
Whipple, Gen. William, 17
Whitemarsh, Pennsylvania, 27, 33
Wildes, Harry Emerson, 46
Wilkes-Barre, Pennsylvania, 106
Willets, James, 87
Williams, Henry, 28, 175, 184
Williams, Gen. James, 158
Williamsburg, Virginia, 243
Wilmington, Delaware, 8, 76, 110
Wilmington River, Georgia, 171, 219, 221
Wilson, Gen. James, 193
Winchester, Virginia, 121, 125-126
"Winged Hussars" (Poland), 193
Wistar's Ford (Brandywine), 9
Witkowska, Teresa, 221
Woodford, Gen. William, 82
World War I, 248
World War II, 1, 64, 170, 222
Wroblewska, Dr. Jadwiga, 223
Wyoming Valley, Pennsylvania, 104

Yale University, New Haven, Connecticut, 190
Yamacraw Swamp, Savannah, 158
York, Pennsylvania, 58, 113, 121-123, 188, 203
Yorktown, Virginia, 75-76, 113

Zebra (ship), 84, 91, 99
Zielinska, Marianna, 212
Zielinski, Capt. Jan, 27-30, 64, 66, 134, 140, 173, 184, 189, 212
Zielinski-Moylan Confrontation, 27-28
Zubly's Ferry, South Carolina, 152
Zygmunt August, King of Poland, 211

· About the Author ·

FRANCIS CASIMIR KAJENCKI was graduated from the U.S. Military Academy and commissioned second lieutenant in January 1943. He served in the Pacific Theater in World War II, followed by staff and command assignments over a span of thirty years. He retired as Colonel and Assistant Chief of Information, Department of the Army, in 1973.

Kajencki earned three Masters degrees: from the University of Southern California in Mechanical Engineering, 1949; University of Wisconsin-Madison in Journalism, 1967; George Mason University in History, 1976. Upon retiring from the army, he took up historical research and writing that led to six published books on American history.

The author was born in Erie, Pennsylvania, November 15, 1918. A widower with four adult children, he resides in El Paso, Texas.

Typography, book design and jacket design by Vicki Trego Hill of El Paso, Texas. This book was produced electronically using a Macintosh computer. The pages were formatted using Adobe PageMaker. Photographs were retouched using Adobe Photoshop, and maps were produced using Adobe Illustrator. Text was set in 11pt. Caslon Book with 14 pts. leading; chapter headings were set in Charlemagne Bold.

Printing/Binding by Thomson-Shore of Dexter, Michigan. The text was printed on 60-pound Writer's Offset B21 Natural, an acid-free paper with an effective life of at least three hundred years. The color plates were printed on 70-pound Huron Gloss Enamel White.